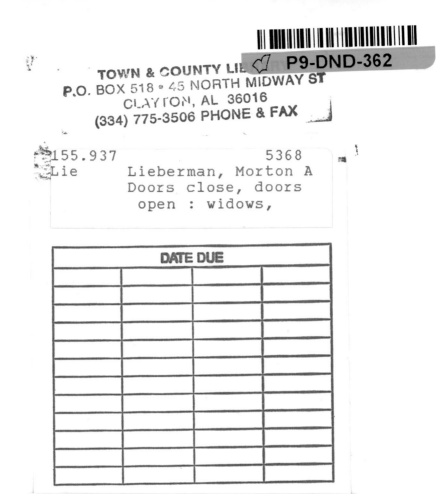

DATE DUE			

Doors Close, Doors Open

MORTON
LIEBERMAN, PH.D.

A GROSSET/PUTNAM BOOK
PUBLISHED BY G. P. PUTNAM'S SONS
NEW YORK

Doors Close,

Widows, Grieving and Growing

Doors Open

A Grosset/Putnam Book
Published by G. P. Putnam's Sons
Publishers Since 1838
200 Madison Avenue
New York, NY 10016

Library of Congress Cataloging-in-Publication Data
Lieberman, Morton A., date.
    Doors close, doors open : widows, grieving, and growing /
by Morton Lieberman.
        p.   cm.
    "A Grosset/Putnam book."
    Includes index.
    ISBN 0-399-14141-3
    1. Bereavement—Psychological aspects.   2. Grief.   3. Widows—
Psychology.   4. Widows—Life skills guides.   5. Life change events.
I. Title
BF575.G7L53   1996   95-48164   CIP
155.9'37—dc20

Printed in the United States of America
1   3   5   7   9   10   8   6   4   2

Book design by Kate Nichols

This book is printed on acid-free paper. ∞

Contents

For my granddaughter
RACHEL SADIE LIEBERMAN

As you grow up in the twenty-first century,
may you open doors we cannot yet imagine.

Preface

This book represents two journeys for me. The first was the more familiar one: It involved putting together and coordinating a large research project. Over the course of seven years, my colleagues and I talked with six hundred widows and one hundred widowers, in an attempt to understand what they were experiencing and how they changed over time. We talked to them soon after their partner's death, a year later, and six years after that. All these people generously shared with me their feelings, sometimes terribly painful, sometimes rueful, sometimes surprisingly upbeat. In the course of my work I became aware of the range of experiences and of reactions to being widowed. I learned what always hurts and what sometimes helps. Over the course of years, many of the women I spoke with found themselves transformed from shocked, angry, helpless, and hopeless individuals into persons of strength and accomplishment. These personal journeys are at the heart of my book.

For me there was also a personal transformation. I began this study with the typical mental health professional's attitude—a male perspective—which I have now come to understand was colored by the myths and half-truths that I brought to the study. I started out thinking of widowhood as an illness and expecting that recovery would be the return to "normality"—a life similar in most respects to the previous one. What I found, instead, were women who discovered in themselves a new way—a way of strength and assurance. The path was never smooth, and many women believed in the dark times that things could never really improve. In the pages that follow you will see that I have emphasized what was surprising to me. I do not go into very much detail about the profound sorrow and pain that these women experienced. It didn't make sense to me to dwell on this, since others have written movingly about their own experiences, and those are the ones we think of as universal.

Doors Close, Doors Open is the product of these journeys. I wrote it for widows and their families. I hope that it will be of help to read about the range of experience, of how widows feel their tragic loss, how they struggle to find themselves once again, and how their inner explorations often lead to remarkable growth.

I owe a considerable debt to many friends, colleagues, and students who helped to make the study and this book a reality. First I would like to thank the seven hundred widows and widowers who, during their moments of profound crisis, took the time to share their feelings with me. Of course, without them there would be no book.

To my colleagues and former students who made critical contributions to my studies and my thinking, I give my thanks. They deserve all the plaudits for the book's strengths and none of the blame for its weaknesses. Foremost is my good friend and longtime colleague, Dr. Irvin Yalom. Without his encouragement and without the model of his writing, I could never have envisaged a book that was both based on my research and written for the prime audience, the widow. Irv Yalom was my close collaborator on studies of the effects of psychotherapy, and I am deeply in his debt for his ideas about viewing widowhood through an existential framework.

Many of my graduate students when I was a faculty member at The University of Chicago enabled these studies to go ahead. I am grateful to Drs. Lynn Videka Sherman, Barry Sherman, Gary Bond, Janet Reibstein, and Elizabeth Bankoff for their substantial contributions to my developing knowledge and understanding of widows and widowers, and to my colleagues Drs. Lomeranz and Guttman, whose sabbatical year at UCSF aided me immeasurably in understanding the inner life of the spousally bereaved. To a good colleague and friend who sadly died all too suddenly and prematurely, Dr. Leonard Borman, who shared with me the studies of support groups, I am forever grateful.

Producing a book is never an easy task. Although I have written a half dozen books prior to this one, the challenge of translating research so that it is accessible and useful to non-academics was aided immeasurably by Joy Parker, whose sensitive editing and calm teaching of how to communicate made the task more a pleasure than an ordeal. I owe a special debt to Jane Isay, publisher of Grosset Books. Her encouragement and gift of language enhanced the readability of the manuscript.

I cannot measure the immensity of the contribution of my wife, friend, and colleague, Mariann DiMinno, to this endeavor. Her warmth, support, and encouragement in reading the early, dense drafts, her recognition of my and my colleagues' "male ears," and her helping us to see the plight of the widow with different eyes went a long way toward shaping the final product.

Doors Close, Doors Open

Chapter 1

Beyond Grief:
The Widow's Journey

A widow, in the throes of sorrow, confused about the present and worried about her future, feels alone in her struggles. She may not be aware that widows are probably one of the most misunderstood groups in America today. Well-meaning family and friends offer advice about how she should be acting and feeling. Doctors place grieving on a timetable of six months to a year, and anyone who grieves too little or too long is made to feel abnormal. Many psychiatrists view widowhood as if it were a disease, requiring therapy and tranquilizers. Society judges a widow "successful" by how quickly she snaps back and acts like her "old self" again.

These misconceptions make it even more difficult for a woman to cope with her loss and grief because she is constantly comparing herself to a hypothetical norm, judging her recovery by the standards of others. Friends and family often view her normal reactions to the loss as simply the self-indulgence, stubbornness, or pathology of the widow. My research into the experience of over 700 widows and widowers across seven years has taught me that there is no norm, no set pattern for healthy grieving and recovery. These new findings should help a widow to see that her grieving is personal, her experience unique, and that she need not—and should not—try to "measure up" to any set timetable of recovery.

Offered sincere advice—"I know just how you feel"; "You'll be fine"; "This will end soon"—from everyone around them, many widows told me how those attitudes often did not relate to their own experiences and feelings. Like anybody held up to a false ideal, widows are more likely to blame themselves for feeling that they are not coping well with widowhood than to realize that friends, family, professionals, and the popular press might just not be right. A widow needs to separate herself from the beliefs and attitudes of others, and to get in touch with how she is really feeling.

This book is the product of my personal journey toward understanding widows. I started out listening with "male" ears. The turning point in my education occurred while I was conducting a study on the effectiveness of psychotherapy for widows and widowers. My three colleagues were all middle-aged, married men, experienced clinicians who had previously studied widows and served as their therapists. Week after week, the four of us listened as widows discussed their marriages, their pasts, their spouses' deaths, their adjustment to widowhood, their personal autonomy, and their strategies for coping with their present lives. As these stories unfolded, it very slowly began to dawn on us that what many of these women were telling us did not fit our preconceptions. Of course these women were describing their pain and loss, but, most important, they were conveying to us a sense of the challenges they were meeting and their personal growth. Some had reached a new and better level of integration and functioning than they had experienced when their husbands were alive.

Looking back, I realize that our male egos, steeped as they were in preconceptions common to our profession, were threatened by this new vision of widowhood. After all, what man wants to hear that his wife might lead a richer and fuller life after his demise?

Months later, I had an opportunity to share our findings with a large audience of Junior Leaguers, many of whom were widows. Several came up to me after the speech to thank me for finally saying out

loud what they, as widows, had known all along. After that first difficult period following their husband's death, they had been able to
grow and develop, establishing new and meaningful lives. The reactions of these women moved me deeply and made me realize even
more definitely that I was on the right track.

For most widows, the challenges they face after the loss of a husband comprise a new and uncharted journey. What perspective can a
widow bring to this potentially devastating experience? Many, of
course, have seen their mothers and friends go through the same experience. But very few women are adequately prepared for widowhood. So they are likely to be influenced by the thoughts, attitudes,
and behavior of others. The world may be filled with people ready to
give counsel, yet each woman's journey is her own.

The research for this book explored the lives of over 600 widows and
100 widowers between the ages of twenty-eight and eighty, many of
whom my colleagues and I followed for more than seven years. It
shows how society's attitudes about being widowed move between
the two stark poles of proper grieving and remarriage. One of the
major burdens facing widows is the net of half-truths, the myths,
that interfere with the search for a pathway not only to recovery but,
more important, to a new beginning. My exploration of their suc-
cesses and occasional failures provides the "facts" that form the back-
bone of this book.

The Widow's Journey:
The Life-Course Perspective

Beyond the sense of deprivation and feelings of grief are a host of
tasks and challenges for widows to face. These challenges can be a
source of unalloyed distress for some; for others, they can provide a
launching pad for personal growth.

Dealing with grief and loss are the paramount tasks during the first months of widowhood. In the midst of mourning, a number of challenges present themselves. Paramount is how to begin to take on a new identity—that of a single person. Many widows face the dilemma of being the sole parent. These women ask themselves: "How do I address my children's grief while I am so immersed in my own?" and "How do I explain their father's death to them?" More often than not, the widows feel so uncomfortable confronting these issues that they end up avoiding discussing the death with their children.

Widows are quickly thrust into confronting their loneliness. They wonder if it is better to get back into ordinary life routines even when they don't feel like doing very much: "Should I even make the effort?" she may ask. "And what do I do about all the advice that my family and friends are providing—even deluging—me with about how to be a widow?"

These are the early challenges. Later, after the grief has become manageable and the initial shock of being single has diminished, other, inner challenges emerge. They are the stuff of widowhood; they will be with you for some time, and they represent the groundwork for meaningful change and growth.

This book is a distillation of the stories of a diverse group of widows and widowers and how they met these challenges. It is about the discoveries they made about previously hidden strengths and talents, and about the inner challenges of widowhood. Listen to how some widows faced the journey into the unknowns of their inner landscape.

The death of a husband frequently challenges beliefs and assumptions about what is important in life.

Jane, a young-looking, forty-five-year-old widow, used to value "feminine" passivity, letting her husband run the family and their affairs. During her grieving process, this soft-spoken mother of two adolescents discovered a new, stronger, and more independent identity, one that takes charge and runs the family business with zest and enthusiasm.

"When I was married, I always used to defer to my husband's decisions in everything, but in the year and a half since his death I've discovered that I really enjoy being in charge. I never knew I was such a self-reliant person. I own an apartment building and enjoy being the boss. I rent out the units, spruce them up, and tell the manager what to do. When I was married I was always torn between wanting to be taken care of and wanting independence. In the past year, I've lived alone and found that I can manage fine. No one is taking care of me financially and I pay my own bills. I even joined Weight Watchers and a fitness program. My self-confidence has really taken off. What a difference!

"I've learned to live very much in the present and no longer postpone things until the future. I've become aware that my life is my responsibility and no one else's, not only now but in the past as well. I was my own jailer, one who wouldn't let herself grow, but now I relish the changes I've already made and those that will come later."

A year and a half after her husband's death, Jane is well on the road to constructing a meaningful life without him. She has asked herself what she likes about herself and what values are important. Independence, being in charge, and learning to take care of herself are high on her list. She is able to take responsibility for the past and face the future with courage, looking forward to whatever new adventures life will bring her.

Much self-image is embedded in a long-term relationship that no longer exists. A new image of the "I" must be separated out from the "we."

If your life has been intertwined with another's for many years, your self-image has been shaped by your identity as half of a couple. A husband's death leaves numerous voids in a widow's life, not the least of which is the requirement that she reexamine herself and move from a "we" to an "I."

Lisa, a widow in her late fifties, told me that all of her adult life she had been shy and reticent in social situations: "When we went to a party, even with people I had known for years, Bob always provided the opening for me. He was the gregarious one." During the course of their marriage, her husband had supplied them both with the extroversion they needed for dealing with their social circle and the world at large. After his death Lisa began to recognize parts of herself that had lain dormant for most of her life.

"You know, when I was a kid, my parents always called me the social butterfly. I haven't thought about it for years. After I met Bob, however, I let that be *his* role. Since his death six months ago, I've begun to rediscover this lost part of myself. It's still hard for me to reach out to others. I feel almost as if I were a kid again. But I'm beginning to find that I don't have to be shy, and I'm enjoying this new feeling.

"I realize now that, during our marriage, I didn't have to deal with my social reticence, I let Bob pave the way—and we faced the world as a team."

Many women explore feelings toward remarriage and relationships to men.

Mina, a thirty-eight-year-old widow, shared her feelings with me about dating and relationships: "I never thought I could live with another man again. After Ralph's death, when friends asked me, 'Will you eventually remarry?' I said, 'Definitely not.' Now I find myself seriously thinking about marrying Frank, though I'm not really sure why I changed my mind. I'm not even positive that I love him, certainly not in the same way that I loved Ralph. Yet I feel that remarriage may be the best thing for me. I've talked and talked to my friends, hoping that their advice would help, but they're just as mixed up as I am. Some of them are enthusiastic. They think it's a good thing for me to do—that it's not disloyal and that I should be getting on with my life. But my best friend Rita is more cautious.

She thinks I should go slow, that I shouldn't rush into this too quickly, and that I would be better off giving myself more time to absorb the shock. I wish my children liked the idea more. I believe they will come around in time."

Mina is receiving mixed messages from family and friends. Some encourage her to remarry; others warn against it.

Most women must confront regrets about their marriage and the aspects of their lives that have remained undeveloped. This leads to intense feelings of aloneness in the face of one's mortality.

Sarah, at fifty-five years old, feels differently about herself since the death of her husband, Tim: "At times, I'm overwhelmed by regrets about the way I lived my life. I think I married the wrong man. I know now that I have to allow the inner me, the real me, choose my life. Now, my choices can match what I want, rather than what another person desires for me. I'm scared of being free! But at the same time it's exhilarating.

"I've learned how brief and precious life really is. I no longer buy long-term subscriptions to magazines. I don't buy one-gallon plants anymore either, but larger, faster-growing ones because there's no guarantee I'll be here in five years. I've stopped postponing things because I know that life must be lived now if it is to be lived at all."

Sarah has realized that it wasn't her husband who restricted her life. She was her own jailer. She is aware of the artificial shape she had given to her existence, the stifling routine of carefully prepared dinners and social obligations. She is frightened by her current lack of structure but also exhilarated by her freedom. Sarah knows that death, her death, is real and inevitable. She has begun to take care of her own body by quitting smoking and beginning to exercise and lose weight. For the first time, she has made a will and provided for her funeral arrangements.

Sarah has become critical of her old materialistic way of life, buying clothes, decorating her home, and having lunch and playing bridge. That existence feels very empty to her now as she searches for meaning in her life. She wants to find a way to make a difference in the world and to leave her mark.

Previously, Sarah's sense of purpose derived from her role as a wife. Now, she believes that, even if she remarries, she will demand much more from life.

One of the major challenges facing widows is how to reconstruct a future. The death of a spouse disrupts plans, hopes, and dreams.

Mary is an articulate, forthright sixty-six-year-old woman whose husband, Roger, died eight months ago. She lives in Seattle, in the same house that she and Roger lived in for twenty years. Her one son, who lives in Los Angeles, plays a fairly important role in her life. She's seen him on several occasions in the last six months and is seriously considering moving near him.

When we first met, she often cried quietly during our time together, and it was clear that she was feeling lost, without an anchor: "My married life was a good one, and I desperately miss Roger. We had recently both retired, and I hate to think that we will never get to do all of the things we were planning together. For thirty years I worked as an office manager. Though I still miss the hustle and bustle of work, and even considered going back to fill in the emptiness of my time, I know that's not the right thing for me to do. I have to find a new path for myself, not just repeat the past. I'm even thinking about moving out of my house, not because it's sad or stirs up painful memories, but because it's falling apart and there's so many things I don't know how to fix.

"I can't say that I enjoy going out or having people over any longer, but I don't know how to relieve this emptiness in me. The past week was a particularly bad time for me, because my dearest girlfriend died from the same kind of cancer that Roger had. Jinny was alone, so I did a lot of the caring for her."

As our talk together drew to a close, I asked Mary what she had learned so far from her loss, and her answer reflected her distress and grief. "I've learned that life is fragile, and that I'm not as independent as I thought I was. In fact, I can't even make simple decisions."

Six months later, however, when I talked to Mary again, much had changed. "In the past I wouldn't spend money, but now I'll go out and spend two hundred dollars on a dress without even thinking about it. I finally made a decision to move to a retirement community in Los Angeles to be near my son George—not to be dependent upon him but to have someone close if I'm in need. I'm also learning to do things alone and enjoy them. I've always wanted to write, and I've started a writing course, which I'll continue when I move. When I was in college, oh, so long ago, I discovered I had a talent, but I've let it lie fallow for many years. Now, I want to honor the talents within myself. I even have a project planned out. Next month I'm going to start on a trip around the country, visiting relatives I haven't seen for years. I bought a tape recorder, so my relatives can tell me everything they remember about our family and I can write the history of our clan."

As Mary has reengaged with life, her distress has lessened and her depression lifted. Now she can envisage a future without Roger and has reconnected with her past dreams and talents. Mary is still lonely, but, unlike six months ago, these feelings no longer overwhelm her. Mary has made great strides toward reconstructing her life and developing a future.

These journeys are very different from the one offered by the traditional grief-loss model. That model doesn't look for growth, but for adjustment. It seeks a return to the way life was lived before the loss of a spouse. The perspective I have gained from my research sees widowhood as a series of "inner" and "outer" challenges. When a woman understands these challenges and can face them successfully, she will not only recover, but she will grow.

I undertook this book because of my conviction that the male perspective exemplified by the grief-loss model unwittingly treats widows shabbily. It leads to the all-too-easy conclusion that many widows are in need of professional mental health care. An industry catering to this "need" has become entrenched in contemporary society. I by no means wish to imply that some widows don't need therapy. I have found that *certain types* of reactions to the loss of a husband *should* be addressed with professional help. These reactions will be described in a later chapter. Still, for the vast majority of widows, neither psychotherapy nor counseling is required.

Genevieve Davis Ginsberg poignantly describes the frustration she felt when her bereavement was viewed through the limiting perspective of the grief-loss model. Her essay in *The New York Times,* in which she describes her search for help and her journey of self-discovery and growth, mirrors the experience of many widows who participated in my study:

> I was looking for something beyond [books on] coping, beyond overcoming, and beyond the generic collection on death, dying, letting go, and saying good-bye to your pet. I was searching for something that would acknowledge widowhood as a bona fide life stage with uncharted potential—more particularly, a stage where the quest is not limited to replacing one partner with another, or remaining a wife without husband forever after. . . .
>
> From the moment my husband died, people thought to comfort me with the assurance that I would one day remarry. "You're young and attractive, you'll see." (I was in my middle 50's, a perfect statistical model.) Anxiously, as years went by and I remained single, I began to feel as deficient as a sorority girl without a Saturday-night date. In response to the repeated warnings of friends, family and friends' husbands, put rather basically, by our 18-year-old niece as using it or losing it, I lost it. . . . Widowhood needs to be reinvented, both for those who live it and those who fear it. Let's bestow on it the status of a real stage of life, not that of a weigh station. I was dragged by my heels into this so-called passage, but now that I'm here, I've come to appreci-

ate the opportunity to find a person buried under so many
layers of daughter, wife, mother. . . .

Genevieve Davis Ginsberg,
"Life After Death,"
The New York Times, December 2, 1990, pp. 34–35.

Success in widowhood requires much more than just coping
with grief. Widowhood is a complex series of events and conditions
involving the real and painful loss of a partner of several decades and
the rupture of two intertwined lives. Widows are challenged to respond to a multitude of tasks, such as developing a new self-image,
reconstructing friendships, becoming the head of household, managing finances, and finding a new meaning in life.

The single focus on "managing" loss and grief so that it will do
no harm or impede recovery stems from a tradition hundreds of years
old. Robert Burton, an English clergyman of the seventeenth century and author of a widely read book, *The Anatomy of Melancholy,*
was a strong advocate of the belief that loss and the associated grief
could adversely affect a widow's health. Burton's view was widely
shared by the medical profession of his day. In 1835 Benjamin Rush,
a prominent American physician, went as far as suggesting that an
individual could even *die* of grief. He based his conclusions on au-
topsies of widows and widowers who showed "congestion in and in-
flammation of the heart, with rupture of its auricles and ventricles."
In the nineteenth century, it was commonly believed that the heart
was the organ of feelings and that a diseased heart could be the result
of emotional traumas.

In the twentieth century many scientists have researched possible connections between widowhood and mental illness. Their work
has been largely inspired by Sigmund Freud's well-known 1917
paper, "Mourning and Melancholia." Freud advanced the idea that
many psychiatric illnesses are caused by pathological mourning.
Both "excessive grief" and the failure to grieve define such mourning. Contemporary thinking about grief still relies on these ideas

published over seventy-five years ago. The widow who grieves too much or two little is suspect. Like Goldilock's porridge, grieving must be "just right."

A recent survey of physicians and psychiatrists illustrates the influence of this point of view. One-half of the professionals surveyed expect most widows to experience anorexia, weight loss, and sleeplessness during their bereavement. Routine feelings, such as resentment, are seen as indications that widows need some kind of therapy. Ninety percent felt that common and transitory feelings of guilt toward the husband were indicative of a problem. Sixty-seven percent of physicians say that widows and widowers should not be encouraged to speak with old friends about their feelings, and the majority feel that the bereaved should be encouraged to relinquish "excessive attachments" to the deceased. Finally, a diehard 30 percent of the psychiatrists surveyed said that it is almost always desirable for widows to seek psychiatric help.

When asked the exact same questions, widows did *not* agree with the professionals. In fact, widows never labeled their emotional reactions to their husbands' deaths as pathological.

The professionals' responses on the questionnaire simply do not match the facts. A national survey of Americans' use of mental health services revealed that only about 4 percent of widows seek psychiatric help. A recent nationwide study of 20,000 adults found that only 2.8 percent of the 4,000 widows studied suffered from any mental illness directly associated with the death of their husbands.

Two of the most pernicious myths about widowhood are that it is only about loss and grief and that most widows require professional help for recovery. Such views are part of a constellation of untruths that denies the reality of women's actual experiences. It discourages widows from the natural process of exploring their inner resources and inhibits them from seizing the opportunity to create a new life for themselves. Most women adapt quite successfully to lives without husbands, even discovering that they relish their freedom. These harmful myths cast a pall on a truth that many American wid-

ows have discovered for themselves: *Widowhood presents a unique opportunity for growth and creativity in women's lives.*

Susan's experience illustrates the dilemmas faced by many widows in
contemporary society. Her world was shattered when the family doctor discovered that her husband, Richard, had a serious heart condition. Three months later he was dead. When I first met her, she was
in a state of shock, going through the motions of making arrangements and "learning how to be a widow." Her children, Linda and
John, were well launched with families of their own, and both lived
less than an hour's drive from Susan's house. Richard had left her
comfortably off, so at least she didn't have to worry about money.

Thoughtful and young-looking, Susan had a soft, well-modulated
voice, and often paused to deliberate before answering each of my
questions.

"I was so stunned during those terrible first few weeks that I really couldn't get things organized. And I'm usually such a competent person. My friends were great. They rallied around me and tried
to help. My kids were great too. My daughter and Rita, my son's
wife, were particularly helpful. My mother, who lives in Florida, flew
up right away and tried to do what she could. She's not as spry as she
used to be, but she was still willing. What more could I ask? I had
loving friends and a family who were really there for me. They kept
reassuring me that things would get better, that the terrible feelings
I was having would diminish in time. It was important to me that
they were there for me—but I just couldn't believe that I'd ever feel
different.

"Now two months have passed since Richard's death, and the
house is quiet most of the time. Mother had to go back to Florida.
Winter is hard on her, and she really couldn't stay any longer. She
tried to get me to come down for a visit, but I just didn't feel like it.
I'm not sure why. Maybe I should have gone. The kids come to dinner several times a week and bring the grandchildren. That helps,
having all that noise around the house, but there are lots of times

when it's just too quiet around here. I can't seem to reach a balance. I have a hard time sleeping and I cry easily, especially when I notice something that reminds me of the life Richard and I shared. Memories just flood over me and I fall into the depths of despair."

Susan began to wonder if there was something wrong with her. When she talked to her friends, they tried to be helpful, but she soon realized that since she was the first widow in her social group, none of them really knew what to say to her. They were advising her to go out more and "get on with her life." But what kind of life? When she went to the library for help, she found shelves full of advice for widows: *How to Meet a Man, Dating Once Again, Managing Your Money, Guides and Signposts to Adequate Grieving, How to 'Know' How You're Doing.* She read everything she could get her hands on, checking out armfuls of books week after week and becoming an "expert" on widowhood. No matter what she tried, the feeling persisted that she would never get over her grief. How could she? It would almost be like having Richard die again.

Another month went by and Susan still wasn't feeling any better, though she seemed to be managing. She had pulled herself together and dealt with all the money matters that were left over from her husband's death. She saw her kids, talked to her mother on the phone at least three times a week, and was sleeping better. On the outside she looked fine, and most of her friends thought she was doing well, but inside she still felt lost.

"My best friend, Cynthia, suggested that I go see a therapist. I talked to my family doctor, who's known me all my life, and he encouraged me to try it out. You know, never before in my life have I felt any desire to go see a psychiatrist and look inside myself. Sure, I had some problems during my first few years of marriage, and Richard and I did see a counselor briefly, but it didn't help all that much. It was so long ago I can't even remember what the crisis was about. We obviously got through it. I wasn't that enthusiastic about going to see someone now, but I guess I was willing to try anything."

In her usual, methodical way, Susan started to ask her friends, her doctor, and anyone else she could trust for names of good therapists. She kept hearing one name, Dr. Alberts, over and over again. He'd had lots of experience working with widows, had written some papers on bereavement, and even had taught part-time at the university. Susan called for an appointment and managed to get one in two weeks' time. Though she wasn't enthusiastic, she told herself she had to do something. What if the way she felt meant that she really was suffering from some kind of mental illness?

Two weeks later Susan showed up for her appointment. Dr. Alberts was a tall, rangy man about fifty years old with nice eyes and a kindly voice. He was easy to talk to and put her at her ease. "I described Richard's death and all the feelings I could remember afterward, particularly the fog I was and still am in, and my feelings of being bewildered and kind of lost. I also told him how magnificent my friends and family were." For thirty minutes Susan watched Dr. Alberts listen carefully and take notes. Finally, she worked up the courage to ask him if he thought there was something wrong with her. She was somewhat disappointed when he only said, "I don't know, we need to talk some more."

He proceeded to ask her how she was eating and sleeping and what kinds of thoughts she was having about Richard. When their time ran out, they scheduled a meeting for the following week.

"The next week when I went to see Dr. Albert, I told him about my life with Richard. Though there were some difficult times, Richard and I had a satisfying marriage. My husband always seemed to be terribly busy building his business and making a living for all of us, but I did enjoy having enough money for a nice house and for educating the kids. We looked forward to a comfortable retirement, but it was a retirement with Richard, not by myself!

"In the last few years, we began to make plans. Richard started to slow down from his frantic work pace and we finally found time to travel. Getting to Europe and having the luxury of spending time in the world's great museums was something I had always wanted to do, and we finally did it last year. I have a bachelor's degree in art history, so the museums really meant something special to me."

Susan had worked for a few years after college in an interesting but low-paying art gallery job. Though she occasionally felt sad about not having pursued her career, she had no doubt that she had done the right thing in staying home after the children were born. "When my youngest entered the first grade, I remember thinking about going back to work, but life seemed so all-consuming. The kids were still small and they needed me. I got active in community organizations and turned into what I guess most magazines would describe as a typical suburban housewife.

"When the kids were out of the house and in college, I thought about going back to school, getting a master's degree, and really getting back on track in a real career. I did take a few courses, but somehow it never amounted to anything. Richard wasn't keen on it. He liked having me around. Yet I know if I'd really wanted the degree, he'd have gone along with me. That's the way Richard was. He never really denied me anything that was important to me, and yet I never wanted to do anything that would make him unhappy."

As the years went on, Richard's business had left them little time to spend together. Though Susan regretted the shortness of their vacations and the fact that they always had to bring along the kids and the burdens of Richard's work, life was still "okay." She kept herself busy taking care of the home, being an excellent hostess to Richard's business associates, and spending lots of social time with friends.

"As the session came to a close, I asked if there was anything I could do to move the therapy along between appointments. Dr. Alberts said, 'Remember your dreams and the images that come into your mind, particularly the ones that set you thinking about Richard. In fact, some of my patients have found it helpful to write these things down.'

"At last, I thought, something concrete to do!"

Susan likes being organized and taking action, and walked out of Dr. Alberts's office with renewed hope. She was on the road to getting well!

The following week, she brought in all her notes on her

thoughts about Richard. After listening briefly, Dr. Alberts said, "Tell me about growing up, about your mother and father. As a child, did you experience any losses?"

Although she hadn't thought about it in twenty years, Susan suddenly remembered the time her father had been away from home in the army and how hard it had been for her mother. When Dr. Alberts showed keen interest in this part of her life, she also remembered how devastated she had been when her dog Skip had died when she was eight. Memories spilled out about friends she had lost, including Lily, her best friend, who had moved away when she was ten years old. Back then it had been impossible to understand how someone could be close and then just leave. The minutes flew by and soon the hour was over. Dr. Alberts had been quiet for most of that time, taking copious notes and gently asking her now and then to remember things or people she had lost. At the end of the session, he said, "Next week, same time."

Susan walked out feeling somewhat funny and a little uncomfortable. "Why bother with all that history?" she wondered. But she decided the doctor knew what he was doing. After all, he was the expert.

Next week's session was the same. More memories of personal loss. Toward the end of the hour, Dr. Alberts said, "Tell me about Richard. What was your life like together?"

During the next several sessions Susan somewhat reluctantly described her relationship with Richard in detail, even though dredging up these memories so soon after his death was "hard and painful."

After two months of this inventory, Dr. Alberts told her that, yes, he thought she had some problems, some stemming from her early life. The absence of her father for two and a half years particularly appeared to be unresolved and was interfering with her ability to let go of Richard. "'I think it would be helpful for you to be in psychotherapy,' he said. When I asked how long, he told me, 'It's hard to say, perhaps once a week for a year.' He told me that my grieving was incomplete and that we needed to examine the reasons for this. Without such an exploration, he said, I would remain in limbo. When I left his office, I thought, 'A whole year! Something must be terribly wrong with me.'"

Susan went back to the library and checked out more books on loss, grief, and stages of grief. She read them all, avidly comparing the progress of her bereavement to what the experts said she should be feeling and doing. Was she behind schedule? Did she get rid of Richard's clothes on time? If following the authors' directives was what it took then, by God, she was going to do it.

Susan was going to be a successful widow!

At the end of that week's session, Dr. Alberts had given her a mild sedative to help her sleep. She was feeling better and her appetite was starting to come back, but she still felt a little confused. "Little things just seemed beyond me, even making a decision about going to a movie. I had always liked 'junk' movies, you know, lighthearted fluff. You could say I was addicted to slapstick comedy. I would read the reviews of a new movie and think it would be just the thing to take my mind off myself. But then I would wonder, would it be appropriate for me to go to such a movie? To laugh? What would the kids say?

"I felt at sea about how to behave as a widow. After all, I'd never been one before. How was I supposed to act? Could I wear bright clothes? What was I supposed to do with my wedding band?"

Susan felt that her weekly sessions with Dr. Alberts were progressing okay, but she still wasn't sure where the therapy was taking her and how it was supposed to end. When doubts crept in, she would console herself by placing her faith in Dr. Alberts. "He's a kind man with lots of experience, so he must know what he's doing." Besides, it was nice to have someone who listened with interest as she talked about her life.

It was even nice in a way to talk about Richard. Yes, their marriage had been good. She had loved him and he had loved her. It wasn't idyllic, but whose marriage was? If she'd had to do it all over again, she would still marry Richard.

On the other hand, there were things that had been wrong. Susan had always put her needs and desires last. Richard, the kids, even the dog had come before her. No one had told her to be that way, certainly not Richard, at least not directly. But if she were to live her life all over again, she knew she wouldn't do it in exactly the same way.

Eight months had passed since Richard's death. Susan was sleeping better, was no longer having so many distressing dreams about her husband, and had given up the pills. Her friends said she was looking better, yet she knew that something was still wrong. She didn't feel complete and she was still at sea after all this time. She reread the books on the stages of grief and measured herself against where the authors said she ought to be.

Gently at first, her friends began to suggest that she get out more. Maggie invited her for dinner and introduced her to a widower slightly older than she was. Everyone said, "It's time to stop thinking about the past and look forward, to get back to a social life, to date, maybe even to consider marrying."

"My friends were telling me to turn away from the past and look toward the future. Yet once a week when I went to see Dr. Alberts, he encouraged me to look at my past. Did I have to choose between the past and the future? What would my kids think if I started dating again? And what about sex? It's been such a long time since I've been with anyone but Richard, I'm not sure I'd even know how to act."

There was no shortage of advice for Susan. Her friends offered it, her children offered it, her mother offered it. Dr. Alberts offered it once a week. The library and magazines were full of advice.

Outwardly, Susan seemed fine. In some sense she was even getting back to her life as it had been before, attending meetings of the organizations she was involved with, even planning for a trip this summer. Though she was lonely, she managed to keep busy, and she did have loving children and entertaining grandchildren. But she worried that she had grown a little more distant from her friends. She sometimes felt awkward at social gatherings, almost like a fifth wheel. It was nearly a year since Richard's death. Life was not painful, but Susan still felt confused and perplexed.

She was still struggling with two things: how to reconcile what she was learning about her past in psychotherapy and how to cope with her barely recognized, but intense, feelings of dissatisfaction and lack of fulfillment. A few months after she told me her story, she decided to terminate her therapy. By this time she was sleeping better and experiencing no major uncomfortable psychological symptoms.

When she left the therapist's comfortable chair, Susan's journey as a widow began in earnest. She decided to take an extended trip to Europe. This was something she and Richard had talked about and enthusiastically planned for their future. Now, she felt that she had to follow through with this dream to help her close a chapter of her life, the chapter of being married. Susan was, in a sense, saying good-bye.

This outer journey proved to be more important than Susan had ever anticipated. "It was the first time in my life that I was really alone," she told me. "The trip was a chance to take time out and get away from all that was familiar and comfortable to me. It was also a chance to get away from the well-meaning deluge of advice from friends and family.

"I enjoyed visiting all the places I had only read about. It was sad without Richard, and I still missed him very much, but I resolved to get on with my life. I even met some eligible men during the trip. I enjoyed flirting with them, and they made me feel like an attractive woman again. Most important, I began to think about my life without Richard. Who am I going to be? I resolved that when I went back home, I wouldn't be the same as I was before."

Being abroad without the props of her familiar world started Susan on a much more important journey, a pilgrimage toward self-discovery and the construction of a new life. For the first time since Richard had died, Susan began to envision a life without him. After three months of traveling, she returned home and began to plan her future. She apprenticed herself to an art dealer, having resolved that what she wanted most in life was to establish her own gallery. To raise the money for this venture, she put her house up for sale. Her children were intensely opposed to the idea, but Susan found the strength to put her own needs first.

While maintaining her close friendships, Susan began to develop a wider circle of people who shared her artistic interests. She also decided to remain single. "I know that for now I don't want to remarry. It was nice to realize while on my trip that I could still be attractive to men, but my priorities are to see if I can succeed in my dream, a dream I've had all my life." Susan was launched.

Susan typifies the dilemma faced by many widows in today's world. Surrounded by a morass of half-truths, good intentions, and "how-to" books, she has done all the right things and yet feels acutely unsatisfied and incomplete. She is not ill, but chose to involve herself in a course of therapy that unfortunately focused solely on her loss and grief. On the other hand, her friends see her problem as the lack of a husband. To them, the obvious solution is to find a man and remarry. These are not the only options available to widows. The pathways through loss and suffering are more varied.

The grief-loss model of widowhood is a male invention, viewed through male eyes. Until recently, the study of spousal loss was entirely dominated by male medical practitioners. In the past decade, the increasing contributions of women scientists have significantly altered the prevailing male view. Sociologist Helena Lopata demonstrated that problems in recovery were often related to stressful economic circumstances and had much less to do with the widow's inner psychological state or pattern of grieving. Psychologist Camille Wortman's studies directly challenge the notion that the failure to grieve leads to poor recovery. Overall, recent studies, which examine widows who did not seek out professional help, have made many surprising discoveries. Intense grief reactions are not universal, nor does the intensity of grieving predict the success or failure of recovery: A widow's economic security, the age of her children, and the amount of emotional help received from family and friends have a big influence upon her recovery, and ultimately, there is no "right" way to cope. A wide variety of coping strategies were all successful in overcoming the myriad of problems and challenges widows face.

The Course of Bereavement

The simplest truth is that most widows reestablish their equilibrium over time. My seven-year study provides clear documentation of this outcome. As time passes, irrespective of professional help, most widows do recover.

Within about a year of their husband's death, many women seem to show a significant decrease in the most common symptoms associated with bereavement—anxiety, depression, intensity of grief, the abuse of alcohol and drugs, and bodily complaints. When we asked widows to tell us what their most pressing issues were and to rate them according to difficulty, however, I found that their greatest problems didn't usually disappear within a year. Most widows simply felt that these difficulties had become substantially "easier" or more manageable.

The widows in my study not only developed a greater ability to cope with their most pressing problems after a year, but they also experienced a significant improvement in their ability to function in the world and in their personal lives. Most showed substantial gains in many important areas, including feelings of self-mastery, and a greater sense of well-being, self-esteem, and life satisfaction.

These changes in symptoms and functioning, however, do not necessarily reflect an overall reduction in the stresses widows experience. When I examined what widows had to say about their continuing economic difficulties, parenting problems, stigma (experiencing the negative views that others hold about widows), and the stresses of assuming the status of a single person once more, the overall picture seemed less optimistic. In fact, within a year of their husband's death, most widows experienced *increased* economic and parenting stress. On the other hand, they showed a substantial decrease in the stresses associated with the way in which their family, friends, and society viewed them (stigma) as well as a small decrease in the strain of being single. The conclusion I drew from this overall picture is that a widow's life does not become less stressful over the course of a year but that most women learn to *cope more successfully* with widowhood and its problems.

This book is the story of what 600 widows taught me about how they negotiated their lives during bereavement and recovery. As I talked to widows over the seven years of my study, I began to see that the traditional grief-loss model, the one I had believed in, did not adequately describe the depth, breadth, and truth of their experiences. This model claims that a widow's principal task is to appropriately grieve so that she can become "whole" again and that the best way for a professional to help her unlock her grief is to urge her to explore the meaning of her loss. Recovery only really occurs when the widow's life is restored to its previous status quo, and failure to recover is a result of inadequate or inappropriate grieving. This model also leans heavily toward seeing widowhood as a "pathology" that needs to be "treated." Its supporters believe that deficiencies in grieving often lead to physical and mental illness, and that many widows fail to recover and require professional help.

The life-course view sees widowhood in an entirely different manner, one that assumes that loss is a normal human passage. Grief is only one of many tasks and challenges facing widows, and the absence of protracted grief is not a sign of pathology. Because there is no "right" length of time to grieve, the successful "resolution of grief" can follow many different pathways. Recovery from bereavement is not the end point of the process. For many women, in fact, widowhood presents an opportunity for growth and meaningful life change. Most important, most widows do not require professional help in their recovery.

In the chapters that follow, using the stories and insights of the widows I studied, I will show how widowhood is one of the normal tasks of life, a difficult and painful passage, but one that also offers rich challenges and opportunities for growth.

Chapter 2

Grief

Grief is a tidal wave that overtakes you, smashes down upon you with an unimaginable force, sweeps you up into its darkness, where you tumble and crash against undefinable surfaces, only to be thrown out on an unknown beach, bruised, reshaped and unwittingly better for the wear. Grief means not being able to read more than two sentences at a time. It is walking through rooms with intentions that suddenly vanish. Grief is 3:00 A.M. sweats that won't stop. It is dreadful Sundays and Mondays that are no better. It makes you look for a face in a crowd, knowing full well, there is no such face to be found in that crowd. It humbles. It shrouds. It blackens. It enlightens. Grief will make a new person out of you, if it doesn't kill you in the making.

Stephanie Ericsson, *Utne Reader* 47
(September–October 1991): pp. 75–79.

Most widows wonder if it necessary to plumb the depths of grief in order to get back on their feet. Many professionals believe that widows must experience profound and intense grief before they can recover and that there is a sequence of mourning that *all* widows must follow. Some even describe the specific stages through which widows "progress," and propose that the failure to follow these steps jeopardizes complete recovery.

Unfortunately, this view of grief and mourning has become part of our culture, influencing the way widows, friends, families, and, above all, health care professionals look at widowhood. These practitioners frequently use a grief time line to gauge recovery, and interpret any departures from the schedule as symptoms of illness. Thus, many psychotherapists believe that if a widow grieves too quickly, she is not really experiencing her loss. If, on the other hand, she grieves too long—beyond some arbitrary point in time—she is seen as emotionally ill.

During their first year of bereavement, I asked each of the 600 widows to describe the intensity of their grief and the frequency of unwanted thoughts about death and loss. I asked them the same questions one year later, and then six years later. The answers were not what I expected.

During the first year, about twelve percent of the widows reported little or no grief and did not experience troublesome thoughts about their dead spouse. Thirty percent experienced mild grief and only occasionally had unwanted thoughts about their husbands. Forty-three percent were moderate grievers. Only fifteen percent were intense grievers, widows who suffered from a great deal of grief. Women in the latter two groups were frequently preoccupied with unwelcome thoughts about the deceased.

Based on the intensity of their grieving during the first year of widowhood, I was able to divide the women into four "grief types":

- LIMITED GRIEVERS—widows who showed little or no grief immediately following their husband's death and a year later.
- AVERAGE GRIEVERS—widows who showed high levels of grief in the period directly following the death, but demonstrated little or very mild grief one year later.
- POSTPONED GRIEVERS—women who reported little or no grief soon after the death, but demonstrated moderate to intense grief one year later.
- PROLONGED GRIEVERS—widows who showed moderate to intense grief soon after the death and at the one-year point. Among the prolonged grievers, only a very small number continued to experience intense grief for longer than three years.

To understand how grieving patterns affect the speed with which a widow passes through her bereavement, and how completely she recovers, let's look at some stories of widows. Gertrude, a limited griever, felt little or no real grief at the passing of her husband.

A Seamless Life

When Gertrude first walked into my office, she seemed a spry, somewhat reserved woman who looked a bit younger than her seventy-two years. She was conservatively dressed in a dark suit with a set of large pearls as her only adornment.

Gertrude told me that her husband, Peter, had died of cancer, at home with all his family and friends around him. She was extremely satisfied with the medical care he had received and said that she herself had never needed the help and support her husband's doctors had offered her. She seemed to take great pride in her strength and self-sufficiency during the course of his illness.

Gertrude has never worked, and her life now is indistinguishable from what it was prior to Peter's death. After attending Catholic mass every morning, she does housework and has occasional lunches with one of her female friends. She is encircled by a large and attentive family composed of seven children and numerous grandchildren. A divorced daughter and her children live with her, and others live close by. It's clear that the center of Gertrude's life, both before and after Peter's death, is the family, whom she sees daily.

When I asked Gertrude to tell me about her life with Peter, she described a marriage that was not unhappy but did not seem very intimate or emotionally passionate: "I was married for forty-eight years, and most of those years were happy ones. Peter was a highly successful lawyer, and I am very proud of him. I'd say that we had a good but limited marriage. We never fought and maybe that was unfortunate, because we were poor communicators.

"Peter and I never talked about his illness and impending death;

in fact, we never really talked about anything that seemed personally important. We were not what you'd call a loving, hugging couple. My life was totally focused on my family. When Peter died, I didn't cry very much, perhaps only a few tears at the funeral. Though I've been to visit his grave four times, I didn't have any particular feelings during those visits."

When I asked Gertrude whether she had any regrets about her life with Peter, she seemed a bit sad and thoughtful: "We were never close, and that makes me feel that I missed something. Not that I think I married the wrong man, mind you. Our first ten years together were very good. And after things cooled down, I can't say that I particularly missed the sex. I'm like one of those women in Ann Landers's column who miss the hugging and kissing more than anything else."

Would she go back and change any part of her life if she could? "I'd pay more attention to the physical side of marriage," she said, but went on to assure me that she did feel fulfilled in her life: "When I was younger, there really weren't a lot of alternatives for women, and having a large family and seeing them grow up was the most important thing for me. I'm fulfilled with my sons and daughters and can hardly wait to have more grandchildren. I certainly don't plan to remarry!"

When I asked Gertrude if she was lonely, she laughed and said that she didn't have time for such feelings: "My family is always around, and I'm always busy doing things with them. Something is going on every day. I might go to dinner at one daughter's home or drop in for pizza at another's. Or a bunch of us will all have a big breakfast together. Although I spend some of my evenings alone, I'm not troubled by that. I still go to affairs and cocktail parties with my married friends, and I don't feel any concern about being the only single person there. But most of my time is spent with my family.

"I do go out occasionally with Linda and Barbara, who have been my friends for years, but we never talk about personal things. I wouldn't think of telling them my problems! I'm sure they'd listen, but I wouldn't want to burden them. I'm not that kind of person—

never have been. My faith in God is very important to me, and that gives me all the solace and support I need."

Gertrude's life seems unbroken to her, flowing on in exactly the same manner as it did before Peter's death. She certainly doesn't feel alone and reports no symptoms of anxiety, depression, or somatic problems. If anything, she's becoming a bit more independent than she was before and is beginning to take over some of the tasks that Peter did. When her children tried to relieve her from worry by taking care of her finances and taxes, she insisted that she was perfectly capable of learning how to manage herself and told them that they should stop being concerned. She told me, "I'm learning I can manage my money alone, and that makes me feel good about myself."

One year later when I interviewed Gertrude again, her life was virtually unaltered. She said she felt happy and had no physical or emotional problems. Morning church attendance and family were still the two touchstones of her being, and she didn't feel lonely because she was never alone. Her views of her marriage have also remained pretty much the same. Although she told me that she regrets that she and her husband weren't more emotionally intimate, she was quick to add that Peter was a great man whom she really loved and respected. Gertrude feels strongly that she got what she wanted out of life—a large loving and caring family.

Gertrude's life is a seamless tapestry, and Peter's death neither shattered nor interrupted her remarkable sense of continuity. She summed up her marriage in the following manner: "Peter and I had a good and long life together. By and large, it was satisfying. Other people might see our marriage as unexciting and unfulfilling, and to some extent that was true, but we had no major ups or downs. I'm grateful for that because I'm the kind of person who appreciates stability."

Gertrude's grieving was neither profound nor lengthy. She has strong ideas about who she is and a firm view of what is most important in her life. Peter's death did not disrupt the main focus of her existence. Pain is not a part of her current experience, nor does she have any agenda for growth or the discovery of a new self.

Many women, like Gertrude, continue on the same path they have traveled for many years, secure in their world view. Some widows, as we shall see in a later chapter, take a very different course. They invest considerable time and effort in reexamining their lives. Though that exploration is often painful, these women are willing to endure the cost because they know that growth and development are important goals.

A Short, Sharp Grief

Anna, a forty-two-year-old widow, is also a limited griever. Unlike Gertrude, however, she did not recover by maintaining the happy status quo. Anna illustrates a different path to recovery—resolution by early remarriage.

Dressed in comfortable slacks and a bulky knit sweater, Anna spoke softly, but her participation in our dialogue was full and enthusiastic. She told me how she felt when Lou, her husband of fifteen years, died unexpectedly of a heart attack.

"I was in absolute shock—total disbelief. I was so numb for the first three weeks that I can barely remember what went on. Even my recollection of the funeral is blurred. I felt as if I weren't really part of the world anymore. Anytime other people were around, I couldn't seem to focus on what they were saying. My life became a large void, and I had absolutely no interest in anything. It was as if the world had become a moving picture on a screen, something out there that was not a part of me. I just watched it go by, but I couldn't care less about what was happening.

"My mother really helped me through this period. A few friends were right there after Lou died, but they were only semihelpful. They floated in and out, sometimes calling when they said they would and other times not calling at all. What helped me most was just having somebody with me. They didn't necessarily have to talk to me or do things for me. I just needed someone there, a warm body who would be responsive and simply present.

"After a while, though, many of my friends began to fade, probably because I was so totally uninterested in doing anything or carrying on a normal life. I think I scared them away.

"About the only thing I really remember doing was attending church once a week. That's where I met Tom, who was also a widower. At first I wasn't at all interested in him. Getting involved with another man was the farthest thing from my mind, but Tom was persistent. He continued to come around and just be there for me. Bit by bit as I became more interested in him, I began to get more involved with life again. He was anxious to get married and I began to feel that maybe it was best thing for me too."

Anna's voice got quiet. "I really didn't love him, but a few of my friends were enthusiastic about my marrying Tom. 'You'll learn to love him,' they said. 'He's so kind and thoughtful and he's really fond of you.' But most of my friends warned me that it was too soon, that I was rushing into things too quickly and needed more time to absorb the shock.

"As I think back now, I can see that it was my married friends who were pushing me to get married, and my widowed friends who were cautioning me against making such a fast move. Fortunately, my mother said she'd support whatever I did. So I took the leap and jumped into marriage, and I don't have any reservations about what I did!"

Anna no longer felt grief or sadness, but she seemed to have traded those feelings for new problems. For one thing, her eleven-year-old daughter, Clara, was not willing to accept Tom as a father: "Clara is very rebellious and feels resentful of his being in the house, but she won't talk to me about it. Most of the time she's sullen and uncommunicative. She comes down from her room for supper and then goes back upstairs. I don't think she ever looks directly at Tom, and they hardly ever exchange words. Tom tries, but Clara won't give him a chance."

Though Anna admitted that the situation was painful for her, she was also sure that she had made the right choice: "After all, I have a life to lead. I can only hope that, eventually, Clara will come around."

Anna managed her recovery by investing in a comfortable but passionless new marriage. Afterward, her grief evaporated; she felt no unrequited longings and experienced no regrets. Her problems with Clara clouded her happiness, yet, despite them, she seemed content with her new life. Unfortunately she moved soon after our talk and I was unable to find out whether her contentment continued.

Anna's pattern of "limiting" grief by a new relationship is one that widowers choose more often than widows. This strategy is not without its pitfalls. Individuals who fall into an early remarriage often appear to escape their pain, but their relief may be short-lived. Some do very well, continuing to feel content with their new arrangement. Others, however, find that the guilt and regrets they experience will interfere with the work required to develop their new relationship into a productive and satisfying partnership. I will discuss the pros and cons of remarriage in greater detail later in this book.

Profound Grief and Recovery

The average griever experiences profound disruption and grief during the first year of her loss, but subsequently shows marked recovery.

Julia was a tall, thin woman who instantly took command of our interview. The mother of five children, she now lives alone. She was widowed suddenly at age fifty-six when her husband, John, dropped dead from a heart attack. His death was a total surprise to everyone. Two weeks earlier, he had had a complete medical evaluation that indicated that his heart was in fine shape. Julia couldn't believe his death, and she continued to feel bewildered and shocked for months afterward.

"I was in a stunned state for at least six months," she told me. "I just couldn't accept the fact that John was dead. I walked around feeling as if I had been hit over the head by a baseball bat.

"Looking back at that time, I think I woke up from this daze only gradually. I realized that I had to make up my mind about what to do with the rest of my life, that things weren't going to change. My grief wouldn't bring John back, and my solitude wouldn't change anything either. Nothing would bring him back! It took me some time to understand this, and for most of the first year, I did very little except sit at home in the evenings and feel very sorry for myself. Thank God for my job. My teaching kept me very busy.

"Finally I decided that life was going to pass me by unless I did something about it. At that point I got involved in everything I could. John and I had belonged to a lot of organizations together. After he died, I sort of dropped out. Now I joined several church groups, a couple of bridge groups, and went bowling once a week. I didn't stay home very often, but I resolved that if I had to come home to an empty house, so be it. I'd do what I could to keep myself involved with life.

"Of course I still miss John very much, but the feeling is no longer overwhelming. I've made up my mind that he may be gone, but that my life is going to go on. I still feel the pain when I think about him. When I'm with my children and they reminisce about the happy times we all spent together, it's very pleasant. When I am alone and think about him, though, I still get sad. I wish he was still here."

I asked Julia what her most pressing problem had been right after John's death. "That's not hard to answer," she told me. "Coming home at night from work and not having him there was terrible. I dreaded the night and going to bed because I had trouble getting to sleep. I'd stay up until midnight or one o'clock, even though I had to get up very early the next morning. This went on for almost a year and then gradually it eased up."

When I asked her what helped, she answered, "My strong desire to start to deal with it, to realize that what I was feeling as a widow was a normal thing, that I couldn't feel sorry for myself forever. I couldn't just dwell on only the bad things, I had to start moving forward again. After this terrible time, my biggest problem was loneliness. There are places I don't go because I'm single.

"There have been times since John died when I thought that I would never have a really fulfilling life again. But I decided that, if I couldn't be happy, at least I could be a contented person, satisfied with my life. Maybe I will never be totally happy again, but I want to be in the world as a living person."

I asked her if she had any helpful advice for the newly widowed. "Yes, go out and get involved with other people and quit feeling sorry for yourself. You can make a good life for yourself but you need to take the initiative. Tell your friends and family not to clam up or freeze. They need to allow, genuinely allow, us to talk, to reminisce, and to grieve openly with them. They should not try and stop that process because that will just make us withdraw even more."

Julia illustrates the pattern of the average griever. At first she was overwhelmed by an intense grief that blocked her from moving ahead. Slowly, during the first year of her widowhood, she crossed a threshold and made a deliberate effort to pull herself back to life. She unequivocally reengaged with life, successfully overcoming the barriers created by her intense sadness.

Six years later, Julia had progressed from being a person who hoped she could at least be "content with life if not happy" to a woman who looked forward to each day with zest for all that life could offer her. She still misses John, but her sadness is completely integrated into her life, and widowhood is no longer a barrier to fulfillment. When she decided that teaching elementary school was no longer meaningful to her, she went back to school and completed an M.A. in business, explaining, "I'm a good teacher, but I needed something else in my life." She now has a stimulating job as an insurance investigator, new friendships, and an active social life. She dates occasionally but does not see herself as needing a new husband. "If the right man came along, I might reconsider my decision, but I'm not holding my breath. My life is packed with work, friends, and my family. I really have accomplished a lot in the last six years."

Putting Grief Out of Your Mind

Helen is a postponed griever, a widow who put off her grieving for the future. One morning, in her fortieth year, Helen suddenly and unexpectedly found herself widowed. The day had started out like any other ordinary winter day. Her husband, Albert, had left for his truck route a couple of hours before, and she had gotten her two adolescent daughters off to school. As she sat relaxing with her second cup of coffee, feeling content and pleased with her life, there was a knock at the door.

"I asked myself, who could that be? My neighbors rarely called so early. When I answered the door, it was Albert's boss come to tell me that Albert had been in a terrible accident. I called the police immediately, and they told me that Albert and his helper were alive, so I still had hope. Before going to the hospital, I called my mother and Tracy, my best girlfriend, and asked them to come over and take care of the children when they came home from school."

When Helen arrived at the hospital, an ambulance had brought Albert's helper in, but her husband didn't appear. "Even then I didn't really think that he could be dead. I just figured that he was terribly pinned in the wreck and that it was taking them a long time to get him out. After about an hour of this terrible waiting, my minister came to the hospital and told me that Albert hadn't made it. I started to scream, 'It's not true. I'm only forty. That's too young to be a widow.' I tried to see Albert when they finally wheeled him in. I wanted to go to him and say good-bye, to see him one last time, but they wouldn't let me because his body had been too badly damaged. After that, my minister took me home.

"When I got there, friends and relatives started to arrive. As all these people sort of shuffled through, all I could do was sob my heart out. The first thing I remember was my son asking me whether we would be able to keep the house. I also remember telling myself out loud, 'Okay God. You've done this to me. You've taken him away. I don't understand why. I won't question you, but now you have to take care of me and my kids.'

"It was strange, but after that first terrible day I felt at peace within myself. This feeling lasted about six months. During this time I did think about Albert's helper, Bob. He survived the wreck but had serious brain damage and was never the same. Though I knew it was ridiculous and that I wasn't to blame, I couldn't stop feeling guilty. I knew that, if Albert had lived, he would have been terribly upset about what he'd done to this friend of his. I guess I carried Albert's guilt because he wasn't here to feel guilty.

"I couldn't even decently bury Albert. You may not know this, but if you live in Montana, they can't bury people in the winter because the ground is frozen. When spring came, I could finally say good-bye to him. After the burial much of my sense of peace was gone. Now that Albert was really buried and gone, I should have felt relief, like I was closing a door behind me. Looking back now, I know that I wouldn't, couldn't admit that he was never coming back.

"After the funeral, I started running, blocking out his death. I began dating and leaving the kids home by themselves a lot. I couldn't even clean the place because every time I was alone in the house more than an hour I'd break down and cry. I had trouble sleeping, so I learned to get by on very little. My life was out of control. I didn't know what I was doing and I don't know to this day how I survived that horrible summer. I just knew that I wanted to be without responsibility. I wanted to be free and have somebody else take care of me. I didn't want to grieve and I wasn't going to! I couldn't allow myself to do any really hard thinking.

"The sense of peace that I'd had since Albert's death was shattered that summer. My mother refers to it as my 'goofy' time. I think the only thing that kept me from falling completely over the edge was all the wonderful people around me. Tracy, my closest friend, was super. Her husband worked a job that took him away from home during the week, so she would come over two or three nights a week. Lots of other people kept calling me, and I was also very busy with my son Johnny's hockey team. There were over 500 people at Albert's funeral. A lot of people were concerned and tried to help. My mom was particularly supportive.

"What bothered me at first was being alone. I handled it well during the first six months by reading a lot. I was frightened about how my life was going to be from now on. Could I do a good job raising my teenagers by myself? I read everything I could to try and comfort myself and to show myself that I could learn how to cope. After I finally buried Albert, my worries changed. The question I began asking myself, plain and simple, was how could I survive? Eventually I stopped running around so much and began to stay home. But I still wasn't dealing with my grief, in many ways I was still blocking it."

Almost a full year after Albert died, Helen began a dramatic journey that turned her life around. It began with a religious retreat: "I decided to go on a weekend retreat that my church was having for the divorced, the separated, and the widowed. The point was to spend a lot of time reflecting, renewing your relationship with God, dealing with death, and just being together in communion with your fellow people. I came away from that weekend a changed person. Before, my life had been empty and was going nowhere. When I found God again, I also found a purpose for my life and received strength. When I came home from the weekend and talked about it with my best friend, she said, 'You still have a long way to go, but for the first time you're happy about something again.'

"Looking back, I realize that I hadn't really grieved for Albert. All that running around was a way to avoid my feelings. I told myself that talking about Albert was a waste of time. Boy, was I kidding myself. When I finally began to let out my feelings, I talked and talked to everybody, all the time. Thank God, they let me talk."

When I asked Helen if she had any suggestions or advice for other widows, she responded forcefully, "Oh yes! First of all, let out more emotions. I had to be strong for my kids and didn't want to burden anybody with my grief. I was afraid that really showing my emotions would scare people, but I was wrong. Widows shouldn't just talk about their grief, they should cry and cry. I didn't do enough of that during the first year. Also, people should talk to each other about what to do when someone dies. Everybody is afraid of death in our culture, so nobody is prepared. If somebody had told me when I was forty years old that I should start making plans for my husband's death or my own, I would have laughed in their faces. But death can come into our lives at any point.

"My final suggestion is that people should realize that time is the best healer and that the healing process can't be rushed. I thought I would feel better after one year, but I didn't. It took me at least two years before I really felt like I was beginning to recover. Now, even after two and a half years, there's still grief and pain. I feel all right most of the time, but people shouldn't expect that everything is going to go right back to where it was in short order."

The next time I saw Helen was almost seven years after Albert's death. Buoyant and animated, she felt satisfied with who she was and how things had turned out. Life had obviously been good to her. She told me that she had never expected, during that awful first year, to feel this good again. Her horizons had expanded, and she was now doing things she had never thought herself capable of. She had undertaken a demanding career in the computer industry and was doing quite well.

Helen's healing process is instructive. Her initial avoidance of feelings about Albert's death clearly postponed her recovery. She denied her grief, hiding it from both herself and others. Above all she felt terror when she contemplated life without her husband. It was only when Helen was finally able to honor her own feelings that her healing began. Seven years later, I found a delightful woman living a richly textured life.

These stories demonstrate how varied are the pathways to recovery. Advice from family, friends, or doctors based on the supposition that there is only one "right" way to grieve is no help. The lives of these widows underscore the extraordinary and often unpredictable by-ways widows take on the road to recovery.

Is intense and protracted grief necessary for recovery? Absolutely not. In fact, my interviews with widows revealed that in many cases the opposite was true. Over the seven years of the study, widows who demonstrated little or brief episodes of grief (limited grief) often did the best. These findings do not fit the expectations of the loss-grief view of widowhood: that intense and prolonged grief is required for recovery. Of course not all limited grievers are identical. Some showed little initial grief after the loss. Others exhibited an "interrupted" grief pattern. Still others manifested intense but very short-lived grief lasting somewhere between a few weeks and several months. For some limited grievers, a new relationship took the place of the old one. Whatever the process, these women adjusted to their loss fairly successfully early in widowhood and maintained that adjustment over seven years. The idea that there is only one right way to grieve and one correct route to recovery has no foundation in reality.

The course of bereavement for average grievers most closely matches our commonsense expectations. These women felt intense grief early on in widowhood, but their mourning had significantly decreased within a year. Several years after their husbands' death, their recovery and adaptation were complete.

Some widows, the prolonged grievers, became emotionally "stuck," finding it difficult to extricate themselves from the spiral of grief. These women suffered for a much longer time after their husbands' death. Over time, however, most eventually achieved a modest recovery.

The last type of widows, postponed grievers, were those who

closed off their feelings early on. Later they became overwhelmed with grief and had to struggle to finally accept the loss. After a lengthy period—averaging two years— however, most of these women were able to achieve a reasonable balance in their lives.

Widowhood is not an illness from which some recover and others do not, nor should society equate widowhood only with loss. To fully appreciate what it means to be a widow, we need to look at the challenges facing these women in contemporary society and to help them navigate the uncharted waters.

There is no one way to mourn. Loss is real and intense. Gertrude's seamless life, Anna's short sharp grief and her remarriage, Julia's profound grief and her subsequent excellent recovery and growth, and Helen's choice to put grief out of her mind for a year all "worked" as strategies for recovery. Not all of these women ended up in the same place, however. Gertrude and Julia recovered the most fully. Both women achieved comfortable and meaningful lives, although each reached her equilibrium along a very different path. Anna and Helen did reasonably well, although Helen's recovery took longer and was more difficult. Anna traded one problem for another.

Does the intensity and length of grieving affect the subsequent mental health and well-being of the widow? I answered this question by examining each "grief type" and comparing two factors: the intensity of symptoms and the adjustment level. Each widow was interviewed directly after the loss, one year later, and seven years later. I defined "intensity of symptoms" as changes in levels of anxiety, depression, substance abuse, health, and bodily complaints over the course of widowhood. The "adjustment" issues I examined involved levels of self-esteem, feelings of mastery, and life satisfaction. Together, symptoms and adjustment are the prime indicators of recovery.

There is no question that different patterns of grieving have profound consequences for both the speed and the completeness of recovery. Regardless of their grief pattern, however, the vast majority of widows did improve over seven years. Limited and average grievers recover fully over time and differ only in the speed of their improvement. One year after their husband's death they were neither depressed nor anxious, nor did they abuse alcohol to alter their moods. Their health was good. In short, when compared to those of women who were not widowed, at the one-year mark the symptoms of the average and limited grievers were indistinguishable. They had, moreover, increased their self-esteem, feelings of mastery, and life satisfaction. Although the postponed and prolonged grievers showed improvement in the year following their husband's death, they rarely reached the level of recovery shown by the first two types. If we examine the same indices of recovery seven years later, however, almost all widows, regardless of type, show marked recovery.

What makes for these differences among widows? Why do some quickly grieve and rapidly recover while others are mired in a seemingly endless recapitulation of their loss? This question will be explored in Chapter 4.

Chapter 3

The First Six Months

$\mathbf{T}$he new widow is immediately plunged into uncharted territory. The challenge of moving from being part of a couple to becoming single is daunting. Everyone needs guideposts to help master new, strange circumstances. People typically look to those around them—family, friends, professionals, and the media—for help. Unfortunately, there are few *authentic and reliable* guidelines in our culture for becoming a widow, and women must often struggle alone with complex questions during the course of their grieving. Frequently, people on whom the widow counts for help are seriously misguided, harboring attitudes and beliefs about widowhood that are distinctly unhelpful. The first part of this chapter examines cultural attitudes toward widowhood and their impact on recovery as well as how well-meaning advice from family and friends can go wrong.

One of the most pressing and important questions I have asked widows is: In what areas do most widows really need guidance after the death of their spouse? The women I interviewed were most concerned about the following issues:

- How should I mourn?
- How long should I mourn?

- What is appropriate behavior for a widow?
- What should I do with the belongings of my deceased spouse?
- How should I address the discomfort of others while I am attempting to deal with my own very real pain and confusion?
- How much of my sadness and hurt is it healthy to let my children see?
- How can I help my children mourn when I myself am having so much trouble coping with grief?
- What do I do about men? Dating?
- Who am I? A widow? A single woman?

Though widows need help with facing the challenges of their new lives, their questions often have no simple answers. This confusion is compounded by the advice and help offered by family, friends, professionals, and the media. The "myths" about widowhood, those powerful collective messages about how widows should be acting and feeling at each stage of grief, often confuse and hinder them. How do the opinions of those close to them and of the "experts" influence a widow's recovery and comfort? And how can family and friends learn to be more sensitive to a widow's *real* needs and issues?

Many of the widows I talked to often felt burdened by cultural expectations of behavior and professional timetables for grieving. Like Susan in the first chapter, some of these women have tried hard to "do the right thing" and be a "successful" widow. The viewpoints of others can become an added burden to the widow as she grapples with the many problems confronting her. Meaningful guideposts are few, and so it is all the more likely that how she negotiates her passage will be heavily influenced by the thoughts, attitudes, and behavior of the culture.

Over the centuries, society's attitude toward widows has run the gamut from respect to distrust. Whether widows were given "special" status and freedoms greater than those accorded married or single women, or whether widows were treated as people who were alienated and bereft, society has always held tremendous power to define a widow's identity and actions. The following example describes two extremes, the golden age of widowhood in medieval times and the dark age of widowhood in Europe's early modern period:

> Widowhood was an ambiguous status in medieval culture. On the one hand, it was regarded as a stage in a woman's life that endowed her with a potential for special grace. . . . On the other hand, widowhood was regarded as a state that freed women to act on the wanton, whorish, and unprincipled tendencies ascribed to women in general. . . . At the heart of many of the ambiguities of medieval widowhood was the perception—if not the reality—that widows had more options than either married or single women. . . .
>
> In many parts of early modern Europe laws specifically singled out the widow for regulation, significantly modifying her authority and rights. . . . In early modern European literature, the image of the proverbial "merry" widow competed with the widow as sadly alienated from her society. Widows, in many works of the period, were portrayed as bereft not only of husbands, but of beauty, wealth and friends.
>
> Louise Mirrer, *Upon My Husband's Death:*
> *Widows in the Literature and Histories of Medieval Europe*
> (U. Mich. Press, Ann Arbor: 1992).

Our modern attitude toward widows is all too clear. Despite the respect for freedom, initiative, and rugged individuality that America prides itself on, widows are by and large believed to be sad and dejected, impoverished in spirit and sustenance, and, worst of all, dangerous and powerless. Here are two examples of what the popular media have to say about widows:

The image of a widow is that of someone who is over-the-hill, pathetic, pitiful, and dependent," said Lynn Caine, "and yet one widow out of four is under the age of 45."

"When my husband died," said one widow, "my kids kept saying, you had a good marriage, but now Dad is gone and you have to get on with your life. I resented being treated as if I had fallen down, skinned my knee, and was refusing to get up. I knew I had to get on with my life, and I did, eventually. But I had to do it in my own way."

Sandy Horowitz, "How to Say the Right Thing,"
Reader's Digest 134 (March 1989): pp 161–65.

An excellent example of the power of society's views about what constitutes "appropriate" behaviors and feelings for widows was voiced by Jill, a fifty-eight-year-old widow. Jill had joined a widow support group in the months since I had last seen her. This decision surprised me because she had often said, "I'm not the kind of person who feels comfortable in groups." The reason behind her change of mind had a powerful effect on me, sensitizing me to an issue I had not yet paid enough attention to in my work: the potential tyranny of the attitudes of friends, family, and coworkers toward widows. What Jill deeply appreciated about her support group was that it provided a setting where she did not have to "be a widow" as defined by her social world. In her own words, "The support group is not only helpful, it's the only place I can laugh."

Attitudes toward women are changing radically, and there is reason to hope that society's archaic view of widowhood is changing as well. The increasing economic achievements of women, the expansion of career roles, and the closing of the education gap will alter beliefs about widows in the future. The empowerment many widows are creating for themselves in today's world is clearly echoed in the lives of many of the women described in this book. Widows are moving toward a new, more assertive self-image. The fact that many of the women I interviewed have made growth and change their priority, rather than a return to the status quo, also signals the changing status of widows.

How Do the Attitudes of Friends and Family Affect Recovery?

When I asked each widow to describe how her family, friends, and professionals regarded widows in general, I found that societal attitudes fell into four general categories: negative stereotyping of widows, feelings of discomfort around widows, widows' need for advice about how to resolve grief, and admonitions about marriage and the need for remarriage. To discover how many widows internalized these views, I provided each woman with a list of characterization statements and asked her to indicate whether or not she agreed with these views on widowhood.

Negative Stereotypes

The most common visions of widows are covered by four statements: Widows are always mourning; it is disrespectful to the dead for widows to have fun; widows are emotionally unstable and present a threat to their friends' marriages; and widows have low moral standards.

Obviously, these statements do not present a very flattering or encouraging picture, but they are often the mirrors held up to grief. They are all the more damaging since there is a substantial relationship between the beliefs and attitudes widows see in their friends and family and how they go on to handle their bereavement and recovery. The widows who internalize these images show significantly poorer recovery. They are more likely to use alcohol and tranquilizers to relieve tension; they suffer from more anxiety and depression, and they have fewer feelings of well-being, self-esteem, and control. These women also suffer from more intense grieving and general frustration at being pushed into confining negative roles.

Feelings of Discomfort Around Widows

Another widespread belief about widows is that "they are uncomfortable to be around," as if their grief has somehow cut them off from the rest of humanity. Most people in our culture are afraid of death and try to think about it as little as possible. Because of this fear, there is a general lack of knowledge about widows. People treat women differently when they find out their spouse has died, as if they can see the Grim Reaper peeking over the widow's shoulder. Even relatives feel uncomfortable around widows. These attitudes make it even harder for a widow to reconnect with family and friends.

Advice About Mourning and Grief

When faced with the immensity of grief, family and loved ones often resort to platitudes and advice aimed at getting a widow back to normal and reintegrated into society as quickly as possible. Some of these platitudes include the following: You should take your mind off your problems; you need to keep busy; you should stop thinking about your spouse all the time; and you should be as independent as possible.

This advice shortchanges the grieving process and limits growth. It completely negates the way a widow feels, her struggle to redefine herself as an unmarried person, and her need for emotional support from those around her. Widows cannot make their grief go away by "not thinking about it" or "keeping busy." Maybe a widow doesn't feel independent; maybe she feels as if she will fall apart if she doesn't have people to lean on. Maybe she won't be ready to go forward or know who she wants to become until she has spent hundreds of hours thinking about her spouse and the pluses and minuses of their lives together. The course of individual grieving must come from within, and no two widows will ever respond to their loss in exactly the same way.

Views About Marriage

Society also holds many conflicting views about marriage, and it is no wonder widows become confused and discouraged as they try to sort out what these viewpoints mean to them. Some of the attitudes family and friends have toward marriage include the following: Married women have little freedom to do as they please; married people are happier than the widowed; widows can have a full life without remarrying; widows are more independent than married women.

Widows who internalize society's view that married people are always happier than women who have lost their spouse tend to have a poorer recovery. In contrast, those who share the beliefs that widows can have a full life without remarrying are usually more independent and recover faster and more successfully.

A Widow Who Saw Herself in Cultural Stereotypes

Sophie, a fifty-three-year-old widow feels a great sense of stigma and alienation. She has bought into society's worst projections about widowhood.

"When you're a widow, you're different. You feel uncomfortable when you go anywhere in public, as if you stick out in a crowd. I can hardly even go to family gatherings anymore. Recently, when I was invited to my nephew's wedding, the whole experience was just too painful. All I could do was think about my husband.

"Widows are different. That's why I could never join a widow support group. I would feel as if I were going there to meet a widower! I have no desire whatsoever to meet or associate with other widows or widowers. The thought of remarrying nauseates me. There's no place in my life for another man and, in fact, there's not much place for widows in the world.

"When widows go out and try and establish a social life, especially with the opposite sex, they're competing with divorced people. I hate that—it makes me feel so ashamed, as if I were a loser. I don't even really enjoy going out with women, because it looks as if you're just spending time with other women as an excuse to look for a man.

"Being widowed means being alone. You might as well be an 'old maid.' Widowers have it easier than widows, that's for sure. They are always getting remarried. As for me, I still wear my wedding ring. If people know that I'm a widow, they're going to think that I'm looking, and I don't want them to think that."

Sadly, Sophie has taken up a number of our society's worst stereotypes about widows. She sees all widows (including, unfortunately, herself) as possessing these traits. She is frozen in time, wanting the warmth and understanding of others, yet fearful about accepting it, lest they misunderstand her motivation. Because Sophie firmly believes that widows are uncomfortable to be with, she avoids the very contact and warmth she desperately wants.

The Challenge of
Becoming Single Again

Foremost among the dilemmas faced by women during the first six months of widowhood is the question of identity. They ask themselves, "Who am I—a widow, a single person, or someone who is still married?" Finding an answer to "Who am I?" is such a long and complex process that I have devoted an entire chapter to it. Here I consider only one common issue, the widow's new identity as a single person.

Developing a Single Identity

A widow must move from the psychological space of thinking of herself as married to thinking of herself as being single again. What to do with the wedding band is a poignant example of the myriad choice points on the road to a new, single identity. A group of widows in a support group shared their thoughts with me about this issue. Although each woman found a different solution, they all agreed that after their husband's death, they were distressed and perplexed about what to do with their rings. For many women the clearest symbol of her marital status resides in that ring. When the women in the group became single again, each one had to go through the agony of deciding how to deal with that symbol.

Linda, a thirty-seven-year-old who had been widowed for two years, told me that some days she wore her ring on her left hand and some days on her right. Francis had different thoughts on this issue. Though she had been widowed only half as long as Linda, she felt that widows needed to acknowledge their "I-ness": "Since we are, in reality, no longer married," she said, "it's better to move the ring to the right hand as a sign of recognition that we are single once more." For Murial, a recently widowed sixty-four-year-old, keeping her wedding band on her left hand for now was important: "I feel comforted just looking at my wedding band. It's a reminder of the love that Joe felt for me."

The length of time that has elapsed since the death has nothing to do with the woman's willingness to embrace herself as a single person again. Each woman, in her own way, struggles with how and when she is willing to let go of the idea of being married, and each moves along the path of healing at her own unique pace. I think every woman did the appropriate thing for herself. Each believes that she has to move on eventually and completely accept the fact of being single, but how she is going to do it, and when, is a personal choice for her.

Finding a Model

To whom can a widow look as she struggles to move from seeing herself as a married woman to being single? Women whose lives during the past thirty to fifty years have been imbedded in marriage and family life find the transition daunting. Whose experience will provide ideas and pathways for her? As she scans her world, three images present themselves. She can easily locate women of her generation who have undergone a divorce and are struggling with what appear to be similar issues. But all the widows I talked to found that their experience was different from the divorced, that their friends' stories were not helpful. The core experience in many divorces is rejection, leading to intense feelings of anger, so that divorced women experience low self-esteem and struggle with issues regarding their womanhood. Not so for the typical widow.

Many of the widows I talked with called up their long-ago memories of being single young women. Most of the time, they all too vividly recollected the fears, insecurities, and awkwardness of that time. They ask themselves in dismay, "Is that what it means to be single again?" For the mature woman who has lived a life full of challenges, raised children, and dealt with the many vagaries of adulthood over the years, the prospect of being single "like I used to be" is unacceptable.

When a widow looks at single women she knows, most of them are likely to be her daughter's age. No wonder then that the struggle to embrace the role of a single woman is so daunting. Most of the widows in my study found that only another widow could provide a suitable model.

How difficult is this struggle? When I began my study of the problems of singlehood, I asked each widow to describe the difficulties she was faced with as she moved toward thinking of herself in this new light, both shortly after the loss and then again one year later. On a scale of "never" to "very often," I asked them to describe how often they (1) feel out of place, (2) have fun, (3) feel fearful of going out, (4) have people to talk to, (5) share experiences, (6) fear not being interesting, and (7) do not have the kind of sex life they would prefer.

Eight out of ten widows experience difficulty with at least one aspect of singleness soon after the death of her husband. One year later, that number was substantially reduced. The experiences most commonly reported as difficult are: (1) feeling out of place, (2) not having opportunities to have fun, (3) not knowing how to manage her life as a sexual person, and (4) having no one to share with. Most, though certainly not all, widows experienced the transition from married to single as very difficult. But the news is not all bad. Even for those who did experience problems living as a single woman, after the first year many of them were feeling much more comfortable. The difficulties of moving into singleness do recede, gradually, with time and experience. When I asked the women what helped, most told me of specific episodes that involved talking the problems over or seeing how others dealt with them. Critical help came from friends as well as the widow's mother, who had passed through a similar problem. The prime source of help was other widows, who helped to put the transition into perspective. They provided a new way of looking at their particular problems.

The Final Good-bye

For many women, an important milestone of moving from a "we" to an "I" is saying a final good-bye to her husband. This farewell is often symbolized by the question of how and when to dispose of his personal belongings. Some widows are able to do this within a week. Others may actually keep most of their husband's effects after as much as five years. But most women find that disposing of the belongings is not done in one step, but is accomplished piecemeal over a protracted period of time. Clothes are usually the first to go.

Several widows from a support group shared their experiences with me. Margaret solved her problem by giving "some of my husband's clothes to my sons. It makes me feel good when I see them wearing them." Rose, on the other hand, gave some to her brother-in-law: "I had no feelings about this at the time, but now when I see him in those clothes, I always think, 'George looked so much better in them than you do.'"

Many widows agonize over what to keep, what to throw out, and whom to give them to. But these strong feelings paled in comparison to the pain of disposing of their trophies and mementos. These were the most difficult objects to give up. Roberta told me how bad she felt when she considered giving away her husband's golf trophies: "I never liked them. They always cluttered up our living room, but now that he's gone, I can't bring myself to pack them up. They are still in their places of honor in the display cases."

Creating a New Social Life

Being single after so many years in a coupled world is extremely difficult. Many widows feel as if there is no one for them to talk to at social gatherings: "You feel as if you're a fifth wheel." The most difficult part of the struggle, however, comes from not being able to tell whether the discomfort they feel around their coupled friends comes from the outside, or from within themselves. It is often difficult for a widow to know if her friends are ostracizing her, or if she is the one imagining the feeling of being "unwanted." This uneasiness is an additional problem, added to the fact that reentering the usual social world as a single woman is never easy.

After the early mourning period is over, many widows feel a sense of distance, at times almost alienation, from their families and friends. For some women, this feeling is enhanced by the differences they perceive between their level of grief and the grief of others. Everyone else seems to be getting back to "normal." She just can't yet, but worries that if she doesn't, her friends and family will eventually drift away. Many counteract this fear by developing a network of single friends and new contacts.

How a widow handles her feelings of distress when she no longer feels comfortable around her old friends has a marked impact on the quality of her recovery. Two widows, Elaine and Wilma, shared their stories with me.

Elaine, a forty-eight-year-old mother of three adolescents, described her disappointment: "Len and I were friends with several couples whom we saw regularly, mostly at their houses since ours was so filled with kids and commotion all the time. After Len died, I tried visiting my old friends, but it became extremely uncomfortable for me, and I think for them as well. Finally, after a few of these terrible visits, I had a frank talk with my closest friends. We cried a lot, but we were also able to admit to each other that everyone really *was* uneasy during these get-togethers. They told me that their husbands felt uncomfortable staying in the room and talking to me, since the wives and husbands used to separate when we visited. After Len's death, when I came over, the husbands had nobody to talk to. When I went to dances with my friends, I hated to sit by myself. If one of their husbands asked me to dance, I couldn't enjoy it even though I love dancing. I kept feeling that I was in competition with my friends.

"The more I thought about the situation, the more I realized that I needed to find a new social circle for myself, to develop friends who are single. It hasn't been easy. I felt sad letting go of all the people I had known and loved for so many years, but I don't blame them. I'm not even mad at them, just sad. I still talk with most of them on the phone fairly often, but we just don't get together socially very much and I don't think we ever will again. My life has to go on in a new way now that Len's gone. I can't always keep looking back at what I no longer have."

Wilma, a forty-four-year-old widow, found it difficult to let go of old friends, even though they were of no help to her. "At the time of John's death, there weren't very many people around who were truly supportive. I lived in New Mexico, and most of my family lived in Maine—on the other side of the country. My children were all grown up and gone from home except for Elizabeth. She and Tim, my five-year-old grandson, were living with me. Elizabeth had gone back to college and was leading her own life, so most often it was just me and Tim at home.

"Before John died, we had many friends, but they were all couples, and I was the first in our group to become widowed. Our friends did offer to help, but I didn't feel particularly close to any of them. More to the point, I had this very strong feeling that my friends and people in general were very uncomfortable around me, particularly when I wanted to talk about my husband."

When I asked Wilma if she needed to talk to someone about John, she replied very emphatically. "Oh, yes, very much so. I have so many bottled-up feelings and thoughts. My daughter lets me talk and talk, and that's helpful, but I just can't seem to do that with my friends. I keep getting the feeling that they feel uneasy and just don't know what to say. They say things to me like, 'Now, now, now, you shouldn't dwell on that.'

"I found one exception to this attitude, however. John and I belonged to a Sunday school class for couples. Since he died, I still go every single Sunday morning. At first it was very difficult for me, but the people in the Sunday school class were very supportive in a quiet sort of way. When they offered to listen, I didn't take them up on it because I can only really talk to people I feel very close to. Nevertheless their offer meant a lot, just knowing that they were there if I really needed them."

Widows often find themselves among friends who are not able to provide the help they need. Elaine was able to accept her disappointment and recognize her friends' limitations. This freed her to search for new sources of help. In contrast, Wilma became stuck, unable to renegotiate with old friends or seek new ones, even when they were available to her.

Fighting the Battle of Loneliness

High on the list of challenges facing the widow soon after the death is loneliness. For many women, loneliness is synonymous with widowhood. Unlike some of the hardships confronting widows during the first months that are quickly overcome, loneliness starts at once and stays a long time. Let's listen to a widows' support group as they compare notes.

When Lois, a short, matronly woman, talked about her struggle with terrifying nighttime loneliness during the past week, Lisa, the youngest in the group, blurted out that she, too, was consumed with loneliness. "But this time," Lisa said, "I didn't try to run away. I looked those feelings right in the face and said, 'I'm not going to give in and always be terrified.' I knew I had to face them and try to get on with my life, so I decided to take action. The first thing I did was to make a list of all the things I could do to overcome my emptiness."

As others shared their encounters with loneliness, most agreed that it was helpful to have a good cry once in a while to let their feelings out, acknowledging that feeling bad once in a while actually helps a person to feel better in the long run. They also shared their survival strategies.

Laura said, "I often listen to the radio, particularly talk shows— even though I never seemed to like them before—to help me get to sleep."

Holidays were especially hard for everyone. Linda told us how difficult it had been during her first Christmas with just the children: "We spent most of our time crying. But by the second or third Christmas, we were able to show home movies of past Christmases when my husband was alive, and laugh and talk and remember him fondly."

Lisa solved her holiday blues by traveling. "I'm not able to stay at home during the holidays. I run away, taking a vacation every year."

Janet told of the difficulty she experienced with her grandchildren around Christmastime: "I really didn't want to have a Christmas tree in the house after my husband's death, but I knew that the grandchildren would be coming over. I had to have a tree for them and carry on with normal holiday activities. Looking back, however, I think this helped me to reconnect with my family."

Anniversaries were the time when the feelings of loneliness were really intense, and most women do a lot of their crying at these times. Tina admitted, "Sometimes it feels good just to throw myself across the bed and cry. After that, I do feel somewhat better." Most widows agreed, however, that feelings of loneliness were alleviated over time.

Connie, who had been widowed for nine years said, "Although I used to dread the feelings, now I don't really feel lonely anymore. When I come home from a social situation, it feels good to be alone. My home is one of the few places where I can kick my shoes off and be myself."

Devastating feelings of loneliness are common to both men and woman who have lost their spouses. Although men and women do not differ in the intensity of such feelings, they picture this loneliness and what they are missing differently. For women, the images of loneliness most intensely experienced are not being thought of, not being held, and feeling unprotected. For men, in contrast, loneliness can be summed up in one devastating image: being lost without a compass.

Coping with Single Parenthood

Widows with children face another set of problems. At the time when they themselves are in the greatest need, they must often tend to the needs of others. This is especially true for the young widow whose children are all still at home. No matter what the age of the widow, however, her need to mourn is made all the more complicated by the needs of her children. A consuming concern for many widows is *how to become a successful single parent.*

Single parenthood is an often-discussed challenge in widow support groups. Joan, a forty-three-year-old widow, told her group about the problem she was having with her seventeen-year-old daughter: "I find it very hard to talk with her. Now that her father is gone, I'm concerned with how I can be both a mother and a friend. There are a lot of things I don't feel comfortable talking to her about, especially Larry's death."

Many in the group shared a concern about how difficult it was to speak about loss and death. Most felt that they couldn't even bring up the subject because everyone in the family was afraid of upsetting each another. Mary, a thirty-six-year-old widow, expressed this fear most eloquently: "If I'm having a good day, my kids won't bring up the subject of their dad's death. If I'm having a bad day, they certainly won't bring it up because they are afraid of upsetting me."

A major frustration for widows is how to adequately discipline children after their husband's death. Many talked about periods when they went very easy on their children, hoping to win more affection or approval, but most soon found out that this didn't work. All felt that the answer, although complicated, was to return to normal discipline.

On the other hand, children can also be a great source of comfort. One of the hardest tasks facing a widow or widower is letting go when it is time for them to leave home. Carla, a forty-eight-year-old widow, said, "It was very important for my son to go to college and vital for both of us that I let him go. He needed to begin his own life."

After her son moved out to get married, Jean, fifty-seven, reported, "My son had never talked much about the death; but even now, several years later, when he comes back to visit, he always notices if any furniture, knickknacks, or anything else in the house has been moved. At first I would get annoyed with him. Then it finally dawned on me that this was his way of remembering his father."

There is certainly no single answer to the complex challenges of being a single parent. Although children at different ages express the loss of a parent differently, the older and presumably maturer children are not any easier to raise alone. The underlying dilemma of how to be helpful to your children when you are feeling empty and devastated yourself knows no boundaries of age.

During the first difficult months the number and variety of challenges widows will face is daunting—and for some, overwhelming. It is not easy to discover who you uniquely are. At a time when you need help the most, the guidance you receive is often colored by old-fashioned attitudes that are no help at all. The advice from family, friends, and professionals is important, yet sometimes it is off target. By paying attention to your own feelings, thoughts, and insights, by following your intuitions, you will gradually find the answers to your questions and the solutions to your problems. But remember: Becoming successful at being single is not done in one easy step. Most widows struggle with these challenges over time. Many are successful in finding a niche of self-definition that is comfortable and right for them.

Chapter 4

Your Past and
Your Recovery

Though most widows recover and go on to live different but full lives, we all know women who have not been able to move ahead—who are mired in perpetual grief. What makes the difference? One of the most critical and fascinating questions was how the widow's relationship to her spouse affected the course of her bereavement and recovery. The following story shows how critical emotions, guilt and anger, affect recovery.

A Very Busy Widow:
Anger and Guilt

Rhoda mourned her husband, but could not resolve her intense guilt and anger toward him. A gray-haired, severely dressed women who appears older than her fifty-six years, she works full-time as a legal secretary.

Rhoda was uncomfortable when we first spoke. While she cried as she described the death of her husband Paul six months earlier, she was clearly an articulate and forceful woman. Immediately after introducing herself, she launched into a raging condemnation of doctors and clergymen. She particularly singled out the oncologist and how he gave them her husband's prognosis. It was brutal: "His announcement of the diagnosis was delivered in a short, clipped, matter-of-fact tone," she told me. "It was conveyed impersonally, without even looking at us.

"It was all downhill from there. I was especially angry that Paul was kept in medical isolation because of a low white cell count. None of our friends could see him, and yet medical students were given free access to him round the clock. And he had to spend his last hours tied to all kinds of machines. During the last few days of his life, the room was so crowded with machinery that I couldn't get close enough to talk privately with Paul. Nurses kept coming into the room to draw blood and do a lot of unnecessary tests. A lot of good those medical marvels did for him! I never even got a chance to say good-bye! He tried to talk to me about his dying, but I just couldn't take it and had to change the subject.

"After Paul died, I had a hard time sleeping, and I still wake up many times during the night. My stomach is constantly upset, and I often feel weak and without energy to do anything. My doctor tells me there is nothing wrong with me, however, that it's all in my mind."

When I asked Rhoda if she was still angry at her doctor, she said that she wasn't sure but didn't want to talk about that because it wasn't important. "What's important is that my husband was a good person. It's unfair that he's dead when so many worthless people are walking around alive. Life isn't fair. I'm very angry toward God and very angry toward the church. I feel as if the people in my church betrayed me. They prayed for Paul's recovery even a couple of days after he died, as though somehow they couldn't quite get it straight! I was so shocked when I heard that. I'm not that religious anyway. I've never been able to accept the Catholic view of the afterlife. I don't go to confession but I still go to weekly mass. Force of habit, I guess.

"Since Paul died, I've been spending all my weekends with friends or with my daughter Cynthia. I also keep myself very busy. I work, and am constantly fixing up my house. I do a lot of gardening. I'm in perpetual motion—that's what's best for me now."

When we met again a week later, Rhoda continued to be very tearful, especially when talking about her husband's possessions: "I don't know what to do with them. I can't keep them, but if I give them away, I'm afraid I'm going to feel disloyal, as if I'm betraying his memory. Getting rid of his possessions would be like forgetting Paul."

I asked Rhoda what her marriage had been like. "It was a good one. A very good one! We weren't the kind of couple who constantly told each other how much we cared. We didn't need to, because we knew how we felt. We never let the sun set on our disagreements and never had a bad year. Ours was a smooth marriage.

"What I've learned from my loss, however, is that life is a bitter pill. I realize now that there is just no justice. I always believed that if you were good, good things would happen to you. Now I know this isn't so, that there's no fairness in the world. If you want something you have to grab, claw, and scratch for it."

Why is Rhoda so angry? Her intense feelings are not solely about the people who let her down. Sadly, Rhoda believes that she too has failed, that she is the villain. These feelings are so painful that she can barely admit them to herself. Thus, she flails at those who did disappoint her. We don't know the full story of Rhoda's marriage to Paul, but the hints that she lets drop indicate that although she see the union as a successful one, at another level there were disappointments that she needs to keep hidden from herself. Rhoda can't let go of her bitter feelings and move on toward a realistic construction of her past, taking account of the good as well as the bad. She's emotionally stuck, spinning her wheels.

One year later, Rhoda was still obviously in the midst of grief. Little had changed since our initial interview, except that her feelings of loneliness were far more intense: "Do you know what I realized after

Paul died? That I'm not number one with anyone anymore. Though I still haven't forgiven the people in my church, I still attend mass every week because Paul would have wanted me to go. But I get no comfort from going.

"I think about all the things we never did, and it drives me crazy. When I remember the last year of Paul's life, I wish we could have been closer. I couldn't offer him enough comfort. Let's face it, I was a failure. I didn't know how to help Paul die, and that damn hospital machinery got in the way."

When I asked her how her health was, she said it wasn't good. "I still can't sleep through even one night and I'm always tired. My stomach is still giving me trouble. Last month I went through a complete medical examination, but they told me that there's nothing physically wrong with me."

The passage of time has not mitigated Rhoda's pain and suffering. Still deeply grieving and carrying an enormous load of guilt and anger, she sees no way out. Profound feelings of guilt and anger following a death often accompany a deep ambivalence toward the person lost. Perhaps if we could uncover the full story of Rhoda's marriage, the negative aspects of the relationship would surface and a truer picture would emerge. Her overly positive descriptions of Paul and their relationship hints at a darker underside, one that Rhoda will have to admit to herself before she can let go and move on.

Not all who carry into widowhood intense feelings of anger and guilt are destined to be perpetually mired in them. Sarah is a sixty-eight-year-old widow whose husband died four months ago. Unlike Rhoda, she was able, with help, to move past anger and guilt.

The Burden of Anger, Guilt, and Regrets

A stony, somber woman, Sarah began our talk curtly: "My life since the death of my husband is comprised of just being alone, each day and each night." More softly, she continued, "I often think of how much time I spend without saying a word to anyone, but it's not as hard as it sounds, because I'm very busy planning things in the future." Her husband's course of treatment was stormy and is still a live issue for Sarah: "When we asked the doctor a question, he was always indirect. He never even looked at us, and he gave us insufficient information and barely any comfort. After almost 100 radiation treatments, I decided to take Richard to an alternative treatment clinic. When I told the doctor, who knew he hadn't helped us one bit, he made fun of me right in front of Richard. He ridiculed me for trying to help my husband!

"I'm still burdened, even after all this time, with regrets about not talking to Richard about his illness. I never really said good-bye. In the last week of his life, when Richard turned to me and said, 'I was thinking about how much I love you,' I didn't respond. I think about that every day and wonder what kind of person I am. Am I made of stone? Right after his death, I couldn't even cry. I thought that something was terribly wrong with me, and I didn't like myself! Later on, I did cry a great deal, but it was frightening, because all through our marriage Richard had regarded me as the stronger one. And I wasn't being strong at all."

A week later, during our second interview, Sarah reported that her widow support group meeting the previous night had stirred up a lot of issues for her: "When we began going round the room talking about husbands, I didn't do very well. All these feelings came rushing back, especially my regrets that I didn't talk to Richard about how I felt. I really loved him, but I'll never forget that I didn't tell him that—never. You know, I really didn't expect him to die, even though I knew he was very sick. I couldn't cry before he passed away, and I just can't stop thinking about it.

"Our marriage was okay, yet I walk around with feelings of having been cheated, of not having done things for myself. I had and still have lots of unfulfilled desires, and Richard couldn't or wouldn't take care of my needs. I was often sexually unsatisfied. Even though I was the mainstay in our marriage, Richard didn't appreciate how much I did. I not only took care of the children but had to work hard all my life so that we'd have enough money. I even had to help Richard with his business. He was never strong. In fact, he was ill throughout most of his life."

At this point, Sarah began weeping. "I never had any real fun or joy, and probably never will. If only I could find myself, I think I would be a woman of great integrity. I would not be the little girl who always tried to please everyone."

When I saw Sarah one year later, I sensed a different person. She appeared more physically animated and more alive in her speech. She had spent some time in psychotherapy and had embarked on a journey of self-discovery, putting much time and effort into this inward search.

Sarah is still very much in the midst of her grief, but she can cry freely now, whereas she couldn't before. Although she is often lonely and despairing, particularly in the evenings, she is starting to get beyond this. She is much stronger since her husband's death and knows that the experience has made her grow and understand more about life. Like a child who had never faced tragedy, Sarah always expected everything to go on as it had before. Now she knows that being alive means having to move on and make changes.

"I've learned about my strengths and I've realized that I can take care of myself. I've even started going to classes and learning about business affairs. In spite of my grieving, I can feel myself growing, like Tennyson said, in the 'depths of divine despair.' I have been enriched by my despair in ways I never dreamed possible."

Sarah's substantial inner changes have not, as yet, found full expression in new behavior. The intensity of her guilt about not saying good-bye to Richard and telling him that she loved him still prevents her from moving ahead fully with her life, but that barrier is gradually dissolving as she continues to honor her own process of self-development.

Although Rhoda and Sarah were both burdened by intense anger and guilt, they followed different pathways to recovery. Sarah managed, with some help from her psychotherapist, to get beyond her initial feelings and to view her life as containing the potential for change, and she even saw the possibility for new growth. Sarah took a risk, a look into the nooks and crannies of her past life, and tried to accept her past marital regrets. Painful as these feelings were, her willingness to examine them made a difference. Rhoda, on the other hand, remained mired in avoiding her past and her feelings about her marriage. When a woman is burdened by intense guilt and anger, the need for inner exploration is paramount. Such inner journeys are often facilitated by understanding, supportive professionals. The role of psychotherapy for widows like Sarah and Rhoda will be more fully explored in chapter 7.

In looking into how a widow's relationship to her spouse affected the course of her bereavement and recovery, I found seven characteristics that describe a widow's relationship to her husband and how she subsequently reacted to her loss. Many widows suffered ANGER at their husbands for dying and GUILT about thoughts unspoken, things left undone, and particularly feelings that they had somehow let their husbands down at the end of their lives.

I measured the intensity of each woman's anger by having her respond to a series of questions: Since your spouse died, have you felt upset with:

- The unfairness of it all
- Your spouse for dying
- Doctors and nurses who cared for your spouse
- The funeral home
- Someone connected with the death
- Your spouse because of the financial situation the death brought about
- God for allowing the death
- God for abandoning you?

Widows who answered "yes" for most of these questions were experiencing a high level of anger.

I assessed the amount of guilt a widow felt by asking the following:

- Do you feel in any way responsible for the death, or that God was punishing you by taking your spouse?
- Do you feel guilty about the way you treated your spouse when he was alive, or that your relationship with him is incomplete in some way?
- Was there something that you said or didn't say to your spouse that you regret?

Again, widows who answered a majority of these questions with "yes" were feeling very guilty.

As Sarah and Rhoda's stories have shown us, when high levels of anger and guilt surface soon after the death of the husband, these feelings greatly hinder recovery. Even a year after the death, widows who still scored high in these qualities were doing poorly. Although most widows were doing well at the seven-year follow-up point, women who had carried a great deal of anger and overwhelming guilt were more likely to be among the few whose recovery was still in doubt.

The other five characteristics that describe a widow's relationship to her husband and her loss are: the extent to which the widow regarded herself as INDEPENDENT or DEPENDENT; whether she felt STUNTED, a sense that her development had been put on the shelf during the marriage; REGRETS, sad feelings about her choices in life; IDEALIZATION of the marriage and the husband, seeing him almost as a mythic hero; and finally, how SUCCESSFUL or UNSUCCESSFUL she judged the marriage to have been.

A word of caution is called for here. In many ways it is foolhardy to try to summarize any marriage, particularly a long one, into a few simple characteristics. In any relationship there are ups and downs— life could not be otherwise. Trying to summarize a marriage within a few categories is like taking a snapshot of a fast moving target. In asking the widows I studied to describe their feelings, thoughts and evaluations, however, I was simply trying to develop a picture of how *they* saw their marriages from the vantage point of the loss. This important perspective tells us something about their outlook and, as we shall see, does have real consequences for how widows progress though their bereavement.

A Sixty-two-year-old "Little Girl"

The following is a story told to me by a widow who showed a high degree of dependency and idealization of her husband:

Linda is a widow in trouble, unable to move beyond the total reliance upon her husband that characterized their marriage. Her adoration and complete immersion in his memory signals a high level of idealization that often spells trouble. Though sixty-two years old, Linda appears remarkably younger than her age. Her high-fashion dress, perhaps more appropriate to a younger woman, and her dramatic makeup enhance this youthfulness. Emotionally, Linda gave off a sensuous ingenue quality.

"Before Len died," she told me, "we discussed his death very openly, wondering why this was happening to us. We couldn't figure out what we had done to deserve this and asked each other if God was punishing us. My husband was a very religious man who insisted that God had a plan for him. He spent the months before his death worrying about others rather than himself, and, up until the very end, he was in charge and made sure that I was comfortable.

"After Len died, no one really looked after me. I put on a big front, but inside I was really scared and hurt. I was very stressed and started to feel very strange. My doctor called these feelings anxiety attacks. I was also very sad, cried most of the time, and had trouble sleeping, waking up several times a night. I still have no appetite."

When I asked Linda how she would describe herself, she said, "Well, I guess I'm still a little girl. Len spoiled me and always took complete care of me. Now I have to be independent and do things for myself. I think I'm learning, but I can't say I enjoy it. Unfortunately, now that he's gone, I have no other choice. I have to be independent, but I feel empty and terribly alone, as if I lived in a big, black hole. No one is there for me any more. I've always been a very outgoing person who makes friends easily, yet, making new friends or even being with my old friends doesn't seem to relieve my terrible sense of isolation. I don't feel *better* when I'm with other people—it just doesn't help at all.

"Ever since Len died, I can't keep my mind on anything for more than a minute, and I am angry, angry at God. Why did he do this to me? It's not fair. I used to go to church regularly, but now I won't, I can't. Just getting close to my church enrages me."

Linda participated in a psychotherapy group for widows and widowers, and was interviewed again one year later. When I asked her how her life had changed since we last talked, she was not very optimistic: "Nothing has changed, and I'm still very alone and sad. I can't seem to get myself moving in the morning, and there's nothing I want to do or accomplish. You'd call that depression, wouldn't you? I thought about trying my hand at a job, but every time I think of this I feel very frightened and panicked."

Although Linda has a number of friends and is engaged in a variety of activities, loneliness is still a severe problem. Loneliness, for her, is synonymous with not being held or touched. Without that, Linda's life feels like a gigantic void.

Linda maintains that her marriage to Len was a good one, but it was a marriage in which her husband, who was older than she, structured and organized her entire life: "I knew just what to do, and I didn't have to worry about making any decisions."

This arrangement was comfortable for her, and I never got the sense that she had rebelled or struggled against it. The only solution she sees now to her present intense suffering is to find a replacement for that psychological relationship. As we talked about her relations to men she said, "I guess you think I'm acting like a naive girl who is just beginning to discover the world of boys. I want to start dating again, but I really don't know what to do or how to act. It's all so confusing."

Unlike many widows who derived pleasure from developing themselves and expressing previously unvoiced goals and desires, Linda is exclusively focused on her need to depend on a man and to be cared for.

To explore areas of dependency and independence, I asked widows to rate themselves on how much they relied upon their husbands in certain vital areas of their lives. These areas included raising children, companionship, day-to-day household decisions, transportation, managing money, and arranging social get-togethers with friends. If a widow answered "very dependent" to more than half of these questions, her relationship had been a highly dependent one.

When compared to the more independent widows, women who scored high in areas of dependency were less successful in recovering. Linda was not only highly dependent upon her husband, she described him in almost mythic terms. Were most women who idealized their husbands similar to Linda, and did this viewpoint affect their recovery?

Unlike the qualities of dependency, anger, and guilt, rating widows in terms of how much they idealized their husbands is not easily reduced to a series of "yes" or "no" questions. Idealization is more subtle and requires sensitive, clinical judgments. My solution was to have trained "evaluators" listen to the interviews and rate widows as to whether they were high, about average, or low in idealizing their spouses. Raters were asked to pay special attention to how a widow described her husband. If all of his traits were couched in superlatives—extremely intelligent, handsome, always generous to others—and there were no negative statements, criticisms, or wishes that he had been better during the marriage, we would conclude that the widow was seeing her husband in an ideal light. If we asked a question such as, "What would you have liked to be different about your marriage?" and the widow responded, "I can't think of anything," we knew it was likely that she was expending energy and effort defending an unreal memory of her spouse. *Four out of ten of the widows I studied had idealized their husbands.*

Somewhat surprising, I found that women who idealized their husbands recovered at the same rate as those widows who saw their husbands in a more balanced light. About the only "negative" aspect I was able to discover about widows who idealized their husbands was that they frequently spoke about him to their friends, who found such talk "boring," a realization that stung widows.

As I listened to the things widows were telling me at the start of my research, it soon became clear to me that one very important issue was how much they felt that aspects of their lives had been put on hold during the marriage. Frequently, parts of themselves that had seemed important, such as continuing their education or developing their talents or careers, had taken a back seat to their husbands, kids, and homes. At times, it was clear that this situation was the result of the husband's active discouragement of their desires. In other instances, though the wife had not been directly discouraged from pursuing her own development, she felt that doing so would "somehow be wrong," as if she were "cheating" her husband or children out of something. It is important to note that such feelings could, and frequently *did,* occur even in marriages that were otherwise good. Susan, the widow I described in detail in chapter 1 is a good illustration of a woman who felt stunted within an otherwise strong marriage. *About one out of three of the widows I studied felt they were stunted during their marriages.*

What impact did moderate to high levels of stunting have on a widow's recovery? Widows who felt that they were stunted in their marriages recovered as successfully as those who did not feel this way. As we shall see in the chapter on growth, however, widows who felt that their marriages had held back their personal development focused on growth and self-exploration in widowhood more often than those who felt that they had been fulfilled in their marriages. Feeling stunted often led to growth!

Similar to ratings of stunting, judges scored regrets about choices in the widow's past life on a scale of (1) no regrets to (5) major regrets. A widow who was seen to express no regrets reported that she was totally and completely satisfied with every aspect of life. No regrets for any choice or decisional direction taken or not taken. No regrets about the relationship with the spouse. No regrets about anything she might have done differently in the relationship or done differently in life. In contrast, a woman who showed major regrets expressed a great sense of unfulfillment in her life. Regrets for such things as not pursuing a career, not having gotten to know one's husband better before marriage in order to have made a more informed and different choice of a mate. Regrets for having married the wrong man or woman. Regrets for having stayed married rather than having the courage to leave the marriage. Regrets for not having expected and demanded more from oneself. Regrets for living one's whole life for spouse or children—regrets for having given so much of oneself with so little expectation (or receipt) of return.

Half of the women I studied stated that they had major regrets about some aspects of their lives. When I examined the impact of regrets on their recovery I found that high-regret widows were more likely to be more anxious and depressed soon after their husband's death, and although lessening somewhat, one year later were still more anxious and depressed than the low-regret women. Not surprisingly, regrets were associated with reduced self-esteem. Although linked to slightly poorer recovery, many of the widows who expressed regrets were able to use these feelings for inner explorations and growth.

"Good" and "Bad" Marriages

When widows are asked to think about their marriages, most try to sum up all those years by talking about how successful or unsuccessful their marriages were. Two women, Tina and Dorothy, whose past histories are similar, described very different marriages.

An Unsuccessful Marriage

Tina, typifies the widows I studied who saw their marriages as unsuccessful. She is fifty-six and lost her husband Jack five months ago from cancer. Two months before his death, they had moved into a new house with her two adolescent sons from her first marriage. Both she and Jack had previously been married, though Jack's daughters are both married and out of the house. They had been together for ten years.

A real estate agent, Tina keeps herself busy with her work: "My life right now is completely taken up with my sons and my job, and when I'm not working, I'm still preoccupied with cleaning up papers from Jack's will. I do see girlfriends over the weekends, so I'm rarely alone, but I don't like it when I am. Last weekend I went to a conference, probably the first time I was really by myself since Jack's death, and I felt extremely uncomfortable. I found myself worrying that there was no one to care for me."

When I asked Tina to talk about the time before Jack's death, she seemed fairly resolved about that period of their life: "We were completely open with one another about his dying. Jack even talked about where he wanted his ashes to be scattered and what should be done with the estate. We spent the last three weeks of his life at the lake, and we all knew that this was the last time the family was going to be together."

Tina was brought up in Arkansas and married her first husband before she was twenty. They lived together for twelve years before the divorce. She had a couple of years of being single, but soon developed an intense relationship with Jack and married him as soon as he was divorced. When I asked Tina to describe her marriages, she seemed troubled: "My life, if you could call it that, started to go wrong much earlier than my first husband. My father and I were not close, and he was very jealous of my mother's attention to me. My first husband was altogether too much like my father. He was overbearing, and we constantly fought. I was so unsure that the marriage would last that I delayed for a long time before having children. As I look back now,

I see that I shouldn't have married him in the first place, but I guess I simply wasn't mature enough to think it through.

"After my divorce, this older man came into my life. Jack was thirteen years my senior, and showered me with kindness. He even encouraged me to have a career and get a real estate license. And yet, I made some serious mistakes with him too. First of all, I never should have gotten involved with him while he was married. He stayed married for the first two years of our relationship, and I realize now that I should have given him an ultimatum stating that he either get a divorce or leave.

"We had a lot of problems in the marriage. Jack was a workaholic. I thought I already knew that, but it was even worse than I realized before I married him. He also had a terrible temper that made me afraid to argue with him or question his decisions. He made it very clear to me that I shouldn't make him mad because he was dangerous—not very reassuring. He never hit me, but I couldn't stand his rages. After a temper tantrum, he would sulk and pout for days. We fought constantly about his not having gotten a divorce earlier, our bad sex life, his being overweight, and his bouts with alcoholism. I'm a very physical person, and it really bothered me that he was not only physically out of shape but seemed hell-bent on making his health worse. I sometimes wonder if he would have lived longer if he had listened to me."

When Tina talks about her marriage one year later, she is of two minds about her husband. There are some things she says about him that indicate a great deal of anger, and others that seem quite positive.

"In spite of how rough our marriage was at times, Jack was a godsend for me—he came at a time in my life when I very badly needed some nourishing. Here I was coming out of a divorce with two children and no one to take care of me, and this older man comes along who is more like a father than a husband. What was really positive about the marriage was that he gave a great deal to the children, and I'm eternally grateful to him for that. At this point in my life, however, I don't want or need any fathering, and remarriage is the furthest thing from my mind."

When I asked Tina whether she thought she had grown in the past year, she seemed quite definite that she had: "I've become much more self-sufficient compared to last year, more career oriented and more effective at business. I've started taking even better care of my body and really getting into shape. I've changed in other ways too. I now understand that life is very fragile and short. Now I'll go out and spend a hundred dollars on a piece of jewelry without worrying about it. I don't mind doing things alone, but I've also joined some community groups and signed up for some college courses just for the fun of it."

Despite a marriage that was certainly not all that she wanted, Tina is well launched into a new life, unburdened, for the most part, of her very real regrets. Ironically, knowing that her marriage was far from fully satisfying gave her the push she needed as a widow. Tina was able to mobilize her energies and interests, sparked by the realization that now she was totally responsible for her own life. She felt herself unburdened by ties and obligations. Regrets about one's marriage can often lead to a decision to make the most of life in the future.

In contrast to Tina, Dorothy, typifies the widows who consider their marriages successful. Also divorced and remarried, Dorothy is an articulate, young-looking sixty-six-year-old woman who addressed all of the questions I put to her very openly, often crying softly during the session. She's still in the same house that she and her husband Carl lived in for twenty years. "The most important person in my life is [my son] Seth, and he just moved to Cleveland after his divorce." She was married to Carl for twenty-five years, and before that she'd been married to her first husband for nineteen years, after meeting him in college. She finally divorced him because she "got fed up with his running around with other women."

"I've worked most of my life as an office manager. I retired a year and a half ago, and Carl was getting ready to retire. I was always good at my job, and people were always surprised at my effectiveness. At first I was happy not to be working anymore, but now I miss the companionship at the office. I'm seriously considering going back. My life is very boring right now, and I miss the friends at work. It's hard to be alone.

"Carl went so fast that we couldn't say all the things we wanted to. We were pretty open, even discussing estates and wills. In many ways, he handled it better than I did: In fact, I couldn't even tell our friends about his illness; he had to be the one who did it. Toward the end, when I asked Carl exactly how he was feeling that day, he said he wasn't angry but that he felt very sad for me.

"After he died, I was exhausted and by myself for the first couple of weeks, the very first time in my life that I've ever been totally alone. When I told my doctor I wasn't sleeping very well, he prescribed Halcyon to help.

"I got rid of Carl's clothes within the first month because my sister, who was visiting, urged me to dispose of them as soon as possible. I kept some items, however, silly things like his comb and razor. I couldn't part with everything.

"During the last fifteen years we had a very good marriage, but it didn't start off that way. Our first ten years were very unsettled, with lots of arguments about his ex-wife, money, and especially his children, who were intrusive and had some serious problems. Carl simply wouldn't talk about the children, even though we saw them frequently, and he could never understand my feelings about wanting to be consulted about visiting them. That was his way of dealing with a problem—to simply ignore it. Then, suddenly, on Friday night I'd learn that we were going to spend the weekend with the children. It was the only area in our lives that we could never really talk about. We could have used some counseling, but Carl would never agree to it. Aside from this, our marriage was a good one, and I never felt stunted in any way. Carl was an interesting and very charming man. He also had many talents, and it's too bad he didn't develop more of them. But I wouldn't want to forget the past fifteen years. We had a very loving and caring relationship."

From the standpoint of two people who loved each other, Dorothy feels that her marriage was a great one. Her only regret, a mild one, is that she wasn't more forgiving of some of his faults. Though there were problems in the marriage, they were not problems with the relationship, but problems related to things outside the relationship, such as Carl's children, whom she still feels intruded too often into their lives.

A year later, a more energized and obviously different Dorothy entered my office. She was dressed more stylishly and colorfully than when we first met a year ago. When I asked her how she was doing, she said that she was feeling more like her old self and had no more problems sleeping: "I decided to go back to work at my old job, and this was the right decision for me. I have a life now and I keep myself busy with the job and my friends. I guess you could say I'm comfortable, but I still miss Carl terribly. His absence still feels like a huge void."

Unlike Tina, who looked inward and began on the road to self-discovery, Dorothy opted to become comfortable but avoided inner explorations: "I don't want to think about the bad parts of my past. I've even put aside all my feelings toward Carl's children because they just aren't relevant to my life now."

Tina and Dorothy saw their marriages in very different ways, but both women recovered equally well, following a different pathway to successful widowhood. An important question I asked myself, however, is: Did the quality of their marriages have an impact on their recovery or the way they reached it? Of all the aspects of marriage that we tried to measure, marital quality was the most elusive. How does a person, particularly one who is still grieving and beset with the multitude of challenges that are part and parcel of widowhood, describe and evaluate a long marriage? How do they fairly take into account the ups and downs typical of all marriages? There is no simple answer to these questions. Though for many widows this kind of evaluation was a difficult struggle, most were both intrigued and willing to attempt summing up their marriages.

Two out of three of the widows we studied had successful marriages. Did this mean that these women showed better or faster recovery when compared to widows who characterized their past marriages as unsuccessful? The answer, surprisingly, is no. The success or relative failure of the marriage did not predict the course of their widowhood. The past is not always with us. It does not lock you into predictable success or failure as a widow.

What about the difference between Dorothy's journey and Tina's? Many widows who, like Tina, spoke openly of regrets about their past marriages, were able to turn inward and use their past pain as a launching pad for growth. Dorothy's approach, becoming comfortable while refusing to analyze the past, does not limit successful recovery, but usually curtails growth. This question will be fully explored in chapter 9.

Did the seven characteristics discussed in this chapter—anger, guilt, dependency, stunting, idealization, regrets, and quality of marriage—affect the success of a widow's recovery? Certain aspects of a widow's relationship with her husband did influence the course of her bereavement long after his passing. Intense anger and guilt in reaction to a spouse's death most certainly have a negative impact on recovery. High dependency in the marriage is also often a problem. On the other hand, the quality of the marriage, how stunted women felt in that marriage, and whether or not they idealized their husbands does not have much effect upon how fast a widow gets back on her feet.

What should these findings mean to you? It is important to understand that the feelings of guilt and anger discussed here and illustrated in the lives of Linda and Sarah are intense and overwhelming. Feeling occasional guilt, having moments of regret, and experiencing some anger do not in and of themselves put you at jeopardy. Most widows have such thoughts and feelings—and many widows whose marriages were not outstandingly good nevertheless had successful recoveries.

A discussion from a widow's support group illustrates how common normal anger is in most marriages. Betty, recently widowed, said, "One thing that I learned about myself is that I'm really angry at my Tim. Many times when I'm feeling anger, and talk about it in the group, I say to myself, 'Where are you Tim?'"

Both Ann and Margaret, widowed much longer than Betty, talked about their own anger and their struggles to deal with it— and both agreed that resolving these emotions takes a long time: "These feelings are normal, and most widows I know encounter them," Ann said. "It's just unfortunate that they remain in the closet, making it more difficult for us all to resolve them." Margaret said, "At times I'm so angry that I look up swear words in a dictionary to find new ways of shouting out my rage."

When, however, anger and guilt:

- become the center of your experience as a widow
- color most of your memories
- seem to "take on a life of their own"
- intrude frequently and are unwelcome in your thoughts

then they signal danger. In later chapters, I will discuss how friends and family, psychotherapy and support groups can aid in resolving these feelings.

Chapter 5

Being Widowed Young

When Ricky, aged twenty-eight, suddenly found herself widowed, she protested: "I'm too young to go through this. It's not fair—widows are supposed to be grandmothers! And what about all the plans my husband and I made that will never be? Now we'll never buy that house we dreamed of, never have all the children we wanted. I feel as if the rug has been pulled out from under my life. I envy my friends who still have their husbands, and I feel cheated out of the kinds of memories that older widows have."

If you are widowed and young, is your destiny fixed? Must you face extreme trauma and a long and arduous recovery? Friends and professionals may tell you that young widows react to the death of their husbands more intensely than older women and are less likely to recover as quickly. But like so many myths explored in this book, this is not really the way it happens. This chapter provides a healthy antidote to these all-too-common misunderstandings.

When speaking with the younger (under forty) widows, I asked myself several important questions: How was the passage through bereavement different for younger widows? Was their recovery more difficult? Were there characteristics of younger widows that impeded or facilitated their success? Were they able to use the challenges they faced to help them grow?

Right after the death of their spouses, younger widows were indeed experiencing more difficulties. The young women were more depressed and anxious, and they tended to abuse alcohol and prescription drugs to manage these feelings. They took less satisfaction in their lives, and their sense of well-being and self-esteem were diminished. Most dramatic were their feelings that their lives were out of control. In the first months, young widows do have a more difficult time adjusting than older women. So it appears that, initially, the general view that they react more intensely to their loss seems true.

Where Do I Fit In?

Mary was thirty-two when she lost her husband, Tom. Her story illustrates the multiple burdens of the young widow who must simultaneously find a way to cope with overwhelming economic deprivation, address the fears and grief of her young children while trying to be both mother and father to them, and yet still find time for her own feelings.

"Tom was diagnosed with cancer one year after he lost his job. From then on, we were constantly struggling—no money and all kinds of bad feelings spilling over. I think his cancer was caused by the troubles we had. He just couldn't find employment, and I finally had to go out and get part-time work. My job made Tom feel useless and humiliated that he couldn't support his family. He was very sad and depressed all of the time.

"As his cancer worsened, our doctor suggested a new experimental treatment. For the first time we began to talk earnestly about the possibility of death, though the doctor kept insisting that Tom would get better. We did try to arm ourselves, but you can never really prepare. The reality of death doesn't hit until later, after it happens. I was completely stunned when Tom died. Even today I'm still very frightened about death. I never thought about dying before, but now I worry all the time about me or my children dying, and I wonder if I'll ever get over that feeling."

Unlike many of the young widows whose stories we have heard, Mary's family let her down badly, failing to support her emotionally: "After Tom died, I turned to my sister Beth for help and encouragement. After all, I figured, when she needed help with her son's cancer, I was always there for her. But she wasn't there for me. In fact, neither was the rest of the family. As an excuse, they said they just couldn't take being reminded of Tom's death, but they hadn't really helped when Tom was alive and sick either. They just didn't give me any support at all. Thank God, I had help from good friends. Tom and I had been close to several other couples, and these people were my lifesavers. They let me talk and they even helped me out financially.

"I also realized during that first difficult summer that I was trying too hard to be 'supermom.' I had to became more accepting of the fact that it was difficult for my kids to admit that their father was really gone. Susie was ten and Timmy was only eight. We all needed to struggle with that as well as with not having enough money.

"As I felt the pressure inside of me beginning to mount, I started to think about finding some extra emotional help. When a friend suggested a widow's support group, I thought, well, maybe something in a group like this could help me. Other widows might give me some useful advice. What I needed most were some suggestions about how to handle my kids.

"By the time I attended the first meeting, I was frequently nauseated and vomited a lot. I was beginning to wonder if I had cancer too. Of course I couldn't tell anyone that. They'd think I was loony. I was stunned when I heard other widows describing the same exact symptoms. Then and there I decided to join. I knew it would be helpful to spend time with other widows facing similar ordeals. When you are widowed, your social life completely changes. All of a sudden, you don't quite fit."

Mary's burden was compounded by the fact that her grief was expressed symbolically through her fear of her own illness and death. Her recovery was made all the more difficult because Mary, unlike many young widows, could not count on the stabilizing influence of a supportive family. She was, however, able to find some of the help she desperately needed from friends and a widow's support group.

To better understand the problems faced by young widows, I asked them to describe the main difficulties they were experiencing as a widow and to tell me how much impact these problems had on their lives. For simplicity I organized what they told me into seven problem areas.

Mourning reactions—missing one's spouse, and struggling with depression, guilt, anger, and grief—were high on the list of difficulties. Many widows I talked to also shared their concerns about *loneliness*—the fear of being alone when the last child finally left, their worries about growing old alone, and their need to find companionship.

A great many young widows had *problems with learning to be the head of the household,* coping with the myriad tasks they had previously shared with their spouses. They found it hard to make all the family decisions alone, and difficult to maintain the home, garden, and car. Dealing with financial concerns, such as keeping up the family business, was also trying. Older widows have life insurance policies and retirement funds to depend upon. Younger widows may not have planned for such contingencies.

Problems with being single were almost universal. Young widows suffered much anxiety about being single, remarriage, sexuality, and finding opposite-sex companionship. *Interpersonal friction,* a burden for many, included problems with relatives and friends and coping with the unrealistic attitudes of others about how their grieving should be progressing. Though some women reported that they felt like a "fifth wheel" at social gatherings, young widows are less likely to lose their "couple" friendships than older women because the generation they belong to does not always separate into "boys" and "girls" at social gatherings as their parents' generation did.

Existential concerns included developing a sense of self and new goals, developing an appropriate life-style, and finding meaning in life. Because younger widows are so busy being single parents and earning a living, however, they often put off the task of intense self-exploration to a later time.

Being a Single Parent

By far, the number one challenge that young widows faced is *being a single parent*. This task was made all the more complicated by the grief reactions of their children. Learning how to set limits for their kids and adequately discipline them was especially trying. The following are the most common problems they faced in raising children on their own.

Helping Children Mourn

At a widows' support group I attended, I heard several young women talk about the problems they were facing in attempting to help their children through their grief. At first, they struggled with how much of their own grief they could let their children see.

Linda said, "I've found that it's important to tell my children when I'm having a bad day, and why it's a bad day." Margaret added, "I've been crying for almost three years. So much so, that my kids make fun of me. 'Oh boy, Mom's crying about Dad again.'"

It soon became clear to everyone, that the first step in helping their children mourn was to allow them to see their parent's grief. Holly said, "If you keep it in the closet, they know anyway, but they will start thinking that feelings like crying are wrong."

Tammy, the youngest widow in the group, admitted, "I wouldn't let my kids ever see me sad. But after two months of my hiding, Cindy, who is only five, said, 'Mom, you always put on a funny face when you think of Dad.' Of course she felt my grief—so much for covering up."

As the discussion continued, Nina, aged thirty-two, added that her younger children were more open to talking about their grief than the older ones: "One day my daughter was very upset and stomped out of the kitchen. When I asked her why, she said, 'I'm mad because I have no daddy.'

Trish echoed Nina's experience: "My eight-year-old, Joey, brought home some books from school to read to me about the death of animals. He's more open about his feelings then I am!"

Myra, a women in her late thirties, added, "That's okay for you to say, but you don't have to deal with the barriers put up by adolescent children. They're much more complicated."

Spurred on by Myra's challenge, the women explored strategies on how to help their children. Several mentioned that they'd been advised to let their children's friends help them. The experience of most group members, however, was that kids could not really help kids: "If you think it's hard for adults to talk with you about your loss," Terry said, "it's often impossible for kids to do it. A couple years after my husband died, I learned that the father of one of my son's baseball teammates had passed away. When I suggested to my son that he try and talk to this boy, he said, 'Boy, I wish someone had talked to me when my dad died.' This was the first time I had any sense that my son's friends did not offer him support. I'd talked to him very little about his feelings, assuming that his friends were helping him get through his grief."

At a time when the young widow is just beginning to cope with her own grief, she is faced with the terrible dilemma of how to help her children understand their loss and begin mourning. Though, clearly, ignoring the children's feelings is not the answer, paying attention only to your child's feelings and ignoring your own will not work. For most of the widows, the first and crucial step to helping their children was to let them see their mother's grief. From that point on, each woman was able to devise a coping strategy that matched their capacities and that of their children. Some relied on other family members to help, and a few found reading material for their children that provided a way of opening up communication at a comfortable level. Still others were able to talk openly to their children early in their bereavement.

Discipline

Grappling with setting boundaries and discipline, almost always a problem area in parenting, is magnified after the loss of a spouse. For all too many parents today, setting limits and maintaining order in the family is an ongoing struggle even at the best of times. The newly bereaved mother faces this problem at a time when she is most vulnerable, trying to figure out how to be both father and mother. Most felt overwhelmed by the problem of how to discipline their children; almost all describe periods when they went very easy on them, hoping to win more affection or approval. It did not take them long, however, to find out that this simply didn't work. Eventually the answer, although complicated, was to return to a normal approach to discipline.

Maintaining Family Togetherness

A common feeling many young widows experience is a sense of distance, almost alienation, from their families once the early mourning period is over. For some this feeling may be enhanced by the differences in intensity of grief between family members and themselves. Everybody else seems to be getting back to "normal," but the widow just can't. Yet she fears that if she doesn't, her family will drift away.

A major challenge is how to celebrate holidays. For the young widow this is increasingly complex because of her children: "Now that the family is radically altered, how do I limit and control my grief when it is being magnified by the approach of what has always been a family time?"

When Marcia described how ashamed she felt about running away during family holidays, many group members came immediately to her support. They confessed that they too felt like running at times, and reassured her that this feeling was normal. Those who had felt like running but decided to stay and stick it out, shared how this decision had helped them.

Georgia explained that it had helped her to keep holiday celebrations exactly the same as before her husband had died: "I wish I could go away on a holiday and do something for myself, but I've found that keeping up the family rituals does help. It's the best time for my kids to reminisce and talk about their father, and that seems to ease us all."

Most of the widows in the group did believe that it was best to keep up some of the usual holiday celebrations. At the same time, most also felt that this had to be done in a way that didn't send the message "Nothing has changed" to the kids. "That would be a fantasy," said Trish, "Everything has changed. I and my children have to help each other accept that."

The challenges for the young widow of becoming a single parent are clear. Beyond the press of these realities are some more subtle and often more pernicious experiences common to young women.

"I'm Too Young to Be a Widow"

Younger widows are often totally unprepared to be hurtled into the void created by their husband's death. Except in time of war, the younger widow rarely encounters age-mates who are also widows. The shock of finding oneself widowed so much younger than expected is one of her greatest hurdles. Ricky, widowed at twenty-eight, illustrates this problem.

Ricky was certainly not prepared for her husband's death. To make matters worse, her husband Duane did not succumb to an illness or an accident, but shot himself in the head one Memorial Day on their front porch.

"At the time of Duane's death, I had two small children and was six months pregnant. We married young, when I was only eighteen. I had my high school degree, but I'd never worked or been on my own before. I was broke and had no medical, life, or mortgage insurance."

Fortunately, Ricky had a lot of help: "My parents and friends pitched in right away, moving into our house to help care for me and my kids. They were all great and extremely supportive. I soon realized, as my pregnancy progressed, that I couldn't make it on my own, so I moved in with my parents and three younger brothers. They did a great job of helping me take care of the children. It was a good thing they were there for me because I was in shock.

"My pregnancy went well and I gave birth to a son a few months later. At the time I still felt stunned with my loss and was taking tranquilizers by the dozen. Though I was still numb from Duane's death, I don't think it had really sunk in yet. Actually seeing the fathers coming into the maternity ward made me realize that my new baby didn't have one. There was a period during those first few days when I wondered if I was going to make it. Then I managed to snap out of it. I told myself that I had my three children and my whole life ahead of me and, by God, I was going to survive somehow.

"When I returned from the hospital, my mother suggested I go to a widows' support group. I thought and thought about getting involved, but I wasn't sure something like this was for me. This went on for several months. Finally, when Christmas came, our first Christmas without Duane, it was terrible, absolutely awful. After suffering through that, I decided to go to the first meeting in January. I figured I'd at least see what it was like and, if it was a bunch of bull, I could always leave.

"To my surprise, it was wonderful. It was a small group—only about ten people—but they made me feel better immediately. One of the first things I realized was that I wasn't the only young widow in the world. When you're under thirty, it's more respectable to be divorced than to be widowed. People seem to think young widows are strange. When they're around us, they act as if they're afraid of death or think it's contagious. When someone asks me where my husband is and I tell them that he's dead, they get this terrible look of shock on their face and then they pull away. Older women have it easier.

"Sharing those kinds of experiences with the widows in the group also helped me to realize that other people were going through the same things I was. When I first joined the support group, I wanted to skip the pain and get on to the good part, but the other members helped me understand that I couldn't do that. You have to live through the grief first. The group gave me a chance to talk, to be open with people who really wanted to listen, and to get my feelings out. They provided me with empathy not just sympathy. These people became my friends.

"I can't tell you how important they were to me in terms of helping me to live with myself, live with my grief, and get through the pain. I discovered that widowhood does not mean grandmotherhood. In our culture, we're shielded from death and we're shielded from widowhood. Those who find supportive friends are lucky."

Ricky illustrates some of the unique psychological experiences young widows face. Though widowhood is always a shock, older widows are at least somewhat emotionally prepared for that eventuality. Most women in their fifties or older have experienced the death of friends and family, and many have thought about the loss of their husband at some point in their middle years. This "rehearsal" for widowhood in many cases enables them to face their loss with less distress. Younger widows are hurled, totally unprepared, into the void created by their husband's death. The shock of finding oneself widowed young is one of their greatest hurdles.

Many young widows feel that people are very uncomfortable in their company, almost as if they carry the smell of death on them. They have no culturally acceptable way to understand being young and widowed since, in our society, being widowed is associated with being old. Compared to older widows, young ones live in a social world comprising more couples, since their age-mates are unlikely to be widowed.

As they attempt to move toward becoming single once again, young widows initially find this challenge more difficult than older widows. They recognize that everyone around them believes that the solution is remarriage and that their age makes this a real possibility. More than older women, they feel pressed to get on with a new life, and being single is often seen only as a way station to remarriage. Young children in the home make exploring the single state even more difficult.

As we have seen, there are important differences between the dilemmas faced by younger widows and those by their seniors. I wondered whether some of these differences, especially the disruptions faced right after the death of the husband, could be a result of the differences in how each woman experienced her marriage. After all, we would expect a marriage of ten to fifteen years to represent a perspective different from one of thirty or more years. As we have seen, feelings and attitudes about the quality of the marriage can profoundly affect the course of recovery. When compared to older widows, I found that younger ones experience more anger, guilt, and ambivalence toward their husbands.

Why would young widows react to the death of their husband with such painful feelings? Though, overall, the quality of their marriages was about equal to those of older widows, young women often have intense feelings of abandonment. Being unexpectedly thrust into widowhood at a point in their lives when the death of a spouse is a rare event throws them into a psychological dilemma. Other researchers who have studied the importance of "time schema" in the lives of adults have discovered that the feeling of being "off" or "on time" for various life events, such as parenthood and career, has serious consequences for an individual's well-being. Furthermore, it has been found that most women at mid-life begin to think about becoming widows. As I mentioned above, such "rehearsals" are not part of the psychology of younger women. Thus young widows are simply less prepared for the loss. The self-blame and rage they experience in the midst of an event for which they have no models or framework may propel them into intense feelings of guilt and anger that make their recovery all the more difficult.

The external stresses faced by young widows and the psychological challenges do appear to take their toll, but this was not the whole story. When I interviewed the young widows a year later, they showed a marked recovery. In fact, they were feeling better, on the whole, than the older widows. While younger women initially do have more difficulty coping, their grief seldom persisted for years, as did the grief of some of the older women.

When I saw Ricky a year later, she was well on her way to total recovery. The panic she so articulately described in the first months after her husband died is totally gone. She is no longer depressed. Most telling was Ricky's sense of being in control of her life: "I have a boyfriend now," she told me, "a very nice solid man. We are good for one another, but I'm not ready for marriage by any means. I'm enjoying my independence too much for that. I bought a new house several months ago. There's only one name on that deed, and that's mine. While that's sort of scary, it's also very nice because I have this feeling that this is mine and no one can take it away from me."

Why are younger widows able to recover so well? Is it because, being younger, they are "psychologically" more resilient? Is it because they can envision rebuilding their lives within a new marriage, constructing a future for themselves? Or, are there characteristics within their environment that facilitate recovery?

Though I found no evidence that younger widows were psychologically more resilient or healthier than the older women, they did get more help and support from friends and family. This help continued long after the husband's death. It is perhaps an overused truism that the right kind of help from friends and family during a crisis in life is a potent antidote to sadness, and studies have consistently demonstrated the power of the support from others for a widow's recovery. I found dramatic differences between the quality and quantity of help available to younger widows and that available to the older ones. There is no question that a widow of thirty lives in a social world different from that of a woman widowed in her sixties. The younger widows have no adult children to depend upon, but they usually receive plenty of support from their parents. This is especially true for women with children under the age of twelve. Ironically, society's inaccurate stereotype that young widows experience the loss of a husband more intensely than older women serves the young widow well. Friends and families are more willing to take the extra step in helping out, particularly when young children are involved.

Young widows also receive frequent and useful support from their friends. Young widows rarely have widowed age-mates. Unless they join a widows' support group, they must rely on their married friends much more than older widows do. In fact, the older the widow, the less support is available to her from married friends. Soon after their husband's death, only 44 percent of the youngest widows had close friends who were also widowed compared to 65 percent for widows between the ages of forty to fifty, 76 percent between fifty and sixty, and 84 percent for widows over sixty. Even seven years after the death, younger widows still remained embedded in their network of married friends and were twice as likely to receive help from old friends than older widows were.

At the end of seven years' study, I also found that most young widows were still receiving generous support from their families. Their good recovery was directly linked to this help from friends and family. When young widows did not receive this aid, their recovery was compromised.

Young widows are also better able to envisage a future for themselves. Even early in their bereavement, when they are in the throes of grief and loss, they can easily imagine that they will someday remarry. Seventy-six percent of the youngest widows believe this, as opposed to 50 percent of those between the ages of forty to forty-nine, 35 percent between fifty and sixty, and 10 percent for widows over sixty. Though the actual remarriage rates for the young widow are much lower than estimated, their predictions are supported by their frequency of dating. Whether or not they do remarry, the belief that they will becomes an important psychological prop, enabling the young widow to see herself someday getting beyond her current very real difficulties.

In their struggles with the realities of their day-to-day existence, young widows do not have the luxury of engaging in meaningful self-examination. Faced with the complexities of raising small children, they do not have the space in their lives for self-transformation. This doesn't mean that none of the young widows ever grew or developed new perspectives on their self-image. It just means that their process was more difficult.

There is scant evidence that young widows experience any more problems in adapting to bereavement than do their older counterparts. Though some of the difficulties they face are different from those faced by older widows, they also have more resources to call upon. On the minus side, their loss is an unexpected event, relatively rare in our society. Young widows also suffer from a high level of stress that comes from learning to be a single parent. Young widows were more likely to carry added psychological burdens from their marriages and to react to the loss of their spouse with anger and guilt. They blame him for dying too early, and they blame themselves for having contributed to his untimely death. On the plus side, young widows are more likely to live in a social world of supportive family and married friends, and they are able, despite their pain, to envisage a more hopeful future.

A younger widow's experience of widowhood is simply "different" from the widowhood of her older cohorts. The belief that her recovery is either easier or more difficult is nothing more than a myth.

Chapter 6

Friends and Family

Friends and family can be of immense help in coping with the many challenges widows face. But they can also cause problems if they do not provide the right kind of assistance, or if they offer help in the wrong way or at the wrong time. In some instances they may interfere with a widow's recovery.

Widows, especially those in middle and late life, almost universally feel alienated from married friends. The old "couples network" that she and her husband used to rely on for social and emotional needs typically fades away. Friends may now perceive a "single" woman as a threat to the stability of their own marriages and so they urge her to begin dating before she is ready. Families, on the other hand, often disapprove of early dating. So the expectations of old friends conflict with what family members recommend. Many women get out of this bind by reconfiguring their social networks. They develop new, less conflicted friendships, often with other widows.

Despite the potential pitfalls of help gone astray, widows whose friends and family provide companionship, consolation, and concrete support during the crisis of bereavement fare much better than widows who receive little or no help. Lack of support can actually affect peoples' physical and mental health, and even their very survival.

Since I knew that not all help is helpful, I wanted to discover what "effective" help is and to learn the pitfalls of help from friends and family. I began by asking the women what kind of help they really needed from friends and family. Assistance is not a disembodied "thing"; it is a service provided by specific people in the person's life. I asked if "effective" help depended on who did or did not give it. Finally, I put all of these answers into a widely flexible time line, since the course of widowhood changes over time. As grief subsides, a variety of new challenges confront the widow. Her needs are not static, nor do her requirements for help remain fixed.

A widow yearns for kindness and understanding while she grieves: a shoulder to cry on; a place to talk freely about her sadness; someone to listen to both her good and bad memories about her husband; someone to go to the movies with; practical help in figuring out finances, fixing the car, or knowing what to say to a troubled adolescent son; or just someone to simply take away the sharp edge of loneliness. The presence of such aid often makes the difference between comfort and distress.

Most of us are lucky enough to have lived all our lives receiving help from others. We may feel this is as natural as breathing, but in reality, widowhood makes what was once a common expectation much more complex. Widows can be emotionally complicated and needy people, and sometimes it's no picnic being around them. At the same time they are dealing with their grief, they need to manage the transition back to being single, with its challenge to construct a new self-identity. They have to become the sole head of a household even as they renegotiate relationships with friends and family. And many widows have to somehow balance their own needs with the special needs of their children.

And so it is no surprise that, if she is to be successful in negotiating these complex challenges, help from the widow's family and friends is crucial. There are many different kinds of help, and a variety of people who can provide it.

As I listened to widows talk about their needs, and the manner in which their friends and families responded to them, I soon discovered that *who* provided the help was as important as *how* they helped.

Nancy, a petite sixty-three-year-old widow, had lots of support from friends during the first few months after her husband died: "One of the things that made a great deal of difference in helping me retain my sanity right after Bill died was that there were so many super people around me. My closest girlfriend was married to a man who worked away from home during the week, and she would come over two or three nights a week. A lot of people called me during the first couple of months. I was also very busy with my son Johnny and his hockey games. We live in a small town and there were over two hundred people at Bill's funeral. A lot of people showed their concern, and my mother was particularly helpful. All I wanted to talk about for those first couple of months was my husband's death, but, thank God, other people let me talk.

"As time wore on, however, my old friends who were very supportive right after Bill died dropped away. I think most of them felt like "Oh, she's doing fine. She doesn't need us now." That wasn't true. I still needed their friendship and help, and a kind ear once in a while. When I went out to social gatherings, the couples I knew were a little stiff around me, and I began to feel like a fifth wheel. Some of my friends did eventually become more relaxed with me, but when they started talking about what they and their husbands and children were going to be doing, I realized that I had nothing in common with them."

At that time, when Nancy was in the depths of her depression and alienation with no one to provide the kind of help she desperately needed, she met Cynthia, a widow she had known slightly. "We soon became close friends. She really could understand what I was going through since she had traveled the same road a few years ago. Cynthia introduced me to other widows, and before long, they became my main source of help. I doubt that I could have gotten through this without them."

Nancy's story illustrates a simple but frequently overlooked truth: *Who provides the help makes a critical difference.* Nancy found several new friends who were like her. All were widowed. She could let go of her old friends who were not giving her what she needed. The kind of help you receive, how dependable it is and how well it matches your needs are all very important in creating an emotional safety net; but just as important is the person who provides the help. Support may come from a wide variety of sources—siblings, relatives, coworkers, married friends, friends who were themselves widowed, and neighbors—but help from parents and grown children is the most crucial of all.

One-half of the widows I studied had at least one living parent. Most said that their parents' comfort and aid was the most effective in helping them cope with the wide range of emotions raised during the grieving process. Often widows find themselves having to resolve feelings of ambivalence about their dead husbands, expressed as anger and guilt. Mothers especially can offer unique help in dealing with these feelings. Many of the widows I interviewed had mothers who had suffered the loss of a husband and could share their experience with their daughters, giving them an anchor to hold onto and a shared perspective.

Adult children, on the other hand, provide "high-contact" help. While a widow's parents, usually her mother, may help her deal with the deeper emotional issues, especially right after the loss, adult children help her by just being there on a regular, dependable basis. Widows recover more quickly when their adult children call them frequently to see how they are doing, make themselves available to solve problems such as fixing a leaky faucet, or just drop in from time to time. For younger widows who did not have adult children, parents seemed to move into the vacuum and fill *both* roles, offering deep emotional support and high levels of contact. When both parents and adult children are available to help, the widow's recovery is speeded along.

Friends and family compliment each other, providing different kinds of help. Though appropriate help from family is important to a widow's recovery, women who also had friends to rely on healed and adjusted to their new lives with the most success. Widows with supportive friends feel much greater satisfaction and a greater sense of control over their lives, are less depressed, and have an easier time moving from the married to the single state. When a widow had no friends with whom to talk about personal problems or to provide emotional support, guidance, or information, it took a longer time to recover.

Both family and friends did equally well when it came to listening to personal problems and providing warmth and affection when needed. Friends, however, were generally more helpful in the guidance and information department than family members.

It is important to point out, however, that not all friends are equally helpful. Widows like Nancy, who tried to hang on to the friends she had shared with her husband took longer to recover. It was only when Nancy was able to let go and find new friends that she was able to get on the path to recovery. Women who found new friends, especially other widows, made a much more successful adjustment.

Catherine, a sixty-two-year-old widow of four months, talked about what she considered the source of her greatest help: "While my neighbors and family were very helpful, only another widow can really know what you are going through. You don't have to wonder if they really understand you, you know they do. When you're widowed, your social life changes completely. All of a sudden, you don't fit into your old circle. You more or less need to make new friends and to adjust to losing old friends."

When Expectations of Who Will Help Are Dashed

Each of us carries within ourselves an image, often barely recognized, of whom we expect help from when we are facing a crisis. When I studied couples who had lost a child, I found that their pain of an almost unbearable tragedy is magnified because of the almost universal difference between the ways in which men and woman cope with tragedy. Though women need to talk and express their feelings, most of the men I studied suffered their pain by withdrawing into silence. The problem was compounded because neither could turn to the other for the help that they needed and had come to expect over the length of their marriage. Often the marriage was torn apart, in large part because of the deep disappointment of not getting the support each had come to expect from their spouse. *Not getting help from those you expect it from is devastating.*

Widows who did not get help from people whom they thought they could count on, or women who received inappropriate responses from friends and family they trusted, were devastated. *It is far more vital to a widow's recovery that she receive help from the people she has always believed were there for her rather than from dozens of people she did not expect help from.* When I examined the type of help widows received from their mothers, I found that widows whose mothers were living and provided support, particularly during the first six months, recovered somewhat faster than those women whose mothers were dead. Recovery was most seriously impeded for widows whose mothers were living but who did not reach out and help.

Trish, a forty-nine-year-old woman whose husband died six months ago, struggled with her disappointment when her mother failed to help her. About six months after her husband Donald's death, Trish moved out of their house: "I just couldn't go on living in the house where Donald died. My son, Don Jr., had just started high school, and I found a new house close by, so he didn't have to change friends or schools. My oldest, Kevin, is twenty-one and out on his own. I'm not working now, but for twenty years I used to be a buyer for a large department store."

Since the death, Trish has suffered from a number of anxiety symptoms. She has high blood pressure that has to be controlled by medication, severe anxiety attacks, insomnia, and uncontrollable crying jags: "I have a terrible time before going to sleep. Sometimes I get so frightened of the dark that I have to get up and turn on the lights. I'm afraid if I open my eyes, I'll see Donald's ghost. I know it's unreasonable, but I feel as if he is still controlling me, even from beyond the grave, that he could somehow prevent me from going forward with my life. I know I love Donald, but there is a great deal of unfinished business between us. At times I feel that I still have to be a good little girl for him.

"I also have to be a good little girl for my mother. I thought I could count on her to help me deal with my grief, fears, and confusion. She went through a stormy bereavement herself and should know how it feels. I keep trying to talk to her about how sad I am and all those terrible thoughts I have about Donald. All she says is, 'Don't worry. I got over it, you will too.' I just can't believe she is doing this to me when I need her so much. I feel as if she is slamming the door right in my face. If I didn't have two close girlfriends I could talk to, my woman's club, and the hospital auxiliary where I do volunteer work, I think I would lose my mind."

One year later, Trish is still struggling with her life and her ambivalent feelings toward Donald. She and her mother have almost stopped speaking, another loss that complicates her recovery. Despite these very real problems, Trish has made some progress, though she still has a long way to go. She values life more but doesn't know what to do with it. Should she ignore the fact that she's affluent enough not to have to work and go to college to become a nurse? Should she stay at home and become more involved with charity work? Or should she simply become a lady of leisure and travel? She prays for guidance in making the right choices, but still has trouble making sense of what's happened to her.

Her life is still filled with anxiety and stress. She misses her husband, worries about her son Craig leaving her when he grows up in another five years, and is fearful of becoming old and unattractive. She's hungry for a relationship where she can be touched and held, but does not quite feel ready for a sexual relationship.

Though Trish has received plenty of support from friends, the shadow of not getting help from her mother has colored her journey through bereavement. She has had to cope with two losses, the death of her husband and her grief for a mother who refused to be there for her. Trish's story mirrors many that I heard from widows in similar circumstances. Her recovery was compromised and delayed because of the added burden of parental abandonment. Though many widows I spoke with had tried very hard, they could rarely elicit more support from the trusted people who had let them down—and this weighed heavily upon them all.

Characteristics of Effective Help

As we have just seen, receiving help from the people you expect to be there for you is critical. Beyond that, there are several other criteria that characterize effective help.

Availability Over Time

All societies develop rituals to address grief and provide emotional support during the early or "acute" period. In fact, almost all of the widows I studied received some help from a variety of friends, family members, and professionals during the first month. Obtaining help from friends and family beyond this time, however, proved to be more difficult.

One widow succinctly summed up her situation: "My friends and family were much more generous in helping with my worst problems right after Phil died, and I appreciated that. What they didn't understand is that widows need help in a lot of areas, and we need it for more than a month or two. I've heard a lot of widows say, 'After the funeral is over, you go home to an empty house and people pretty much leave you alone.'"

Josephine, a sixty-two-year-old widow, had this to say about her experience: "My children were always there for me, but the friends who had socialized with Peter and me as a couple pretty much left me alone. A few called on me once or twice after the funeral, but that was it. I was hurt. After all the years we had spent together and all the things I'd done for them, they abandoned me when I really needed them.

"But then I realized that I'd done the same thing to other friends whose husbands had died. I'd reached out to them at first, but then life went on. I guess that's more or less the way things are. Thank God I have my sons and daughters-in-law. They haven't let me down. Tim, my oldest, calls me every day. He always says, 'Mom, can I do anything for you? I'm here if you need me.' My youngest doesn't call as frequently, but I know he cares. Their wives are busy raising children and working, but they drop over after work to chat. Sometimes they bring me something to eat that they cooked the night before. I feel cared for and cherished."

Dependability

More important than the amount and kind of help provided by friends and family is the consistent availability of help when it's needed. *If help can't be counted on, it's not helpful.*

Linda, a fifty-three-year-old widow, described the dependability gulf between the kind of help available right after the funeral and the help that came later: "When John died, a lot of my friends really helped. Suddenly, not long after the funeral, they weren't there anymore. A few friends were semihelpful, floating in and out and saying they would call me. Well, sometimes they did, but most of the time they didn't. Thank God my mother was there for me. We had never been very close, and she wasn't someone I could talk to easily. Her health wasn't great, so I couldn't count on her to help me very much with the house or the kids. Yet, looking back, if it weren't for her, I would have been a basket case. Just having somebody with me who really cared, a warm body to fill the void and listen to me if I wanted to sound off, saved me. I'll be forever grateful.

"I knew, without her ever saying it out loud, that she understood because she had gone through the same thing when my father died.

All I seemed to need was to have someone just be there, someone who could be responsive and simply present. When my friends began to fade away, I felt hurt, but maybe it was partly my fault. I was so totally uninterested in doing anything or carrying on a normal life, I might just have scared them away."

The Type of Help Needed and the Type Received

If a widow really needs a shoulder to cry on, a friend or family member who offers to help with tasks around the house might do more harm than good. Neither is it true that the more help you receive, the speedier your recovery. Not all help is the same. Everything depends on the *type of help* you receive from family and friends.

As I listened to widows talk about how their loved ones had reached out to them, it became clear to me that help comes in different packages.

Contact—Many widows talked about the importance of simply being with or talking to others. They needed someone to attend social or recreational activities with. Simply talking on the phone or getting together with another person was also helpful.

Emotional Support—Many of the widows rated having someone to support and comfort them when they were feeling down as very important.

Guidance—Widows need someone to help them get a perspective on their problems. They also need information and advice about the problems and challenges of widowhood.

Intimacy—Widows need people who are willing to share thoughts and feelings about loss or to talk about personal problems with. Sometimes they just want to share a good laugh.

Sanctioning—We all need to be valued and approved of for who we are and how we act. For widows, caught up in a maelstrom of change, the approval of friends and family is doubly important. Simply being appreciated, getting encouragement about the future, receiving approval for having (or wanting to have) an active social life or for how they are leading their lives mean a great deal to widows.

Two widows, Ellen and Magrath, were distressed when they found that the kind of help they were receiving from old friends did not match what they needed. How each woman handled the situation had a marked effect upon their recovery.

Ellen, a fifty-year-old mother of three teenagers, talked about the sadness she felt: "The social life Lee and I had together was mostly seeing our married friends in their homes. After he died, I felt very uncomfortable trying to continue spending time with them in the same way, and I don't think they had a much better time with me. Finally I just sat down and talked to my closest friends about the problem. Although they hated to admit it, they told me that it did make them uneasy to have me over by myself. Without Lee to talk to the husbands, the old easy interaction we had was gone.

"I decided the only thing to do was to cultivate a new circle of single friends. After all, I had to figure out how to be a single person, and I thought other single people might have some insight that would help me. Plus, they'd be able to tell me I was doing it right—my old friends had known me too long as part of a married couple to be able to give me the reassurance I needed that I was handling all my new problems well.

"We keep in touch now, mostly by phone, but I don't see them socially any more. It's been hard to let go of the people who have known and loved me for so many years, but I don't think I had a choice. And I don't blame them for it—I understand it, but I can't help but feel sad. I do have new friends, and I think they are an important part of moving on and changing my life to fit my new circumstances. They've helped me look forward instead of back."

Magrath, a fifty-six-year-old widow, found it difficult to let go of old friends, even though they didn't help her. "When Bill died, all of my family were living far from California. My kids were all grown and had families of their own. As a couple we did have lots of friends, and I naturally turned to them for help. I was the only widow in our group. They were very nice to me right after the death, helping me make the funeral arrangements and seeing to it that I had plenty to eat. Of course my kids flew in and were there for a week. Then they had to go back home.

"My friends were there for me at first, but after a month of reaching out, they stopped—it was as if, 'That's over, it's time for you to get back to your life.' What life? How? I was confused and disappointed. Maybe they would've helped more if I'd asked, but I couldn't ask! Somehow, I didn't feel particularly close to any of them. I thought they seemed uncomfortable around me, especially if I started to remember Bill."

When I asked Magrath if she needed to talk to someone about Bill, she replied very emphatically, "Yes, I need to get it all out and there is no one listening. One widow at work that I've known over the years did approach me and offered friendship and support. That felt good, but I didn't take up her offer, I really didn't know her that well. I wanted my friends to be there for me and they weren't."

Widows commonly find that old friends are not able to provide the help they need. Elaine directly addressed her disappointments, accepted them, and recognized her friends' limitations. This enabled her to search for new sources of help. Magrath, in contrast, was stuck, unable to tell her old friends what she needed, or to seek new ones, even when they were available to her.

It is rare that a single source of help will address all the issues faced during a successful journey through widowhood. Families are good at offering a shoulder to cry on when you're down, but learning to negotiate the transition from being married to becoming single is often best met by widowed friends of your generation who have gone through the experience already.

The Two Faces of Advice

Friends and family think that giving good advice is the way to be most helpful to widows. Unfortunately friends and family members often cannot penetrate the cloud they cast on the widow, as if she were suffering from a mysterious, dangerous, and communicable disease. Death makes people uncomfortable, and most people are uneasy around a widow, projecting their own anxieties onto her. Rather than listen for what she really needs, they freely and frequently give advice that is not helpful. Almost every widow I talked to described how she was flooded with suggestions about what she needed to do, but useful advice was rare.

In a recent study widows were asked what advice was helpful and what wasn't. Here is the list of advice they said was not useful and often made them feel worse.

The Fourteen Most Unhelpful Statements Widows Hear

- You're standing up well to it.
- It is the will of God.
- I know just how you feel.
- You'll be fine.
- This will end soon.
- Life is for the living.
- It is time you got over it.
- You're lucky to have the children.
- You're lucky the children are grown up.
- At least you're young and can remarry.
- Time heals everything.
- You had a good life with him.
- One can't live with the dead.
- You're lucky to have had him for so long.

Widows found that platitudes and rationalizations did not match their feelings. They don't want to be told that life will be better, or that what they have lost can be replaced. They resent someone who has not suffered the death of a husband telling them that she or he can understand their feelings.

Widows are also bombarded with advice from doctors, lawyers, and the media. It's hard to turn to a newspaper or magazine without finding some column advising widows on how to cope. Not all of this information is bad. Some of the women I interviewed found some meaning in what they read, but many stated that the media advice didn't fit their special circumstances. Still others were looking for personalized insights into widowhood that aren't readily or easily available in the press, or even in the library.

If you are having difficulty finding the right kind of advice in the media, you are not alone. Most common is *philosophical advice* such as "See life as larger than the individual, extending into future generations," or "See widowhood as a challenge rather than simply as a loss. Find ways through your personal religious beliefs to accept the inevitable." There is no dearth of *advice about time* such as "Give yourself time to grieve."

The bookstores are also full of treatises on *practical advice* with titles such as *How to Manage Your Finances.* Pop psychology articles in women's magazines often emphasize *advice about negative attitudes* such as "Avoid self-blame and anger," for example. And finally, all media sources are replete with *advice about seeking out help.* Media messages might include statements such as "Find people to talk to, seek out other widows," "Join a support group," "Psychotherapy can help," "Let your friends know how you feel," or "Don't hide your feelings from your children."

Why does such advice often feel empty to a widow? There is no simple answer to this question. Most often, widows said that the information didn't speak to them, didn't match their feelings. Others found that something that had left them cold when they read it six months ago suddenly made sense. Some found that they were enormously helped by what they heard or read. There are no general rules on what will help, but it clearly doesn't hurt to look at what is out there. Remember, advice is not fixed in stone. You need to evaluate and try it on for size. It may fit; it may not. The danger is to accept all information as if it were the revered truth and then blame yourself for not following it.

Your Changing Needs

Relationships with friends and family almost always change during the first two years of bereavement. To try to keep things the same is both ineffectual and impractical. As I talked to widows over the first seven years of their bereavement and asked them to look back and reflect upon their relationships to family and friends, almost all of them spoke of the changes that had occurred in these relationships.

Widowhood has a marked impact upon friendships. Six out of ten of the widows I interviewed said that they saw their old friends less after their husband's death. Only one out of ten told me that they saw these friends more. Within a year or so of the death, a surprising 15 percent of the widows had all new close friends; 26 percent had mostly new friends; 32 percent still counted mostly on their old friends; and 27 percent depended totally on those with whom they were friends prior to widowhood. Twenty-nine percent had no widows among their friends; 47 percent had a few; and 24 percent had friends who were mostly, or all, widows.

As time passes, widows frequently report a decrease in the availability of help from both friends and family. If this change is too abrupt, it can cause serious problems. Widows whose families spend less and less time with them have less of a sense of well-being, fewer feelings of being in control of their lives, and more difficulty moving toward becoming single. A similar pattern prevails when old friendships fall by the wayside, especially if insufficient new friendships are formed.

Negotiating the challenges of widowhood is not a static process.

Since the various "inner" and "outer" tasks that confront widows extend into future years, it is unlikely that they will require the same kind of help, or even the same helpers, right after the death as those they will need a year or two later. It is a dangerous oversimplification to think solely in terms of good and bad friendship groups, or good and bad quality of help. For example, research has shown that during the initial grieving period, while a widow is taking her first tentative steps toward adjusting to her loss, a group of people who have known one another for a long time is the best choice for providing emotional support and reducing initial loneliness. Later, as the widow begins to reorganize her life as a single person, new friends may be needed, particularly if she is trying to create a new life-style or identity. During this period, when her role is changing, she may need a new social circle to help her resolve the problems associated with this transition. At this stage of her recovery, she may be better off having a group of friends who do not all know each other. This wider resource base can provide her with information and opportunities that a single, ingrown social circle cannot.

There is no question that the right kind of help from the people you expect to be there for you is critical for quick recovery. Most of the widows I studied managed, sometimes through a considerable struggle, to find such help. Support is often there, but obtaining it takes effort and persistence. Remember, as widows change over time, so do their requirements for who can help and what kind of help they need.

Chapter 7

Do You Need Psychotherapy?

If you are feeling depressed, sad, and irritable; if you find yourself crying frequently, having trouble sleeping and eating, occasionally being confused, making silly mistakes you usually wouldn't have, feeling the presence of your husband, or thinking that you saw him yesterday in a crowded shopping mall, do you need therapy? On the other hand, if you are able to get on with your life almost immediately, immersing yourself in the many new tasks you need to accomplish in the wake of your husband's death, and if you seem to be able to put your grief behind you, are you suppressing your grief? When friends and family encourage you to seek out the help of a psychotherapist, saying, "It won't hurt and it may help," should you follow through? If you see yourself in this paragraph, should you seriously consider the services of a mental health specialist?

This chapter will attempt to give you some answers to your questions about therapy: Will it help me? What happens in therapy? How does it work? What are the attitudes of psychotherapists toward the problems of widows? Does therapy help widows? What are the signs I should look for to tell me that I need professional help?

Mental health professionals look at psychotherapy as an important resource for those struggling with the loss of a spouse. Typically, they offer help by encouraging widows to explore their grief. The questions they ask most frequently are: "How intense and prolonged is your grief?" and "Have you been able to 'appropriately' mourn?" From the psychotherapist's point of view, these queries provide touchstones for helping to restore you to your previous level of functioning, which they consider to be *the* optimum state of recovery. Many mental health experts believe that true mourning entails an inner struggle between intense yearning for the lost husband and the reality of his absence. Of particular importance to them is helping you negotiate the journey through mourning, which they generally define as the widow's gradual surrender of her psychological attachment to her husband, in order to liberate her feelings for investment in new relationships. Psychotherapists assume that many psychiatric illnesses are expressions of pathological mourning, which they define as "excessive grief as well as its opposite, failure to grieve, and denial of emotional feelings." This viewpoint assumes that there is an "ideal" intensity and duration of grief that should be the standard for all.

Because of this "proper grieving" approach, many psychotherapists feel that it is critical for a widow to follow a prescribed time line of mourning, which delineates the changes in intensity of grief that a healthy widow should be experiencing and the predetermined stages that her grief should pass through. Adherence to this schedule is a measure of a widow's success. Departures from the "expected" are often seen by therapists as strategic guides in addressing the problems associated with the loss of a spouse. Thus, failure to grieve or a brief period of grief are seen as failures in "appropriate mourning." Similarly, "protracted grieving"—beyond some point in time—is seen as equally troublesome, requiring professional help. We did learn, however, in chapter 2, that women who experienced brief or limited grief showed the best and fastest recovery. Even after seven years they were doing very well.

This traditional view, which begins with the belief that reactions to the loss of the spouse frequently lead to the development of "problems" needing the attention of a mental health specialist, has had profound effects on how widows are perceived by the professional community. At a conference of mental health professionals specializing in working with grief, I asked the attendees to estimate the percentage of widows nationally who are suffering serious enough reactions to the loss of a spouse to require their services. Their answers—estimates that ranged from as low as 10 percent to a high of 90 percent—were both surprisingly inconsistent and disturbingly out of touch with actual statistics. The real figure, based on a National Institute of Mental Health survey of 20,000 randomly selected adults, ages eighteen through ninety-nine and drawn from all walks of life, reports that only 2.1 percent of the 2,648 widows they studied were classified as ever having had a psychiatric disorder associated with the death of their spouse. This is five times lower than the lowest estimate and forty-five times lower than the highest estimate!

Of course, mental health experts spend time only with widows who seek their help and so their view of widows comes only from patients. In addition, many mental health experts admitted that not all the widows they see really need psychotherapy. These women enter therapy to explore, in a comfortable and nonjudgmental setting, issues that have been stimulated by their loss and new status.

How do widows "use" psychotherapy? What do they talk about? I recently studied widows who "volunteered" to enter a therapy group conducted by professionals who were trained to approach spousal bereavement as a series of constructive challenges rather than to place their focus solely on grief and mourning. A common theme in this group was *change*—the transition from being a "we" to becoming an "I." The fears and difficulties of learning to live as a single person were high on the list of subjects these women discussed, and many shared their deep loneliness and their sense of no longer being special to another person.

Rebecca, six months after Sam died, was still in deep grief. Her loneliness was intense. This seventy-two-year-old woman was still living in her much too large suburban house, where she had lived all her married life. She cried a great deal when she talked about being alone: "I've never been without a man in my life; when I was growing up there was my father and my older brothers. They were always around. After I married, Sam was always there. We shared everything throughout our lives. Now that he's gone and my brothers are long since dead, I'm not special to anyone anymore. It's not the same; my children are attentive, but they have their own lives. I need to be special and I will never be that again."

From the opposite end of the spectrum, others spoke of experiencing a sense of liberation and exhilaration with their new freedom.

Despite a good and lengthy marriage, Mary always felt that many parts of herself had been left behind: "Andy was a good and kind man, but he filled all the space in our life. He took care of everything, telling me I shouldn't worry myself about decisions, even one involving our three children. He was a good provider. I never lacked. Now here I am, sixty-eight and having to start to think for myself. It's scary and exhilarating. I like taking responsibility for myself. I've learned many new things: paying taxes, going on vacation by myself, testing my limits. I know I can do this."

Many women expressed fear that, if they were to change, grow, develop a new relationship, and enjoy their life, they would be betraying their relationship with their dead spouse.

Sally, a vivacious sixty-one-year-old widow, told me how she went to pieces after Leonard died: "I cried all the time; it just came over me when I would think of him. It's been eight months since Leonard passed away. Two months ago I met Robert, and we are beginning to get close. He wants to marry me—I don't know. Sometimes I think it's too early. I keep thinking if I do, it's like really forgetting Leonard. Then I think, maybe Leonard was meant to die and that Robert was meant to come into my life. I'm confused.

"Last week I had a dream about this. I was in some place where there's a kind of building and all these men were going into the buildings. Something was going to happen there. I don't know, perhaps an interrogation. I saw Leonard go in and saw a lot of men come out, but Leonard was not with them. I looked for him up and down the streets; I walked around; and then I stopped and said to myself, 'You're not going to find him, he's dead.' Suddenly I saw a man come out; it was Robert. I got the powerful feeling that it was the right thing for me."

Sally, in her dream, is struggling with a feeling very common among women who start a new relationship. Despite a new and meaningful beginning, she struggled for another year with the feelings articulated in her dream of how to start again with a man who clearly was important to her. They finally married two years after Leonard's death.

Often widows discussed the tyranny of the "shoulds," the social expectations confronting them. At one meeting the widows were compiling a list of the most outrageous advice they received.

"My friend told me: 'It's only eight months since your husband died; you haven't mourned long enough.'" Another woman said that her mother shook her finger at her: "It's not right to show happiness so soon after your husband died." "How can you go out with a man? It's only six months since Tom passed away," was Emily's contribution to the list. Ramona told the group how her daughter-in-law was telling her that "you must get rid of all Ron's personal things right away." Several women in the group said that many of their friends told them, "It's best to hide your feelings of grief from your children." Valeria stated that her doctor told her, "Don't make any important decisions for at least a year." Clare said that her mother criticized her for wearing a dress that in her words "was too colorful for a widow."

Some widows shared an increased appreciation of the randomness and contingency of the world, but most were more aware of their personal mortality and of the value of living one's life in the immediate present rather than postponing life to the future. Many were greatly troubled by a sense of life's meaninglessness.

Martha, a fifty-four-year-old widow, talked about her struggle to find a new purpose in her life. One year after a brief course of psychotherapy, she described her progress with the journey toward meaning: "I still think a lot about it. I often wonder how I fit into the design of life; more often than I like, I feel just like a drop in the bucket. I want to be more than that. I know that sounds a little overblown, but it's important to me. Ever since Paul died I know I need more in life. My teaching young people is part of the answer, but I'm still searching for something more to fill the void I still feel."

Most who participated in the therapy found it a stimulating and useful experience.

What do we know about the ability of psychotherapy to help widows? There is no good scientific evidence that psychotherapy is any more effective in helping a widow recover than help from family, friends, clergy, or support groups. The reason for this state of affairs can be attributed to the way psychotherapy is studied. Many of the studies are based only on widows who actively seek out psychotherapy. Others rely on identifying "vulnerable" widows, those whom the researcher believes "require" psychological intervention. Still other studies evaluate programs that are offered to all widows. As might be anticipated by these descriptions, findings depend upon which widows are studied. Those who seek out a psychiatrist and are viewed as suffering from an "illness" associated with the their husband's death are obviously different from widows who have recently lost their spouses and are experiencing the typical feelings of grief and sadness. Furthermore, the studies differ in what kinds of control groups they compare their therapy to. Some researchers develop elaborate procedures for evaluating therapeutic effectiveness by comparing a group of widows who did not receive help beyond their family and friends to a group who attended therapy; others compared the results of one-on-one professional help to those of support groups. Most studies, however, do not bother with any comparisons whatsoever and only evaluate the effectiveness of their approaches by providing evidence labeled "before therapy" and "after therapy."

A recent study of mine illustrates the confusion that characterizes studies of psychotherapy efficacy for widows. I compared volunteers comprising a random control to those of another group who were receiving brief group psychotherapy specifically tailored to their problems. When I reevaluated these women one year later, I concluded that the results failed to provide clear-cut evidence of the effectiveness of psychotherapy on recovery. *Most of the widows studied improved during the year of study, but so did the randomized control group, who received no treatment.*

Overall, only a minute number of widows require professional mental health help because they are suffering from a specific psychiatric disorder caused by the death of their spouse. Nor is there convincing evidence that the current level of professional help is uniquely suited to modern widows struggling with the complex challenges generated by the loss of their spouse. Evidence from a number of studies indicates that other helpful settings, such as support groups, work just as well as psychotherapy for such widows.

When faced with the death of a spouse, who should seek out a mental health professional? To help you decide whether or not you need psychotherapy, I will first describe the widows I studied who felt the need for professional help. We should remind ourselves that just because most studies do not conclusively show that widows benefit from psychotherapy does not mean that professional help is never called for. The vast majority of the 600 widows I studied found help with their problems from many different sources—friends, family, support groups, clergy, and physicians. Most relied solely on help from their family and friends; one out of five relied on help from physicians and clergy; and one out of seven sought help from a psychotherapist.

Who were the widows who turned to psychotherapists? How did they differ from those who turned to physicians and clergy or from those who relied solely on their friends and family? What kinds of feelings and life circumstances propelled them to seek out psychotherapeutic help?

Many of those who turned to professionals for assistance felt that they *could not* rely upon their families or friends, reporting diminished contact with these sources of support since becoming widowed. They were experiencing considerable difficulty moving into the single role, and frequently reported high stress during this transition. Some were struggling with the problems of raising children as a single parent; others sought out therapy because of their struggles with regrets, meaning in life, identity, and existential despair. Still others sought therapy because of what they felt were unyielding conflicts with people in their lives. One widow named Sophie shared the following with me: "Although my mother-in-law and I never got along well, we at least had an armed truce while Larry was alive. As soon as he was buried, however, everything she had kept to herself came spilling out." Devastated by this unfair attack when she was at an all-time psychological low, Sophie sought help in psychotherapy.

Two Women Who
Went to Psychotherapy

In chapter 1, I described the challenges facing Susan and her experiences in psychotherapy. After the sudden death of her husband, Susan was in a state of shock, going through the motions of making arrangements and "learning how to be a widow." At the urging of friends, she sought out a psychotherapist, but at the end of a year of therapy she found herself struggling with two major problems: how to deal with what she was learning about her past in psychotherapy and how to cope with her barely recognized, but intense, feelings of dissatisfaction and lack of fulfillment in her life. Finally, Susan decided to terminate her therapy since it didn't seem to be taking her forward. By this time she was sleeping better and experiencing no major uncomfortable psychological symptoms.

When she left the therapist's comfortable chair, Susan's journey as a widow began in earnest. She decided to take an extended trip to Europe. This outer journey proved to be more important than Susan had ever anticipated: "It was the first time in my life that I was really alone. The trip was a chance to take time out and get away from all that was familiar and comfortable to me. It was also a chance to get away from the well-meaning deluge of advice from friends and family. I began to think about my life without Richard. Who am I going to be? I resolved that when I went back home, I wouldn't be the same as I was before."

Being abroad without the props of her familiar world started Susan on a much more important journey, a pilgrimage toward self-discovery and the construction of a new life. For the first time since Richard had died, Susan began to envision a life without him. After three months of traveling, she returned home and began to plan her future. She apprenticed herself to an art dealer, having resolved that what she wanted most in life was to establish her own gallery.

While maintaining her close friendships, Susan began to develop a wider circle of people who shared her artistic interests. She also decided to remain single: "I know that for now I don't want to remarry. It was nice to realize while on my trip that I could still be attractive to men, but my priorities are to see if I can succeed in my dream, a dream I've had all my life." Susan was launched.

Susan typifies the dilemma faced by many widows in today's world. She was not ill, but chose to involve herself in a course of therapy that unfortunately focused solely on her loss and grief. Therapy wasn't especially useful to her and may even have delayed her ability to face and productively use her own experience to move beyond grief.

In contrast, Lydia, also in her mid-fifties, was a widow who did need psychotherapy and who ultimately benefited from the experience. Lydia's husband, Bob, had died the previous fall after developing a rapidly metastasizing cancer. Leaving her high school teaching job, she nursed him night and day for six months, right up until the last week of his life.

Lydia was clearly suffering after Bob's death, so severely that her friends and children felt helpless in the face of her profound grief and incapacitating sadness. An active person before Bob's death, she literally took to her bed, withdrawing from others and her previous round of community organizations. Advice from her friends to get reinvolved with life simply bounced off her. Finally, her family doctor of twenty-five years suggested that she seek professional help and recommended Dr. Wicks, a woman psychiatrist who was about the same age as Lydia. At first, Lydia resisted the idea, but with the prodding of her children and friends, she finally called for an appointment.

Initially, Dr. Wicks explored the circumstances of Bob's death. She found that Lydia was a hyperresponsible woman, a characteristic that had dominated her life since early childhood, when she was growing up in a strict and coldly religious family. Despite her heroic nursing of Bob, she could not find solace in what she had done for him during those painful six months. Bob, often angry during the twenty-five years of their marriage, constantly raged at everyone and particularly at Lydia during his illness. He resented needing her and being dependent upon her. After Bob died, Lydia was flooded with feelings of guilt and doubt about the effectiveness of her nursing. She endlessly made the round of doctors, asking for absolution. Did I do the right thing? Could I have helped Bob more? If only . . . Despite their reassurance that "no man could have asked for a more devoted and caring wife," Lydia could find no comfort.

Guilt and recrimination overwhelmed her during her first months of widowhood, and she could neither mourn nor express her grief. This was the therapist's first important discovery.

After this revelation, Dr. Wicks clearly felt that some exploration of Lydia and Bob's twenty-five years of marriage was needed. At first, Lydia presented a portrait of a spouse who could do no wrong. Bob was "a wonderful man" and "the best of all husbands." Over time, however, with Dr. Wicks's patience and persistence, a different Bob began to emerge—a man who was exceedingly demanding and aggressive throughout the entire marriage. Sexually exacting, he viewed Lydia as an unresponsive woman, causing her much psychological pain. From the very first night of their marriage, he had little patience with her. Many times, when Bob was traveling, Lydia would lie awake thinking about him being in an auto accident or some other calamity that would leave him alive but totally dependent upon her. Despite the many difficulties in their marriage, there was a strong bond between them. Both were enmeshed in a mutually dependent relationship, and both took considerable pleasure and pride in raising three children together.

As the therapy progressed, Lydia's anger toward Bob emerged more clearly. During one session she suddenly burst into tears, saying, "I could have killed him. I don't mean that literally, but I was so angry with him all of the time." Her expression of these deep feelings of rage was a turning point in Lydia's therapy. For the first time, she could look at her marriage with Bob from a balanced perspective, fitting their relationship into her life experiences.

Once her therapy had enabled her to see her life in this manner, especially during the last three months of her year of treatment, Lydia began to reengage with life. She managed to return to her teaching and to tentatively reenter her previously busy club activities. Still fragile, she had not quite integrated her new, complex, and contradictory feelings and memories about her husband, yet she clearly was moving on and discovering, ever so tentatively, who she really was. At this point, she and Dr. Wicks felt that her therapy could comfortably end.

Lydia exemplified the widow who needs and can effectively use psychotherapy. Her utter dependence on Bob and her intense anger and guilt frightened her and those around her. Though concerned and willing, children and friends could really find no way to help. Her therapist recognized these barely suppressed feelings and patiently but consistently sought to bring them forward, enabling Lydia to finally put them into a perspective that released her from their tyranny.

Susan, on the other hand, represents those whose history and reactions to the loss of their husband are typical. Her experience falls within the broad range of widows whose journey through bereavement and responses to the challenges of widowhood are usual. In these cases, psychotherapy is unnecessary and occasionally can even divert women from developing their own, unique resolution of grief.

The differences these two women experienced in therapy are not a product of the skills of their therapist. Both therapists were highly experienced, and both viewed their client's "problems" in a similar light. The different results can be traced to the difference in their real psychological needs.

Psychotherapy is most effective for widows who feel intense anger and guilt about the death of their husband. Those who report high ambivalence toward their lost spouse, experienced as anger toward him and guilt about the circumstances of his death, not only enter therapy more frequently, but also improve more frequently over time.

Psychotherapy uniquely enables widows plagued by these "irrational" and obviously painful feelings about their loss to address them productively. For a widow overwhelmed by intense feelings of anger and guilt, the simple offering of understanding and friendship that can be found among family and friends, within support groups, and from other professionals, such as the clergy, appears to be insufficient. Psychotherapy is a system geared to healing irrational and overwhelming feelings not easily dealt with in other help settings and, as such, is most effective when a widow feels overwhelmed by distress and rage.

Chapter 8

Support Groups: Havens of Understanding and Comfort

It was a warm spring evening in a pleasant suburb of Chicago. Twelve women and two men had come to a meeting in a community center basement. Several of the women stood in a loose circle, chatting amiably with the familiar ease of old friends, and a few were engaged in animated and intimate conversations with one other person. Others stood alone, lost in their own thoughts.

Francis, recently widowed at fifty-four, entered the room apprehensively. She had only reluctantly dragged herself to a meeting of this local widows' support group at the urging of a friend. Despite countless reservations, Francis had promised herself and her friend that she would at least try it out, but she wondered what she could really gain from this diverse assortment of widows and widowers. They did not seem to be from any particular social class or background or to have anything much in common. Some were soft-spoken and reserved, while others were loud and boisterous; some were young and others old; some were well-dressed and others not.

After the death of her husband, John, Francis was frustrated when both her doctor and minister, who had been friends for many years, just didn't seem to understand her real problems. They were always too busy to listen. Old friends had been a little better. Ultimately Francis felt unsatisfied and alone. Friends were all too ready to pile on endless advice—take a trip, find a husband, get on with your life, see a therapist—but none of these suggestions matched Francis's real concerns. Although she found it hard to put what was troubling her into words, she knew instinctively that her friends' counsel was not what she needed. Finally, Francis had reluctantly decided to take the frightening step of attending a support group. "If I don't like it," she had told herself, "I can always leave."

Now as she looked around the room she felt like an outsider: "I don't see how these people can really help me," she thought. "I don't know any of them, and they all seem a bit odd, as if they weren't one hundred percent comfortable with themselves. Or maybe," she thought, "it's just me." Ever since John had died, Francis had felt like an outsider, as if she didn't quite fit in anywhere. She wondered whether her experience with this group would be a repetition of those painful social outings with the friends she had known for over thirty years. Would she always feel like the proverbial fifth wheel? "But perhaps," she told herself, "since these people were all widows and widowers, they'll understand these kinds of feelings. Maybe the group could help her after all."

Trying not to stare at this roomful of strangers, Francis took a chair in the back. Almost immediately, a woman detached herself from a small group of widows and came up to Francis to introduce herself. She told Francis that she was the group leader and that the meeting was about to start: "Would you like to take a seat in the circle of chairs at the front of the room?" she asked. When she saw panic flash across Francis's face, she quickly added, "It's okay if you prefer to sit in the back." Relieved that she could blend into the background if she wanted to, Francis stayed where she was.

Soon everyone quieted, and those still standing drifted to seats in the large circle. The woman who had greeted Francis began the meeting by suggesting that everyone introduce themselves since there was a new member in the group. One by one the men and women stated their names and how long they had been widowed or widowered. Some added how their spouses had died.

As the introductions moved around the room, Francis sat quietly. She did not dare talk, but she listened intensely, watching each person as she or he spoke. "Am I the oldest in the group?" she wondered, but decided that she wasn't, since the widow sitting in front of her looked older. Francis also began to wonder if she was the most recently widowed. No, one youngish-looking woman had lost her husband just one month ago. Another woman, she was surprised to note, had been widowed for almost five years.

The group began in earnest as Louise, a short matronly woman, talked about her struggle with terrifying nighttime loneliness during the past week. Lisa, obviously the youngest in the group, blurted out that she too had been consumed with loneliness. "This time," Lisa said, "I didn't try to run away. I looked those feelings right in the face and said, 'I'm not going to give in and always be terrified.' I knew I had to face them and try to get on with my life, so I decided to take action. The first thing I did was to make a list of all the things I could do to overcome my emptiness."

Soon the whole group was engaged in an animated yet thoughtful give-and-take as others added their own stories about their struggles with loneliness. Martha, aged sixty and widowed for two years, talked about how she had grappled with this problem during the first year and what it was like for her now. Listening to her, Francis was enthralled and intrigued. She wondered if she would ever have the courage to tell these strangers her innermost feelings. "How do they do it?" she wondered. "They make it look so easy. I'd like to be able to talk about the things that are troubling me, but I know I'm not ready. Maybe some day . . ."

After about an hour of discussion, the group was ready to stop. It dawned on Francis that even though these people seemed at ease when telling about their problems, their failures, and their victories, most were emotionally spent and needed a respite. People broke up into smaller groups and twosomes to enjoy coffee, cake, and conversation.

Tina, a recently widowed woman about the same age as Francis, came over to talk. Later, Francis told me about their conversation:

"As we chatted, I began to feel that somehow there was a chemistry between us. Tina's problems were so much like my own. I left the meeting bewildered yet curious and almost optimistic. I definitely decided that I had to come back, although I wasn't quite sure why. Somehow or other I felt that maybe this group could be helpful to me. And before the next meeting, Tina even called to see if I wanted to get together for lunch. I had already made my first new friend." And so the support group began for Francis.

What are support groups? A variety of labels can be used to describe them: self-help groups, mutual aid groups, or simply support groups. Whatever they are called, they are made up of people banding together to address a shared problem, be it a physical or emotional illness, a feeling of being stigmatized by society, difficulties in negotiating the normal transitions of living, or something as ordinary as the challenges arising from the stresses and strains of modern life. Whatever the source of the trouble, what unites the people who join these groups is a desire to seek help from people who know how they feel because they have "been there" themselves. The diversity and ubiquitousness of such groups is astounding. I once did a study, based on a national sample of 20,000 adults, and estimated that over 8 million people attended a support or self-help group during 1994.

Unlike "professional" help, which is steeped in theory and has professional customs, support groups evolve from the members' collective experiences and shared problems. Most of the people in such groups neither need nor want professional help, believing that personal experience is the best teacher. Support groups are self-governing and self-regulating. They emphasize self-reliance and are generally available without charge.

If we were to attend the group I described for six months, we would hear members talk about a wide variety of issues: coping with the feelings generated by the death of a spouse—anger, grief, guilt, loneliness, and regrets; moving into the role of being single again; sex, dating, and remarriage; being a single parent; and dealing with one's children, relatives, and married friends. These are grist for the mill in support groups, as are other common problems of everyday living. They may talk about new untested challenges, such as keeping the car and house in good repair. Discussions of financial arrangements and personal growth and development are also usually part of the widows' support group agenda.

The Value of Support Groups

"Do support groups work?" widows ask me. "Will one really help me feel better? Will a support group speed up my recovery?" The answer is definitely yes. During my seven-year study, I talked with 400 widows from across the country who had joined seventy different support groups, and compared them with a control group of 100 widows who were invited to participate in the same groups but chose not to. The widows I interviewed were from all walks of life and economic circumstance. Some were barely out of their early twenties and others were well into their seventies. Some had not completed high school, while others were well-educated professionals.

Regardless of their backgrounds, ages, and circumstances, widows who joined support groups recovered much faster. After one year, members of support groups felt less depression and used less medication and alcohol to alter their feelings of sadness. The more deeply involved they became in the groups, the greater their signs of recovery. They became less anxious, had a greater sense of well-being, higher self-esteem, and rated themselves as much improved.

One fifty-year-old widow named Eleanor talked about the importance of a support group in her recovery. Eleanor's greatest challenge was the struggle to become "single" again: "The support and encouragement of my group worked its magic. Since joining, I've learned to live for today. My future was taken away from me when Al died, and it took me a long time to build it up again. But now I know I can be happy as a single person.

"When Al was diagnosed with cancer, the doctors gave him six weeks to live. When he died nine months later, I felt as if the rug had been pulled out from under my life. He was the head of the household in every way, and I had always relied on him for everything. During the thirty years of our marriage, he made all the decisions, managed all the finances, and had the final say-so about everything, even about how we raised our three children. Al always took good care of me until the very end of his life. When he was gone, I felt as if I were having a bad dream. My first feeling was sorrow, but I very quickly began to feel cheated. I had expected us to grow old together. I never wanted to be the decision maker in the family.

"After Al's death I went through the motions of getting dressed every morning, going to work, and taking care of the kids. I was in a complete fog the whole time. I couldn't bring myself to make any decisions, even something as simple as buying a new rug for the dining room or getting car repairs done. After about six months, I began to force myself to become a tiny bit more independent. Surprisingly, I gradually began to feel more comfortable about taking charge of things. Now it only takes me a couple of days or a week at most to make a decision instead of three months, as it did at first.

"I didn't get to this place on my own, however. I had help. Months after Al died, I realized that I still hadn't really accepted his death. Around then, I noticed a local newspaper story about a widows' support group. I thought, a group for widows, that's strange. I wondered what it would be like to go to a meeting, but at the same time told myself that I had no need for such a group. A few weeks later, I decided to try one meeting, just to see what it was like. I never dreamt that I would enjoy it or that I would ever go again. At the beginning of that first meeting, everyone introduced themselves and then briefly told how her spouse had died. The moment I made my introduction, it dawned on me—I finally had to admit that I was a widow.

"At the end of the evening, I still had the feeling that I didn't really need this group of people, but something kept drawing me back. Soon I realized that I was getting involved. I really liked the gatherings and I began to get to know the other widows.

"My new friends in the group helped me get over my disappointments with my old friends. At first, I felt very rejected by the friends with whom Al and I had socialized for all those years. After his death I really made an effort to visit and keep up with them. After all, they were people I had known practically my whole life. Soon, however, I realized that my visits were extremely uncomfortable both for me and for them. When I realized this wasn't going to change, I sat down and had a frank talk with them, and we all admitted how ill at ease we were. My friends confided in me that their husbands no longer felt comfortable staying in the room and talking to me. They didn't know why, and I wasn't about to press them. I wasn't angry and I don't think they were, but I realized at that moment that I needed to find a social circle of single people.

"Being listened to by the other widows in the support group took away a little bit of my hurt. For the first time in a long while, I began to realize that I had a future. I even quit going to the cemetery. Before then, I'd find myself at Al's grave at least three times a week. I'm not even sure now why I went so frequently. The cemetery is a very long way from my house, and it took me hours to calm down after each visit. Now that I was able to put some of my sadness behind me, I began to relish life again. I started getting together socially with the other widows from my group, and I even began seeing a man regularly. I was growing more self-reliant all the time. Most important, I could once again take up my full family responsibilities and be both a mother and father to my children.

"Before Al died, I was friendly and outgoing, but after his death I became withdrawn and very depressed. I felt half dead, completely unattractive, and drab, as if my life were over. My friends in the support group drew me out. Molly, my best friend from the group, said to me, "You're not a bad-looking woman. Why don't you try wearing a little blush and a little eye makeup." At first I was dumbfounded by her suggestion. In my whole life I had never worn makeup, but one day I got brave and went out and bought some. I felt like a kid again—I didn't even know what to select—but I picked some out and started wearing it. I was thunderstruck when people started complimenting me on how I looked."

When I asked Eleanor to sum up what the group meant to her, she said, "I have four families now: my regular family, my support group, the church, and my friends at work. Each contributes something unique to my life. My job gives me a purpose in life, the church gives me spiritual guidance, my biological family gives me a feeling of confidence that somebody's always there, and my widows' group provides a place where I can take a long look at myself and begin to plan a new life."

Eleanor has clearly become a happier women who has reinvested herself in living: "Of course I still have my bad days," she says, "but all in all I feel that there's purpose and enjoyment in my life again."

Seven Principles of Support Groups

Here is why support groups work:

- They enable a widow to get in touch with her painful feelings.
- They provide an antidote to the all-too-common conviction that widows are alone and unique in their experience of their loss. In support groups, a widow discovers that she is not the only person ever to have had these feelings or thoughts.
- They provide an opportunity to see how other widows have dealt with their problems, supplying new information and models for change.

- They give a widow permission to find her own pathway through the challenges and dilemmas she faces. Unlike friends, family, and, all too frequently, professionals who are likely to prescribe the "right" way to do things, support groups accept and encourage diversity in problem solving.
- Support groups accomplish their work by helping people to experience hope, develop understanding, and feel loved.
- They provide a setting where people can form new relationships and find additional sources of sustenance, understanding, and comfort.
- They encourage widows to help one another, an experience that frequently aids the "helper" as much as the person being helped.

Support groups supply large doses of compassion and acceptance of the unique ways in which each widow addresses the problems of her loss. Let's take a closer look at how these groups help women find their way through the challenges of widowhood.

While passion, pain, anger, and profound sadness are not uncommon, the loss of a husband brings out these uncomfortable emotions to a high degree. Throughout our lives, most of us have learned to sit on these feelings and keep them hidden, even from ourselves. Support groups arouse strong feelings in their members, and they empower their members to "discover" and express such emotions. Some widows are stimulated, perhaps for the very first time, to acknowledge the death. Eleanor, described in detail at the beginning of the chapter, illustrates this kind of realization: "At the beginning of that first meeting, everyone introduced themselves and then briefly told how her spouse had died. The moment I made my introduction, it dawned on me—I finally had to admit that I was a widow." Some widows find the emotional intensity overpowering and leave their groups, but the majority of widows appreciate the opportunity to express those painful feelings because expressing them helped.

Support groups also enable widows to voice their innermost concerns. One of the most important issues discussed in support groups is how to cope with the specter of loneliness. Here is an example of a group I visited with. Feelings of aloneness strike widows at different times of the year.

Nancy related how anniversaries were her hardest times: "Every April I'm a basket case. As Tom's date of death draws closer, I go to pieces and can't stand being alone. Thank God, it only lasts for a few days."

Judy said, "Sometimes, when I'm faced with admitting that I'm really all alone, it helps to let go of all my anger and frustration."

Rita reported that she read trashy novels to put herself to sleep at night.

Carmen, the oldest widow in the group, whose husband had died three years before, said, "Although I used to dread being alone, I don't really feel that way anymore. In fact, coming home from an evening out feels good. My home is one of the few places where I can kick off my shoes and be myself."

Diane, a new member of the group who had lost her husband two months ago, had not yet spoken during the three meetings she had attended. This evening she began, with considerable difficulty, to tell the group that tonight was the first time she could admit to herself how lonely and sad she was: "Peter's death was a complete surprise to me and I guess I had to hold all the hurt inside."

The capacity of a support group to elicit formerly unspoken and perhaps hidden feelings makes an important contribution to a widow's recovery. This self-expression is especially critical for widows who are uncomfortable with intense feelings, attempt to suppress them, or even refuse to admit their existence. Being present in a support group where others are freely expressing their most intense emotions is beneficial for widows who feel emotionally blocked. After such meetings, widows often report feeling swept up in the general feelings, realizing that they feel them too. Most reported an initial sense of panic when this happened to them but that their panic soon melted away to be replaced with intense relief.

Support groups provide members with a setting in which they can learn from one another by enabling them to contrast their own feelings and attitudes with those of others in the group. These comparisons facilitate a widow's struggle with that all-important question, "Who am I now that my husband is gone?" By offering new possibilities of feeling, perceiving, and behaving, the group provides valuable information about forming a new identity. Support groups also provide new information and "models" for dealing with particular problems and challenges. Typically, support groups are composed of new widows and those who have been widowed for years. Those most recently widowed often find the experience of the more "senior" widows one of their most valuable resources. Support groups not only contribute concrete strategies for handling problems, they also provide hope and inspiration through example. The "senior" widows find the experience of helping others both exhilarating and liberating. It marks a turning point in their recovery.

At times practical problems are discussed, such as, "Should I give up my home of several decades to live in a smaller, less-expensive, easier-to-maintain dwelling?" At one meeting I attended, the women were discussing the pros and cons of living in a condominium.

Tess was concerned about the ramifications of moving out of her home: "I've lived in that house for over thirty years. How do I give up such a big part of my past? It's almost like renouncing all my memories of my marriage and the place where I raised three kids. The children are all grown, but I wonder if they would ever forgive me for selling their home. On the other hand, taking care of it and paying for the upkeep is a burden I don't want, and it seems to get harder all the time."

Several other group members echoed Tess's story, sharing how hard it had been for them to even think of selling their homes. Marcia said, "I had the same feelings that you have, Tess, but after much soul-searching, I took the leap, sold the house, and moved into a condominium. It was the smartest decision I ever made. I have never looked back—not even once. My life is so much easier now, and I've even found new friends. Above all, the move gave me more time. Because the condominium association takes care of all the maintenance, I don't have to worry about endless yard work. I also no longer have a huge place to clean and keep repaired. I have so much extra time, I've started taking college courses and may even finish the education that my marriage interrupted more than thirty years ago."

Others in the group also offered practical advice and support: "In a condominium you never feel scared of being a woman alone." "You always feel safe. In our complex, we have a locked lobby and no one can get in unless we buzz them in." "At this stage of life, not having to do yard work is a blessing." Later, the discussion turned to finding an appropriate condominium complex, how to identify and avoid young "singles'" condominiums, and other specific advice on how to rate good and bad living situations.

This information was invaluable to the women in the group who had been contemplating such a move themselves. Ironically, many of them had already received great quantities of unsolicited advice from their children, but the difference was that the other widows in the group provided real information based on their own, relevant experience.

Support groups provide a good way for widows to discover that, despite their own problems, they can reach out to others in distress. Explanations of why support groups "work" often begin with the idea of helping others. Some of the widows I talked to told me that this really helped their own recovery. They also felt gratified that what they had to share was received by other widows as welcome and useful.

A widow of several years named Martha attests to the curative powers of altruism: "We who are no longer grieving must remind ourselves that the group is for new widows—not for us." The group helped her most by making her feel useful: "I like to keep active by doing something worthwhile, reaching out to other widows. I especially feel a sense of kinship with the two women in the group whose husbands committed suicide. I've helped them both work through their despair and mental anguish."

Support groups equip widows with a new perspective by showing them alternatives to their problems. Over the years, the thousands of widows who attend support groups have evolved, from the crucible of their experiences, a new way of thinking about bereavement, its problems, and its challenges. These ideas provide a map for approaching the universal problems widows face. When a widow attends a support group, she learns to open up her thinking and examine the different alternatives and perspectives the group has to offer.

During one group meeting I attended, the members shared "war stories" about their attempts to develop a new social life. They recounted the ordeals and barriers they had encountered in being with old friends, inviting new friends into their homes, and, above all, venturing out into new social situations. All agreed that the most difficult part of the evening was coming home alone or, if they were hosting, the moment after the last guest had left: "After everyone leaves, you're alone again and there's no one left to talk to." "When you attend a social gathering, everyone you see is part of a couple and you feel as if you're a fifth wheel."

Being single after so many years in a world of couples is difficult. The women in the group struggled with the question of whether these feelings came from outside of them—the discomfort that their coupled friends felt when they were with them—or whether they came from within. After a long and energetic discussion, most of the women in this group concluded that the feeling of being a "fifth wheel" was one that they themselves had brought to the situation by sending out the message "I am the one who is out of place."

Many widows who feel as if they are standing alone following the death of their spouse find a high level of identification with the group. The feeling of solidarity that comes from realizing that there is a "refuge" from the world where people often don't understand enhances the feeling of participating in something worthwhile. Support groups often become like a family, giving members a sense that

they are understood and accepted. And since widows feel hurled outside of their comfortable, secure frame of reference, realizing that
their problems are part of a larger experience shared by many helps a
widow to feel "normal" again. The loneliness of widows, their feelings of being stigmatized, and the almost universal complaint that
the considerable emotional support they received soon after their loss
failed to "last long enough," can all be voiced and given emotional
release within the accepting and helpful setting of a support group.

What brings a woman to seek out a support group, despite her initial apprehensions? About three-quarters of the women I spoke with
told me that they had joined to learn how other widows coped with
their problems and to talk with others who had had the same experience. Many felt the need "to be with people who I could feel comfortable with." Some hoped to find supportive people who understood
them and could even become their friends. Many others anticipated
that the group would provide a setting in which they could embark
upon a journey of understanding and exploration to find new meaning in their lives.

Very few, however, joined a widows' support group because they
were looking for a new spouse, because they couldn't afford professional services, or because they wanted to escape thinking about their
loss. A surprising 90 percent of those who became members of a support group said that they had invited other widows and widowers to
participate in their group.

When I asked what they disliked about their support group,
most women said that there were not enough men in the group, and
about a third said that it was not social enough. When I asked the
same question of widows who had been invited to join a support
group, had attended a few meetings, and had subsequently decided
it was not for them, about a quarter said they had found the group
too depressing; a quarter felt it was not social enough; and half stated
that the group did not give them the help that they really needed.

The hundred widows I interviewed who were invited to join a
group but chose not to try it gave a variety of reasons for their deci-

sion. Some felt that they could get adequate help elsewhere; some thought they could handle the problems they were experiencing by themselves; and about a third said they did not want the obligations they believed belonging to such a group implied. Other explanations for not attending were that the members of a particular support group were too different from oneself or that lack of mobility or the length of time needed to reach the meeting place precluded consistent participation.

Though these are all good and understandable reasons not to join a support group, I still encourage widows to find and join a compatible group. Participants in support groups recover better and faster than widows who do not choose to join. If you think such a group might be helpful to you, the appendix provides information on where to find a suitable group.

Chapter 9

Growth: Beyond Grief
and Despair

My husband was only forty-nine and we never had a chance
to say, "good-bye" to each other. I was hearing I'm going to
become an old woman. . . I had not only grown up, grown
old, as I expected, I had died in my own way and been reborn a different human being. This new person crawled
out, waited with sadness, then weak in the knees, began
walking towards the future. By now, I feel like a middle-
life adolescent; confused, sometimes angry, frightened, yet
amazed by my shaky independence, I had the same in-
choate longings, those wild curiosities, and romantic
yearnings, the needs to find meaning and connection in the
world. But what I know now is that even if you love them
inordinately, people are not ours to possess; they are only
loaned to us. In fact, we barely own ourselves, and we need
to keep re-inventing our lives in order to keep moving.

Rhoda Tagliasozzo, "The Legacy of Widowhood,"
The New York Times, July 31, 1988, pp. 12 and 21

Betty, a spirited sixty-two-year-old, came to my office two
months after her husband's death. She complained of difficulty
sleeping and a general listlessness, much in contrast to her previous
life: "After Art died, all I could manage was to take care of the essentials. Other than attending to the practical problems of life, I did
nothing but mope around, and I didn't want to see anyone. Friends
would call me, but I would put them off with some lame excuse."

One year later when we talked again, I immediately sensed a different Betty. When I asked her what had happened, she said, "About

six months ago, I woke up one morning and took a good look at my-self in the mirror. I told myself, 'I can't go on like this. Either I do something about me or have the decency to do away with myself.' I looked myself straight in the eye and said, 'Art's dead and gone, and you can't change that. So what are you going to do about you?'

"My first priority was to rediscover who I was. During most of my life as part of a 'we,' I had lost touch with myself as an 'I.' My search began with a pilgrimage back to where I was born, to Ireland. The trip was both invigorating and a little scary because I wasn't sure why I was there and I didn't quite know what I was looking for. I began by searching for the house where I had been born. I even spoke to old townspeople and relatives. Slowly, as I began to put to-gether my roots and my childhood, I realized why I'd come. I needed to find me!

"When I returned home, I began to do lots of new things. Some of these activities involved parts of me that were interrupted long ago when I was in my twenties. Others were things I had always yearned to do but never done. I even put braces on my crooked teeth. I took swimming and piano lessons, and I began to attend poetry writing workshops.

"Finally, I managed to get up the courage to sell my house. I had never liked it and had just gone along with my husband when we bought it. Now, I'm designing a new house that will meet my needs. I've also enrolled in the freshman class of the university's intergener-ational program. I start in a month. Sometimes, for half a second, I wonder if I'm doing too many new things, but then I think, no, I'm enjoying every moment."

Is Betty's experience unique, or can personal tragedy lead from pain to transformation? Can tragedy produce growth? Researchers have found that patients who are fatally ill with cancer may undergo pos-itive personal changes: They communicate more openly with family and close friends, experience fewer fears, rearrange their priorities, are less preoccupied with trivia, and live life more immediately rather than putting off experience and pleasure. Can the death of a husband be a similar spur for change? Listening to the hundreds of widows I interviewed talk about the losses they had suffered and the challenges they faced made me realize that many use widowhood as an opportunity for growth. After the shattering experience of death, they reintegrated themselves, changing both their relationships and their self-concept. Such transformations often enhanced their lives. In fact, many felt that they were living more successful and fulfilling lives as widows.

In the early part of my seven-year study, I saw the importance of developing some type of "growth" scale to help me understand how much or how little widows' lives were changed over time. I soon realized that a widow who grows is one who is obviously stretching—doing new things, taking educational courses, and struggling to find her own identity and her roots. She is more aware of herself as an "I" rather than as a "we." She has developed new interests, visited new places, and is willing to explore new relationships. She may be more self-sufficient than other widows, learning how to successfully take care of her finances, car, and house, or she may be engaged in some form of creative expression such as painting or writing.

Not all widows were like Betty. At the opposite end of the spectrum were those who were living their lives very much as they had done before their husband's death. Some of these women felt mired in a repetitive sameness from which they were unable to break out. Others clung to their prior lives out of desperation, fearing that change would throw them into an unknown abyss. Other widows were so afraid of change that they clung to their spouse's clothes and possessions for years, leaving all personal effects in place, untouched. And others were genuinely comfortable with their lives as they were and expressed no desire for change or self-renewal.

Still, I was both surprised and delighted to find that over one-third of the widows I interviewed showed clear-cut evidence of growth. To be honest, I had not anticipated such an overwhelmingly positive finding. After all, I was raised in a culture and work in a profession that view widowhood as a profound crisis in which the best that can be hoped for is a return to a status-quo level of adequate functioning. But many of the widows I interviewed were engaged in an active search for their forgotten selves. They frequently discovered new strengths and talents. Many of them took big risks, trying out new things and entering fresh relationships, and some even returned to their distant pasts to develop long-dormant abilities. Most made a decided effort to live in the present rather than postpone their lives for a vague tomorrow. The struggle to grow was not easy, nor did it occur instantaneously. More often than not, growth was achieved slowly and arduously, over long periods of time. Nevertheless, many of the widows stayed with the process.

Two widows, Clara and Donna, illustrate diametrically opposite responses to the challenges engendered by the death of their husbands. Clara used this opportunity to develop and grow; Donna did not.

Growth Through Liberation

Clara is seventy-six. Her husband Bob died ten months ago. Short and round, she has a somewhat owlish appearance because of her very thick glasses. Clara came to her first interview dressed in a simple, unadorned wool sweater and straight skirt. The absence of makeup and jewelry emphasized her stern demeanor.

Clara had been a high school teacher for most of her life, until her retirement at age sixty-five. She has lived in the same house in a small town close to Boston for over fifty years. One son, David, lives in the same city, but offers little solace or help. The other son, Jonathan, lives far away. Clara feels closer to Jonathan, talks to him on the phone at least once a week, and insists that he would be much more helpful than David if he lived nearby.

"You know what my son David had the audacity to tell me last week? He said that he would much rather I spend money on hired help like gardeners and decrease his legacy than call him up. I had an argument with him about it and afterward felt that there were no supportive feelings coming from him at all."

Clara's style of interaction is direct, blunt, and very open, but her directness belies the intense sadness that frequently breaks through her calm demeanor. Although she attempts to push away her depression by being as busy as possible, she knows it isn't working: "I'm still grieving because of Bob's death, but what I'm really angry about is the aloneness of widowhood and the fact that I see no light whatsoever at the end of the road. After Bob died, I was in a state of deep shock for a couple of months. It was almost as if my brain had gone numb, and I just stopped thinking. I'd burst into tears, and yet, somehow, I knew that wasn't enough.

"Since I buried Bob, I haven't been able to visit the cemetery. I haven't gone for almost a whole year. Are you shocked? Do you think I'm cold and unfeeling? It's just that I'm not ready to do it. Visiting the cemetery would tear me apart right now, and I've really got to take care of myself. I got rid of his clothes as fast as possible. Two days after he died, everything went. The only things I kept were some pictures of him to remind me of our travels together."

Clara had been the prime caretaker of her husband, nursing him throughout his final illness until he became too impaired to stay at home. Bob spent the last month of his life in a hospice: "My husband was a noncommunicator. I tried many times to talk to him about his illness and what was happening to us, but he didn't want to. Toward the end I remember grabbing him and pleading with him not to leave me. He responded by buying me a present, a new luxury car. I was touched that he was still looking out for me. He knew I'd be too cheap to buy a new car for myself. At the same time, I regret that I didn't participate in the decision of which car to buy. That was so typical of Bob. During the last week of his life, he did reach out to tell me he loved me and that I'd been a good wife and good nurse. That felt good. Before, he was never able to tell me explicitly that he loved me. I treasure the fact that he could tell me in the end."

When I asked Clara what her marriage had been like, she said,

"The early years were okay, but about twenty years ago when Bob turned fifty-eight, he decided to retire. The best thing about that was the traveling we were able to do together. During most of those last years, it was as if I were a part-time widow already. Bob would go to sleep at eight o'clock every night and I'd be left alone. My husband, was a great giver-upper. Why, he even gave up sex at the tender age of forty-two! But actually, our sexual life was never that good to begin with.

"I think I wasted my life by marrying him. We had no social life, we never entertained, we had no sex, and I had no real companionship from Bob. He was good to me, but oh so boring. I'm too bright and energetic to have retired at the age of forty. Bob neglected me emotionally, starved me, actually. I was, and still am a sexy woman even though I'm seventy-six. He never saw that. I know I could have married a lot of different men, but somehow I think I didn't make myself available enough. I could have had a much more challenging career, could have been a successful business woman, but perversely I kept myself in an unsatisfying marriage. I never thought about me, I just marched along in life. At one point, my doctor even suggested that I ought to think about leaving Bob, but I simply couldn't entertain that thought. I don't know why. I just couldn't think about ending our marriage, ever!"

A year after sharing these sad confessions and regrets, Clara bounced into my office and announced that her grieving was over. Her dress was new and stylish, and she wore a hint of makeup that enhanced her bright new image. Animated and lively, she told me that the despair she had felt a year ago had disappeared: "I don't grieve for Bob any longer and I've visited the cemetery only once since I last saw you. I just don't think about my past life very much, except every so often when I remember how much of it I wasted.

"The best thing that has happened to me since I talked to you is my new boyfriend. I see him about twice a week and we have dinner together. Thank God, Larry is the complete opposite of Bob. He's extremely affectionate and sees me as a sexy lady. We enjoy being together. I'm not at all interested in marrying Larry, but it's a very nice relationship and it makes me feels good. It makes me realize how much I missed.

"I think I've changed in a lot of ways over the past year. I've become much more autonomous, and I even had a fight with the city government over a house that I own. When Bob was alive, he tried to fight the city and win, but he never could. After he died, I took over this problem and was really able to assert myself. I found out what to do, did it, and finally won. I've grown so much. Never in my wildest dreams could I have done this before. I see myself now as a much more effective person. I'm also more serene, more generous, and calmer. I've learned to accept things much more gracefully, and I've taken on disputes and won them."

Clara has found a way to confront the deep, unyielding depression and overwhelming regrets that she experienced after her husband's death. At the age of seventy-six, she has been able to develop into a much more comfortable, lively, and commanding person whose notions of pleasure in life have certainly increased. The death of her husband initiated feelings of profound regret and loss but, at the same time, it freed her to pursue aspects of herself that had long been restricted by her less-than-adequate marriage.

A Comfortable Sameness— No Growth

Donna, a young-looking sixty-two-year-old whose husband had died four months ago, marched into my office. She was stylishly dressed in a powder blue crêpe dress adorned by a multistrand set of pearls. Taking a seat, she promptly began to tell me about herself: "My husband Jonathan owned a small manufacturing company that was always good to us. Jonathan hated doing paperwork, so I took care of that part of the business and did much of the bookkeeping. About two years ago, when Jonathan became ill, we decided to sell the company. That's done, but I still spend a good deal of time coping with a large mass of work that needs attention. I'm busy completing the papers on my interest in the business as well as the estate.

"The final few months of Jonathan's illness were very, very hard. I did most of the nursing until the last couple of weeks. Those weeks were hell. Jonathan deteriorated mentally, constantly hallucinated, and lived in a world filled with delusions. I was up almost every five minutes of the night with him, and it really wore me out. I finally had to hire a nurse to be with him at night.

"Jonathan and I never talked about the seriousness of his illness. He was very brave and never mentioned these things. During the final month, we talked about the past and the good trips we had taken together and all the things we both liked doing. His last words to me were that he loved me. He was a very thoughtful and affectionate man, and I miss him very much. I haven't felt a lot of grief since his death, but I think I did most of my grieving two months before he died. I've visited the cemetery only twice, but I have a real sense that Jonathan is looking down on me as I work on our business papers. I sense him saying to me that I'm doing the right thing by getting on with my life as usual.

"We had a good and happy marriage and were almost never separated. We both spent much of our time together, either at work or at home. All the years we shared were good years, but perhaps the last fifteen were the best. We had no real disagreements; in fact, the only one I can remember happened when the children were younger and we argued about discipline. I was the stricter one. I can't think of anything I would have changed about Jonathan and our marriage. Maybe I would have liked a little more social life. He liked people on a one-to-one basis or in very small groups, but he never liked large collections of people. I have no real regrets about any single thing that I've done in life or regrets about things that I haven't done. It was a happy life, a happy marriage. I feel I've really lived the life I wished for.

"I miss him, but I don't really feel lonely. I have two sons, John

Jr. and Robert. My son John was living at home before Jonathan died, and he's still there. We have dinner together every night, and I rarely go out any more. It's easier to visit with my friends on the phone. I don't have a great deal of interest in meeting new people, engaging in new activities, or joining clubs. I never really did. I have a few good friends. They call me or I call them, and I don't seem to have any need to enlarge that group. I like the company of men very much, but I haven't decided whether or not I'm going to ever have a relationship again. I think it's still too early to worry about that.

"My beliefs are very important to me. I've never been a regular churchgoer, but I believe in God and the afterlife, and I do feel I will see Jonathan again. God has a plan for each of us and His plan for me now is to test me and see whether I can cope with the loss I have to face. I think God's plan for Jonathan was to take him in order to ease his pain."

I asked Donna if her husband's death had stimulated her to think about her own life and the closeness of death. "I had a dream about my death: I was in an airplane and suddenly I saw that it was going to collide with another plane. I woke up just before the impact. I've also noticed that I'm becoming more concerned about my health. I've decided to stop smoking and take better care of myself. Jonathan's death made me think about my own limitations. I know now that I'm not invincible. I think about my own demise and I've started preparing lists of instructions for the children about burial, distribution of goods, where the money is invested, and things like that. I never thought like that before Jonathan died, but I have to now.

"I also ponder the fact that I've become a single woman again, even though I see myself as still married. No one else seems to treat me that way. I haven't really considered remarriage, although sometimes I worry about who would take care of me if I became ill."

Donna is a bright, articulate woman who was extremely forthright during the interview. Her intense grief was limited to the months before Jonathan's death. Although she misses him very much, she has managed to find a dependable equilibrium. She feels satisfied with her life and is particularly comfortable with her nearly thirty-eight years of marriage. It was a good, stable marriage, and each day those memories sustain her. She is highly self contained and able to work effectively and plan for the future. Economically comfortable, she feels ready to engage in volunteer work for good causes. Unlike Clara, the stimulus for looking inward and changing is not present in Donna's life, nor would she see any reason to change even if someone suggested it to her. She has no regrets. She liked the life she lived and feels comfortable with her current circumstances. Although loneliness is sometimes a problem for her, she doesn't seek out new friends but simply accepts that her life is limited now and that she herself is closer to death. She readily faces these limitations but is not driven to use them for inner or outer changes.

Why did Clara confront her regrets about her life and her relationship to Bob and use these painful memories for a launching pad for growth? Why, on the other hand, did Donna not pursue a similar search? Both women have made excellent recoveries. A year later each had put grief and intense sadness behind her and had achieved comfort and personal equilibrium; yet their methods of doing so were distinctly different.

Clara embarked on a long, arduous path of self-exploration addressing the profound regrets she had experienced during her marriage. This exploration enabled her to develop a new and meaningful self that engaged in life. Her relationship with Larry provided both companionship and a reaffirmation of the kind of woman she always knew she was capable of being. Donna's life after Jonathan's death continued on the same path. Her self-confidence and comfort, together with her good memories of the marriage, did not generate a need for intense self-exploration, a search for a new identity, or the rediscovery of talents or interests long buried. Although Donna did begin some inner exploration of what it meant to be alone, her process never reached the compelling intensity of Clara's.

Existential Explorations:
Processes Leading to Growth

What facilitates growth? Why are some widows able to create a new beginning from the pain of loss and the anxiety of an unknown future, while others struggle but can't get beyond the status quo? What are the psychological processes that promote growth? The answer to these questions can be found by looking at how willing widows are to investigate their inner world. Spurred on by their husband's death, do they explore existential life issues? I found that widows who were engaged in exploring their inner selves displayed several similar qualities. First of all, they looked inward, asking themselves "Who am I and what is the purpose of my life?" Clara uncovered a deeply buried sensuality and new capacity for receiving affection. She also discovered that it was important for her to be assertive, to fight her own battles and win. Widows like Clara, who welcome growth, aren't afraid to reexamine the past and take personal responsibility for their lives and their choices. Growth also involves the courage to confront thoughts about life's brevity and, hence, its preciousness. Clara grew because her husband's loss made her realize how much of her life she had already wasted and how important it was for her not to waste what time was left to her.

Donna, on the other hand, came to grips with her loss, but was content to maintain the status quo of her former existence. She has no regrets about her marriage or the choices she made with her life and therefore no impetus to search for a richer, fuller existence.

Looking Inward

Debby, a fifty-five-year-old widow whose husband Tim died seven months ago, illustrates the qualities of a widow involved in growth and inner exploration. Because her husband was a successful lawyer who provided the family with a comfortable suburban life-style,

Debby hadn't worked since the early days of their marriage. She kept busy by raising three children and by being a competent social hostess and a committed charity volunteer. Tim's death created a profound upheaval that catapulted her into an exploration of her past and current life. The question uppermost in her mind was "What will I become in the future?"

"I think differently about my life since Tim died," she told me during our first interview. "At times, I'm overwhelmed by regrets about the way I've lived. I think I married the wrong man and, what's worse, I realize now that I always used to put what Tim thought of me and what he wanted me to do before my own desires. Now I have to let the inner me, the real me, make life choices that match what I really want rather than what other people desire for me. I'm scared of being free! But at the same time it's exhilarating. I've realized how brief and precious life really is."

Debby knows now that it wasn't her husband who restricted her life but that she was her own jailer. She is now aware of the synthetic structure she gave her existence in the past, seeing these habits as stifling routines, and she no longer believes that satisfaction can be obtained from a life of carefully prepared dinners and social obligations. Frightened by the lack of structure in her life, she is also exhilarated by her freedom. Because she knows that death, her death, is real and inevitable, she has begun to take care of her own body by quitting smoking, exercising, and losing excess weight. She has, for the first time, made a will and made her own funeral arrangements.

Debby is critical of her old materialistic existence, in which she wasted much time playing bridge, having lunch with friends, shopping for herself, and decorating her home. That way of living feels very empty to her now, and she is searching for some way of giving meaning to her life, of making a difference in the world. She realizes that previously her sense of purpose derived from her role as a wife. Today, she believes that, even if she were to reassume that role, she would nevertheless demand more. Debby struggled with these questions for almost three years. When I next talked to her, she was a changed, calmer person whose zest for life was clear from the onset of our interview. She had embarked on a program of study at her local university and found the challenge intriguing and energizing.

Confrontation with Death

Though written 350 years ago, John Donne's admonition, "Ask not for whom the bell tolls; it tolls for thee," endures with astonishing freshness. It speaks to a truth that is self-evident to many who have experienced bereavement—that the death of someone close has the potential to hurl the survivor into a confrontation with his or her own death.

Many of the widows I interviewed were forced to confront their own mortality when they lost a spouse, and many reported a powerful new awareness of life's transience. Linda, a fifty-eight-year-old widow, told me, "When my husband died, I suddenly realized that everyone who's alive right now could just suddenly stop living. Death can come at any time, and, as I've gotten older, I've begun to see it happening to my husband and my friends. Eventually, my time will be up. This is obvious. Who doesn't know it? But somehow I'm aware of everyone's mortality in a way that I never really was before. I honestly feel as if I could die almost any minute. Because I know that, I can't shrug off my aches and pains as I did in the past. I think about them."

Life Review

The loss of a husband encourages widows to reevaluate their lives, deciding which areas they feel satisfied with and which feel incomplete. Many are filled with regret when they realize how many aspects of themselves have been postponed or ignored. Some widows, who were distressed about the things they hadn't done, realized that they had restricted themselves by choosing a partner who was not sympathetic to some of their goals, such as pursuing a career. Others lamented that they had not expected and demanded more from themselves.

When evaluating the past, many widows focused on their marriages. Some regretted not getting to know their husband better before marriage. Some were distressed to realize that they had probably married the "wrong man." Others were sorry they had stayed married, choosing to live their whole life for their spouse or children rather than finding the courage to leave. Some expressed regrets for having given so much of themselves with so little expectation of return.

The Search for Personal Meaning

Barbara, a fifty-seven-year-old widow, was overwhelmed when her husband, Len, died: "My life was totally immersed in Len. We had a good, perhaps ideal marriage. How can I ever replace that?" Though she began to feel distressed by the static nature of her existence three months after Len's death, she couldn't seem to find the energy or the motivation to change it: "I feel no sense of purpose," she told me. "The world and my life feel empty. Previously, I'd gotten my purpose from being a wife and companion, but since my husband died, I don't feel as if I have anything left. I don't have any goals, and I'm not even sure what I want to accomplish. I'm just standing in neutral, marking time."

One year later, Barbara's loss propelled her on a search for personal meaning. Although still depressed, she began to intensely scrutinize her previous well-ordered life as a mother, wife, and social secretary. Barbara found that she regrets having lived in the shadow of Len and is searching for some way of giving fresh meaning to her life: "I realize that during all those years my total sense of purpose revolved around being a wife and mother. I know now that even if I could wind the clock backward, I wouldn't choose to totally locate all of my identity in the marriage. I want more from life." During our early meetings, Barbara clearly hadn't found a new center for her life. Though she had not yet reached her goal of finding new meaning and making a difference in the world, however, I saw that her commitment to change was strong, determined, and genuine. For women such as Barbara, creating a new life from the challenges of widowhood is only a matter of time. Slow recovery and obvious distress often accompany the path to growth. Not until two full years after Len's death did I begin to see a new Barbara, confident and engaged in life.

For the widows who vigorously questioned their purpose in life, who reexamined their past and confronted their existence, there was a payoff. In the long term these women experienced greater joy, excitement, sense of challenge, and growth in their lives. Every single widow who grew in response to the loss of her husband engaged actively in an existential exploration. On the other hand, not all women who confronted the meaning of their lives grew, but the likelihood was high that once they began such an exploration, they would reap some real benefit. In fact, seven out of eight widows who actively pursued the search manifested remarkable personal growth.

Once I realized that intense self-exploration was critical for growth, I wondered what role this search could play in the process of recovery. We know that the journey into the self significantly alters the course of bereavement. It leads to a rediscovery of who one is and what one wants out of life. Do these explorations help with the feelings of grief and also enhance adjustment, or are growth and recovery two independent paths? In other words, can a widow make a successful recovery without embarking upon a quest for a new identity? To answer that question, I compared widows deeply involved in self-exploration to those who weren't by examining their course of recovery in five different areas: symptoms of grief, intensity of mourning, personal effectiveness, the stresses and strains experienced in becoming single again, and the amount of stigma they experienced—in other words, their perception of the negative views toward widows held by friends, family, and acquaintances.

Although there are definite benefits to be gained by a search for the self, it turned out that not embarking on an existential journey did not hinder a widow's ultimate recovery. Good adjustment and growth are separate and independent paths, as Donna and Clara have shown. Both women made excellent recoveries, but only Clara engaged in a painful but productive journey that led to growth, an enhanced self, and a fuller engagement with life.

Widows who embarked on an existential search, compared to those who chose not to search for new meaning in life, reacted to the death of their husband more intensely. Soon after their husband's death, the searchers experienced more turmoil than the nonsearchers—feelings that were part of their inner journey. They were more depressed and anxious, and reported more intense feelings of loneliness. Their sense of isolation was not based on the absence of companionship, however, because they had the same level of social activity and family contact as the nonsearchers. Both groups also showed similar dating patterns, although there was an interesting difference in how each of the two groups viewed these relationships. Widows who embarked on an inner journey were less likely to use their friendships with men to evade or diminish their grief. They looked into, rather than away from, their loss and were willing to endure and fully experience their aloneness.

Betty, whom I introduced at the beginning of this chapter, illustrates the turmoil associated with the existential journey. For the first six months she described herself as a "basket case" unable to do anything but "the bare essentials." After looking at herself, she embarked on a trip that began her journey: "It was scary, going back to Ireland. I never traveled alone before. What would I find there? Maybe no one remembered our family?" Her distress was real and potent. During the first year of her widowhood, Betty was in a constant state of anxiety, at that time not having the pleasure of hindsight and seeing that her search would lead to a new and different Betty. Men are still an unknown for her: "I'll cross that bridge later; right now I've got to keep going. I'm not really running away, just postponing that part of me until later."

. . .

The sharpest differences between the searchers and nonsearchers can be found in how they viewed their marriage. The status-quo widows were more likely to idealize their spouse, often describing their husband and their relationship in superlatives, even though they also suffered considerable guilt and anger toward their husband.

We met Linda in chapter 4, where I described her as a woman in trouble, unable to move beyond the total reliance upon her husband that characterized their marriage. Her adoration and complete immersion in his memory signals a high level of idealization; though sixty-two years old, Linda appears remarkably younger than her age. She views her marriage as "made in heaven." Her husband, who was older than she, structured and organized her entire life: "I knew just what to do, and I didn't have to worry about making any decisions." This arrangement was comfortable for her, and I didn't sense that she had rebelled or struggled against it. The only solution she sees now to her present intense suffering is to find a replacement for that psychological relationship. Linda never looked inward and was not able to envisage a life where she could be different. Personal growth and development were not part of her language. In contrast, Barbara, described earlier in this chapter, also idealized her husband, but she was able to embark on a personal exploration that promises a productive new self.

Most searchers, on the other hand, were clearer about examining the flaws of their marriages, viewing their spouses in realistic, non-idealized terms. Although they evaluated their relationship with their husband as good and generally satisfying, these women also stressed that they had felt stunted by marriage and that important aspects of their self-expression and interests had not been permitted to flourish. They fully realized that their loss offered them an opportunity for psychological freedom.

The searchers were also distressed about real situations they were facing. Their attention was focused on questions about the meaning of life and on the opportunities and challenges of their new-found freedom.

Clara, the seventy-six-year-old widow we met earlier, faced her past and present disappointment with considerable courage. Regrets about her marriage and her life were compounded by a distant, non-supportive son who mirrored her husband's patterns. Her struggles were real and all encompassing. We learned that Clara, a year later, was a much changed person who was able to find pleasure in her self-development and new relationships.

Often people mired in chronic grief tend to become fixated on their loss. Instead of focusing their energies on themselves, they become fixated on the anger they feel toward their spouse. Two of the widows we met in chapter 4 illustrate the role anger and guilt can play in stimulating growth. Although both of these women, Rhoda and Sarah, were burdened by intense anger and guilt, they followed different paths to recovery.

Rhoda mourned her husband, but could not resolve her intense guilt and anger toward him. A gray-haired, severely dressed woman who appears older than her fifty-six years, she has this to say:

"I think about all the things we never did, and it drives me crazy. When I remember the last year of Paul's life, I wish we could've been closer. I couldn't offer him enough comfort. Let's face it: I was a failure. I didn't know how to help Paul die, and that damn hospital machinery got in the way."

The passage of time has not mitigated Rhoda's pain and suffering. Still deeply grieving and carrying an enormous load of guilt and anger, she sees no way out.

In contrast, Sarah, a stony, somber woman, began our talk curtly: "I'm still burdened, even after all this time, with regrets about not talking to Richard about his illness. I never really said good-bye. In the last week of his life, when Richard turned to me and said, 'I was thinking about how much I love you,' I didn't respond. I think about that every day and wonder what kind of person I am. Am I made of stone? Right after his death, I couldn't even cry. I thought that something was terribly wrong with me, and I didn't like myself!

"I walk around with feelings of having been cheated, of not having done things for myself." At this point, Sarah began weeping, "I never had any real fun or joy, and probably never will. If only I could find myself, I think I would be a woman of great integrity. I would not be the little girl who always tried to please everyone."

When I saw Sarah one year later, I sensed a different person. She appeared more physically animated and more alive in her speech. She had spent some time in psychotherapy and had embarked on a journey of self-discovery, putting much time and effort into this inward search.

"I've learned about my strengths and I've realized that I can take care of myself. I've even started going to classes and learning about business affairs. In spite of my grieving, I can feel myself growing. I have been enriched by my despair in ways I never dreamed possible."

Sarah began to view her life as containing great potential for change, and even saw the possibility of new growth. Sarah took a risk, a look into the nooks and crannies of her past life, and tried to accept her marital regrets. Painful as these feelings were, her willingness to examine them made a difference. Rhoda, on the other hand, remained mired in avoiding her past and her feelings about her marriage.

The searchers did suffer from more anxiety and depression, but they associated this distress with realizations of their own mortality. They possess a certain type of internal strength—a sureness about themselves, a relative inner freedom that enabled them to gaze inward. They have taken time out from external concerns to pay attention to their inner needs and identity, often even delaying important decisions until their self-exploration is well on its way.

The fact that many widows are able to pass through their pain and not only reestablish their equilibrium but move ahead and develop is heartening. This vibrant growth calls into question our society's preoccupation with seeing widowhood solely in terms of loss and grief. Proponents of the loss-grief model of widowhood assume that bereavement is a stressful situation that disrupts a widow's "normal" life and that the best way to judge a widow's recovery is to see whether or not she returns to her previous level of social adjustment after grieving for an "appropriate" amount of time.

But loss has a powerful and highly personalized meaning. Within each individual is a great capacity for self-exploration and personal change. We all know that one of the tasks of widowhood is to face loss, but widows also encounter a significant number of challenges beyond this traditional confrontation, including confronting the major questions of existence: mortality, freedom, responsibility, isolation, and meaning in life.

These existential challenges always confront widows, but not all women choose to attend or to respond to them. Those who have the ability to respond ultimately receive a meaningful payoff: personal growth. Obviously, not all widows experience the same degree of growth, but every woman I met who seriously engaged in an existential search reaped some important benefits.

The death of a loved one hurls us into a confrontation with the fundamental questions of existence. Taking up the challenge is not an easy process, nor a quick one. Investing the time and energy it takes to thoroughly examine our lives is clearly not for everyone. Many widows, such as Donna, view their lives as comfortable and satisfying, and feel no inner calling to embark on such a journey. Others are deeply involved in their day-to-day lives, taking care of children and pursuing careers. These women often feel that their lives should be lived in the present and that they have neither the time nor desire to invest in an inner search—nor should they, for recovery is not contingent upon such explorations. Although it is more likely for an active existential search to begin soon after the loss, some widows do return to the search many years after their husband's death. These women felt that time was needed to heal and organize their lives before they could face themselves so honestly and so deeply.

Chapter 10

Who Am I?—A Painful
but Valuable Journey

W hen you look into a mirror, who do you see? Is the person
staring back at you the same individual you saw when you
were twelve? When you were first married? Or is it a new you? The
death of a husband thrusts the widow into a vortex of conflicts, competing thoughts, and intense and strange feelings. She is compelled
to ask herself questions about her identity: "I know my life is different, but am I the same person I used to be—just facing new circumstances—or have I changed into someone different? If so, how have I
become different? Does the mirror really reflect a new me?"

Beyond dealing with the early flood of grief, one of the most
challenging tasks a widow faces is the struggle with the question
"Who am I?" Everyday life, with its rush of events and its commitments to career, children, and social relationships, rarely allows self-
examination. It often takes a major life crisis, such as the death of a
spouse, to motivate intense self-scrutiny. Many women experience
this first at the time when all of their children are out of the house.
The window of opportunity opens, enabling many "empty-nest"
women to make substantial transformations in how they see themselves and how their lives need to change to accommodate their new

self. Some women go back to school; others start new businesses; and some find new interests in creative fields.

Why Does a Widow's Reflection in the Mirror Change?

As two lives become intertwined over many years, the husband and wife's self-images often merge. When a woman is widowed, she can't escape from an examination of who she is. Two conditions are pivotal in starting widows on this exploration: the earlier self-image embedded in the "couple" identity and the dramatic change in the way others see you because you are a widow. The reliance upon this "joint self" is more frequently found among women than men. Maggie, a widow in her fifties, illustrates how one widow confronted her couple identity.

Maggie had relied upon her husband's high competitiveness to get them both through confrontational situations. During our second meeting, she told me about the changes in herself since his death: "I never had to be aggressive when Arthur was alive because he provided all the combativeness we needed to face the world. Now that he's gone, I'm discovering that I'm becoming more assertive—and I kind of like it."

During the first year, Maggie struggled to sort out who she was now that Arthur was gone. During her marriage, many aspects of herself could not find expression and so had been hidden from her view. According to Maggie, being competitive and assertive was "not the way a nice women behaved." If a situation called for being forceful, Arthur was always there, and Maggie didn't even have to consider expressing those feelings. As she reentered the world after Arthur's death, Maggie began, hesitantly at first and then later with more confidence, to discover qualities she never dreamed she possessed. If she found herself in a situation that called for assertiveness, she could handle it: "I needed to replace my old car, but I kept putting it off. I didn't or wouldn't face the barrage of car salesmen. I know you have to be firm when dealing with them. In the past Arthur always took care of big purchases. Finally, I couldn't delay it any longer and marched into a dealer. I surprised myself. I was firm and outspoken, and I did get a good deal. More important, I found that I could assert myself." After some initial adjustment, Maggie began to shift her self-concept and to enjoy her new self.

The loss of the joint self-image is certainly not the only reason why widows reexamine their identity. Our view of who we are is the product of countless interactions with people who are important to us. As children, our earliest identity grew out of the reflections we received from our parents, brothers, sisters, relatives, and peers. The self, however, is neither fixed in time nor unyielding. It does not exist in isolation, but it is to some extent formed by the reflections we receive from others.

Throughout a marriage, a spouse provides a unique source of information. He or she is the mirror for many of our most important and central qualities, both positive and negative. Our children, our friends, and our coworkers give us feedback during our adult life, but the length of the marriage and its intimacy means that marriage is the single most important source of information about who we are.

This does not mean that our identity is in constant flux. Our self-image rarely changes in response to our countless, daily interactions; if it did, we would live in constant turmoil. The self does grow and develop over long periods of time, however. The process for developing and maintaining a self-image is a splendid mechanism. Although our identity is ultimately dependent upon our social relationships, we do make choices about who we connect with. From the countless reflections from others, we select those that are important to us.

We know from numerous studies that in all of us there is a strong, perhaps overriding need to maintain a coherent and consistent self-image. It is essential to our existence that we see ourselves as being the same from week to week and from year to year. When people are challenged by life crises or major changes in their environments, the sources of feedback used to maintain their coherent and consistent self-image may be dramatically altered. People in such circumstances are faced with a crisis, and this is the crisis that widows confront.

What Happens When the Spouse Dies?

When a husband dies, the mirror suddenly changes, and widows begin to ask themselves important questions:

- Who will replace those reflections of my self-image that I have lost with the death of my husband?
- If these reflections are not replaced, what will happened to the way I think about myself?
- What do I do with those qualities that were embedded in my identity as part of a couple?
- How can I meet the challenges of creating a new identity for myself?

Two other life passages, going to college and leaving home to join a retirement community, may help us understand the identity changes that accompany widowhood. Very often, teenagers find the first year of college very stressful. Many studies attest to the damaging effects of such stress on a student's physical and mental health. The main reason for such stress is the struggle with developing a new identity to go along with the new life circumstance. Moving from the comfortable world of family and friends who provided reflecting mirrors to a new and initially strange world where the reflections are undependable can be disturbing. So "the football star," "the class president," "the talented lead in high school plays," "the popular friend," and "the outstanding student" who knew who they were and how their abilities were rated may meet a variety of people from different backgrounds—people who may be just as bright, gifted, or talented. Locating reflections from others that will confirm your identity often takes time, and such confirmation may not come as easily in a more competitive environment.

When the elderly move from their homes into a retirement community, a crisis is often precipitated. People ask themselves: "How do I maintain who I am? Who will provide the reflections that enable me to see myself in ways that are comfortable for me? What am I really like now?" For the elderly, these challenges come at a time in their lives where change is not so easy. Some cling to an identity that reflected them at a much earlier time; others manage to find activities, roles, and people that enable a slow but sure transformation into the new circumstance. This is a difficult process, and not everybody achieves the transition. Some elderly individuals experience a precipitous decline in their physical and mental health when they move into a new environment.

One way of facing this destabilization of identity is to give up those parts of ourselves that are no longer supported by reflections from others. The athlete from a small high school who enters a big-ten university and finds that people no longer treat him or her as a gifted athlete may alter his or her self-image to emphasize other aspects of the self that *are* valued. The "excellent athletic self" previously supported by peers and parents may fade away, replaced by "the good sport" or "the good student." The athlete can maintain the same self-image by a variety of internal maneuvers, such as ignoring the reflections of others or reaching into positive memories as a way of saying, "See, I am still an excellent athlete." Some go further, asserting this aspect of the self by maintaining the conviction without confirmation. Other psychological mechanisms, such as declaring that the coaches or the other players at the college are not really recognizing a unique talent, may come into play. In all these ways, people can invest psychological energy into maintaining the familiar self-concept, despite the current absence of mirroring.

For widows, the problem of changing and maintaining their self-image is vastly more complicated. What happens to widows when important parts of their identity, such as being kind, loving, and affectionate, can't be expressed because there is no husband to acknowledge these qualities? How then can a widow hold on to these important views of herself?

This problem is agonizing. Either giving up important views of ourselves or using a variety of psychological strategies to ensure that our self-images remain intact entails great psychological costs. In fact, I found that people who use psychological maneuvers, such as ignoring the reflections of others or reaching into the distant past as a way of maintaining their identity, risk psychological difficulties and even physical illness. Among the elderly, such psychological maneuvers are frequently linked to shortened survival.

Altering your self-image to fit the new circumstances also poses risks. Studies show that high self-changers are frequently also troubled people. A study by psychologist Jack Bloch illustrates the impact that radically changing one's self-image has on psychological health. He used the famous University of California at Berkeley longitudinal study that followed the lives of over four hundred people from preschool to their sixties. Bloch found that those more prone to changing their self-image were less psychologically healthy than those who did not change their view of the self so often. In a different study of 2,000 adults aged eighteen through seventy-five, I found that both men and women who altered their views of self in response to life crises were psychologically less healthy. There is considerable evidence that keeping our views of ourselves consistent is an important mental health safeguard.

No wonder widows often go through such identity stress. You

cannot avoid having to confront who you are when your husband dies, but that doesn't necessarily mean that you need to always change who you are. So what can you do? The obvious, but often very difficult, solution for a widow is to find new mirrors supporting her old self-view. Here are some stories of widows who faced this dilemma, exploring how they dealt with changes and maintained their self-image, sometimes successfully and sometimes not.

To study changes in identity, each of the 600 widows was interviewed soon after the death of her husband and then again one year later. Initially, I asked each woman to describe herself using forty-eight statements such as: I enjoy being in charge of things; I am somewhat of a dominating or bossy person; I believe that I am an important person; I am proud and self-satisfied; I can reproach people when necessary; I am short-tempered and impatient with mistakes other people make; I am frequently disappointed by other people; I am rather timid and shy; I am a cooperative person; I am somewhat tender and soft-hearted; I am an affectionate and understanding person.

I asked each woman to divide the list of self-descriptions into two categories: these are like me now; these are not. To help me understand which present qualities were new since widowhood and which past qualities had been lost, I asked widows to give me examples from their current life.

Giving Up Past Identities

Cary, a fifty-seven-year-old widow whose husband died six months before our meeting, discovered several characteristics that once described her but now no longer did. For example, she was used to giving frequent advice and counsel to others, but now felt a huge empty place in her life where that quality had been: "How can you avoid giving advice when you've raised four children? It's impossible! But when the children grew up and moved away, I focused my advice-giving talents on my husband. Now listening to the problems of my family and helping them isn't an important part of my life anymore. My husband, Ken, tolerated, even liked, my penchant for being liberal with advice, but who else would accept that from me now? Certainly not my children, who became fiercely independent once they moved out of the house."

Cary also placed "When necessary, I can complain about things that bother me," in the past, remarking, "I guess my husband was the one I talked to about my problems. Now that I don't have any one to confide in, that part of myself no longer exists."

Before Ken died, Cary was able to be rebellious or feel bitter about things. She sadly told me, "I guess at my age you don't really feel that way anymore, and it wouldn't do any good anyway." Though Cary was trying to rationalize this lack in her life, it was clear to me that she no longer had anyone who would really listen to feelings about what was wrong with the world.

Cary also felt that she could no longer say with confidence, "'I'm often helped by other people.' I don't see as much of other people as I used to. My husband always filled that role, and who can I turn to now?"

Cary has a clear view of who she was during the years of her marriage. Although some of the ways she described herself might be irritating to some people, apparently they worked in her marriage. Now, with no one to advise, complain to, confide in, or help, she feels lost. Giving up these qualities is very hard for her, and she has not been able to adapt them or tone them down enough to make them more acceptable to others. Nor has Cary been able to locate a new relationship for their expression. She is in limbo, unable to change her self-image and unready to comfortably relinquish certain aspects of it.

When I saw Cary a year later, however, these tensions were well on their way to being resolved. By joining a widows' support group and finding an outlet for her distress and frustration, people who needed her advice and help, and people who were willing to listen to her when she talked, Cary was finding ways to "fit" back into a comfortable identity. Most important, however, she was also learning, from the responses of others, the value of some new qualities: tact, patience, and restraint. Though she had been able to express herself unrestrainedly with her children and her husband, Cary was beginning to learn the value of listening and holding back. She was discovering that when she wasn't pushy and overbearing, others would appreciate her advice and support.

A New Self

Mary, a sixty-two-year-old widow whose husband, Bill, died four months ago, found the strength and flexibility to let go of her past qualities and limitations and begin to make positive changes. She was discovering that she enjoyed being in charge of things: "Before my husband died, I never had the opportunity to be in charge of anything. I was always overshadowed by someone else, but now I feel as if I really do run the family estate." She was also glad to feel that she could be frank with people: "In the past I could never stand up for what I really felt. Now, I'm a lot more willing to be honest. Before, I felt my opinions didn't matter, but now it's important for me to speak my mind. After all, I'm an intelligent woman, and my insights count, too. When my husband was alive, I was afraid to speak up and always agreed with what everyone else said. It was hard for me to form my own opinions. Now I've changed. I'm more into self-realization—being able to know and explore who I am. I'm not just playing the role of keeping Bill happy all the time."

One of the most important things I learned from the women I studied is that widows who revised their self-image by uncovering new qualities recovered faster and better. I also found that most of the widows I interviewed moved from a more dependent self-image to a less dependent one. They saw themselves as becoming less passive and deferential, and more assertive and aggressive. Interestingly, many widows' new self-image incorporated traits that are more stereotypically characteristic of men in our society. After the first year of bereavement, most widows view themselves as much more assertive, stronger, and warmer.

I also learned that a healthy new self-image is usually a product of "subtracting" some aspects of the personality that no longer work and adding others that were perhaps always there but found no proper self-expression.

Sometimes, developing a new identity involves recapturing a lost part of the past self. Consider how Karen, a fifty-five-year-old widow, came to view herself.

Karen's husband Tim was a successful owner of several clothing stores who provided the family with a comfortable suburban lifestyle, making it unnecessary for her to work. During the years of her marriage, she was busy raising two children and being a "good wife." Tim's death created a profound disturbance in her life. Beyond her grief and sadness, however, was a strong desire to explore her past and current life. The question that was uppermost in her mind was: "Now that my husband is gone, what will I become in the future?"

Describing herself after her husband's death, Karen said, "I found out that I enjoy being in charge of things. I decided not to sell the business just yet. Each of the managers is competent, and I discovered that I enjoy being the boss and solving business problems and issues. Previously, I had always deferred to my husband's final decisions about everything, but now I find that I can take care of things quite satisfactorily.

"I have rediscovered the independent and self-confident person I was learning to be when I was young. When I married Tim, I pushed this independence down, feeling that it was somehow inappropriate. For the first few years of our marriage, I struggled with the double feeling of wanting to be taken care of by my husband and straining for independence. In the past year, however, I've become independent again and find that I can manage fine. No one is taking care of me financially, and I've accomplished a lot. I supervise the managers, pay my bills, and take care of car and house repairs. I even learned to do my own income taxes. I've also started getting in shape and have joined Weight Watchers and a fitness program. In every way, I'm doing a great job of taking care of myself."

One year later, Karen had made even greater strides toward recovery. She exuded confidence and a sense of clear self-possession, describing herself as being in touch with many previously hidden parts of her personality: "I'm exhilarated by my freedom. I live in the present now rather than postponing things for the future, as I used to. I'm really responsible for my life, and for the first time I realize that it's mine to do with as I please. That's scary, but I'm not going to turn back. I know that I used to blame Tim for my problems, but I now realize that they weren't really his fault. Whatever limitations there were in my life, I put them on myself, I'll never make that mistake again!"

Lora, a forty-six-year-old with three teenagers, two sons and one daughter, is struggling to find an independent identity. Although comfortably off financially, Lora has been contending with a mountain of business paperwork left in total chaos after Roger's unexpected death.

Lora described her newfound self-image to me: "After Roger died, I realized that I enjoy being in charge of things. Handling the paperwork during the last six months and dealing with the complex issues of estates and taxes has given me a real sense that I am competent and can manage.

"I also discovered that I'm a very good leader. Being a single parent and managing the complexities of a household full of adolescent children have forced me to take on a new role, that of being totally responsible. My husband was always very competitive, and, now that he's gone, I think I've taken on this quality and am really enjoying it."

When I saw Laura a year later, she had clearly gone a long way toward finding a stronger self-image. Because her husband's death has left her with a much greater sense of her mortality, she has become more aware of how precious life is and how important it is to live every day to the fullest, not postponing the things that she really wants to accomplish. She communicates a powerful sense of purpose and a strong desire to continue to evolve a new, more acceptable self-image, one that is unburdened of her restrictive past.

It is not enough to simply throw off aspects of your old identity as if they were out-of-fashion dresses and take on the new clothes of a changed identity. These changes must be rooted in reflecting mirrors—people and experiences that give you feedback. I found that widows who found others to mirror and maintain their new self-views recovered rapidly and well. Widows who maintained their old self-image by using feedback from current relationships also made a good recovery and positive adaptations.

Let's listen to someone who discovered a new reflecting mirror that supported an identity that had been ignored for too long. Rona, who recently celebrated her sixtieth birthday, had been widowed one year. She talked about rediscovering that she was still a valued person who had much to offer others. When her husband of thirty-five years died, she felt at sea: "All my life was spent as a behind-the-scenes advisor helping Paul's political career. I never wanted recognition from anyone but Paul. He was very generous in recognizing my contribution and always said that he never could have become mayor and been reelected without me: 'You understand people and are the diplomatic one in our family,' he said. I complimented Paul's talents and provided a critical anchor for him. It was a good partnership.

"After Paul died, I felt much of who I was rapidly slipping away. Soon I began to doubt myself. Was I really a competent, talented person? Or was the way I saw myself just a wishful dream that had never been? Mary, my closest friend, intuitively understood my problem and my need to feel valued again. She suggested that I volunteer at the university museum. That was six months ago. Now I'm running the whole volunteer program, and I feel confident that I am still the person I was. It's nice to feel valued and appreciated." Rona had successfully discovered a substitute reflecting mirror that supported parts of herself that she felt were central to her identity.

Sadly, not all widows are able to realign their identity by adding new qualities and locating new mirrors. Women who changed their self-images by letting go of important aspects of their previous selves did more poorly than those who held on to valuable characteristics. On the other hand, widows who maintained a completely unchanged self-image by basing their self-view on the distant past or on unsupported beliefs about who they really were jeopardized their recovery. Cary, the fifty-seven-year-old widow described earlier in this chapter, illustrates the problem of attempting to hold on to parts of the self that aren't working any longer. As she gradually learned to modify characteristics that were important to her, such as advice giving and expressing her opinions of the world, by learning restraint and tact, she was able to find new outlets for her basically caring and interactive nature. Though the first year of widowhood was a very distressing time for her, a year later Cary was beginning to understand the need to rework some parts of her self-image. This was the first step to building a new, more realistic identity.

The struggle to maintain a coherent and consistent self-image is important for everyone, but especially for those passing through the shattering and vulnerable psychological state of widowhood. One of the greatest challenges of widowhood is to successfully forge a new identity, a struggle that can go on for years. Developing a more authentic identity based upon new realities need not be accomplished all at once. Now that the "mirror" of one's husband is gone, new sources of support are needed to provide feedback. Many of the widows I interviewed negotiated this difficult task successfully. The search for a new identity involves a delicate balance between maintaining some characteristics from the past while adding, or rediscovering, fresh ones. This is a significant part of the overall challenge of widowhood. Eventually, many women find themselves becoming more "their own person."

Chapter 11

The Myth That Remarriage
Is the Best Solution

O f all the complex decisions that widows face, remarriage is perhaps the most difficult. Almost all of the women seriously considered remarriage. How long they should wait following their husband's death, what kind of person to marry, and how to meet a potential spouse are all questions they face. All of the widows were aware of the demographic imbalance facing them: Since women outlive men by an average of seven years, fewer men are available. But the issues go far beyond demographics. Widows deal with the confusing advice of friends and family, the psychological cost of remarriage, and the probable loss of newfound independence and freedom if they choose to remarry.

Perplexing Advice

Eileen, a fifty-six-year-old widow, struggled with confusing advice. She told me of the conflicting messages: "I don't think I'll ever get married again. It's not that I haven't given it a lot of thought. I've even talked to many of my friends about it, but they were about evenly split on the issue, and that didn't help much. Some were very much in favor of my remarriage and urged me to do it quickly. Others warned that it was too soon and that I should wait: 'You need more time to absorb the shock of Herb's death,' they said. What I found interesting was that my married friends were the ones pushing me to get married again, while my widowed friends cautioned me against making a fast move.

"My immediate family is also divided into two camps. My mother is extremely supportive and told me that she'd stand behind whatever I wanted to do, but my married daughter, Cindy, is resentful and said she was dead set against my even considering remarriage. My daughter's views really troubled me, but I finally had to tell her that it was my decision, not hers. After all, I have my own life to lead. But I also feel pretty sure that if I ever seriously took the plunge, Cindy would eventually come around."

The views of others can range from disapproving to all-too-approving. Either extreme can make a widow feel uncomfortable and confused.

No matter what her friends and family say, each woman has her own feelings to contend with. Many women equate remarriage with disloyalty to the dead husband and find themselves in an unbearable psychological dilemma. This tension can become so great that a widow will seek professional advice, but here she runs into another set of "rules" and absolutes. Most mental health professionals believe that emotional reattachments that occur "too early" interfere with the "normal" grieving process and that early remarriage exposes the widow to a future risk of distress.

For some widows, of course, remarriage is a necessary and practical solution to economic problems and to the need for a replacement father for young children. Kitty, a fifty-year-old widow remarried to solve her survival problems. Unfortunately, she paid a high psychological price for her decision.

A Practical Marriage

Kitty's husband, Scott, found out that he had cancer in June, and before Christmas he was dead. "Until the very end," Kitty told me, "I thought for sure a miracle would happen and that he wouldn't die. Scott was a Rock of Gibraltar about his illness, and he never so much as complained or cried. In fact, we didn't talk about it much and never really spoke of his death until it was imminent. Up until that moment, I hadn't come to grips with the fact that he had terminal cancer.

"When it was finally over, I felt completely stunned—totally unprepared for his death. I was numb and felt as if I were living in a vacuum. I went on listlessly with my day-to-day responsibilities, which mainly consisted of taking care of the children, but I was completely oblivious to the world around me.

"At first, people helped me out. Scott's brother was always very close to us, and he was very supportive and available at the time of the funeral, as were most other family members. But as the weeks and months passed, all of a sudden his brother stopped coming by or calling very often. This hurt, because I really needed his help with Pete, my oldest, who was having a very difficult time."

Kitty was thirty-four years old when she married Scott, and they were together for fifteen years. During that time, they had four children. When Scott died, the youngest child was seven and the oldest was fourteen.

"I felt overwhelmed by being a single parent with four young kids," Kitty told me. "The girls adjusted pretty well to Scott's death and were able to talk about it and to mourn openly. I also know that their relationships with friends at school went on much as they had before. The boys, however, were suffering terribly, especially my son, Pete, who decided he would only hang around with 'troubled' kids—children of divorced parents or children who were having problems in school. Pete and I fought all the time.

"I was so used to my husband taking care of everyone and everything, but now I had to do it on my own. I'm learning, but it's an up-hill battle. I think if money were not such a problem, I could make it, given enough time. I haven't worked since we married, and I don't have any skills. I went out and tried to find a job, but all the places I applied turned me away, either because I was too old or because I had too many young children and they knew I would miss a lot of work taking care of them. This kind of discrimination is supposed to be il-legal, but I knew why they weren't hiring me. Finally the husband of a friend who was president of the library board got me a part-time job at the local library. I thanked God, because I knew I couldn't stay home and dwell on Scott's death any longer."

I asked Kitty what the rest of her life was like. "Other than work," she told me, "I virtually never go anywhere. You see, when you're a widow, you're different. Because you stick out in a crowd, you feel uncomfortable when you go out in public. Even family gath-erings are a problem.

"Things might be different if I ever got married again, but the thought nauseates me. There's no place in my life for another man, and there's really not much place for widows in the world. When widows go out looking for men, I always think, 'How pitiful.' In spite of this, I hate being single, and I just don't know what to do. Before I married Scott, I found being alone painful. Being a widow is almost like being an 'old maid.' I sometimes find myself resenting men because they have it so much easier in life, even if they are widowers.

"I still wear my wedding ring because I'm afraid that, if people know I'm a widow, they're going to think that I'm looking, and I don't want them to think that."

Kitty recognized that the pain she felt as a single parent and her very real financial distress would be assuaged by remarriage, but she resisted this solution. Being single may have been overwhelming for her, yet she felt that it would be shameful to be perceived as looking for another man. She couldn't see herself ever seeking male compan-ionship because it would force her to acknowledge her loneliness and sadness.

. . .

When I interviewed Kitty one year later, however, I found that her life had changed radically: "I met Art at a family wedding, and now we are planning to get married. Although I really like him and feel that he's very kind, he's not Scott! At times I even feel disloyal because I know it'll never be the same with Art as it was with my husband. Scott and I really loved each other, but Art and I are just very comfortable together—there's no real passion. On the plus side, he's wonderful with my children, especially the boys, and I need that desperately because this last year has been very hard. With Art we'll all have a comfortable life. I'm not really sure I'm doing the right thing, but the few friends I still see occasionally are enthusiastic. They all believe I'm making a good choice."

More than almost any other widow I talked to, Kitty experienced intense stigma as a woman alone in the world. Her shame at being a widow also reminded her of an earlier time when she was afraid of winding up an "old maid." Kitty saw even a "cold" marriage that promised comfort and relief as a way out. Her intense ambivalence portends future difficulty. She has not let go of Scott and appears unable to make room in her affections for Art. A year after our last interview, I received a brief note from Kitty telling me that she and Art were moving across the country. She said very little in her note about how her life was progressing. My guess is that without some intensive help in sorting out her complex feelings and finally saying good-bye to Scott, she will remain stuck, neither satisfied with her life nor able to move ahead and develop a more meaningful relationship with Art.

After the early shock and grief are addressed, many widows, especially those in their middle and later years of life, begin to revel in a renewed sense of independence. They enjoy the opportunity for growth and self-development. For them, remarriage can be a threat to this transformation and newfound freedom.

Some women expressed strong feelings about not wanting to

take care of another man, especially if their husband's illness had been a lingering or a painful one. Many widows desired male friends, and even close intimate relationships, but they established distinct boundaries, clearly communicating to their partners that they were not looking for marriage.

How do widows view remarriage? Most struggled with trying to reconcile "being free" and "being happy." It was almost as if they were attempting to "square the circle," asking themselves "How can I keep my new feelings of independence and freedom if I remarry?" This ambivalence was dramatically expressed in their views of married life. Four out of ten felt that their married friends had less freedom than they did. Even more (seven out of ten) believed that widows could live a more independent life than married women. Many told me that, despite grief and sadness, they were also experiencing, some for the first time in their lives, a liberation. This feeling was frightening, yet most woman were challenged to struggle with this newfound freedom: "I now know that I have to decide what I want to do with the rest of my life," one widow told me. "I can't hide behind all those obligations I had when Len was alive. The kids are all grown and don't need me at this point. It's not easy taking responsibility for me after all those years of being obligated to others."

Exhilaration and heady feelings of freedom were mixed with other images. For most widows, marriage was a pathway to happiness. Seven out of ten told me that they believed married people were happier than single ones. Surprisingly, this view was mitigated by their belief that women could certainly live a full and happy life without being married. Seven out of ten widows assured me that life was certainly not over for them. Even if they didn't remarry, they knew there was much to "this business of living life." This view was more pronounced in the older widows who firmly believe that they *could* have a full life without a husband. More often than not, younger women equated fullness of life as only possible with a husband.

These complex and sometimes contradictory beliefs have a marked effect on how widows approach the issue of remarriage at different stages of life.

· · ·

To begin with, I needed to know what the women expected soon after the death of their husband, so I asked each for a prediction as to whether or not she would remarry. I found it fascinating that a woman's expectation that she *would* remarry seemed to be the single most accurate predictor of whether or not she actually *did*.

In spite of these expectations, intention was not the only deciding factor. Even for those women who strongly predicted remarriage, the question of timing was often critical: "How much time needs to pass following my husband's death before I can become serious about another man?" Across all ages, remarriage predictions were substantially lower during the first year of bereavement than they were during the second year of widowhood.

As you might expect, the younger the widow, the more likely she was to see herself as eventually remarrying. Fully three out of four widows under forty years of age believed that they would remarry, but the proportion of women who believed this went down with age. Of the oldest group, widows over sixty, only one in five firmly believed that she would remarry. Differences in expectations reflect not only the stark demographics of the proportion of available men beyond mid-life but differences in attitudes and desires as well.

To understand the psychological and social indicators connected with a widow's choice to remarry, I compared the widows who planned to remarry to their age-mates who didn't. When I looked at the quality of their previous marriage, one sharp difference stood out. Widows who feel more anger toward their dead husband and more personal guilt about his death are much more likely to remarry. This may seem surprising. Why would someone with negative feelings toward her dead husband be more likely to give marriage a second try? Perhaps for these women remarriage represents—though it may not necessarily deliver—relief from unreconcilable grief. This seems especially plausible in light of the fact that these widows report higher levels of grief than the widows who did not "plan" to remarry.

I then asked myself if the problems widows experienced during the first year of bereavement had any relation to their plans for re-marriage. The most telling factor here was that women who found it extremely difficult to be a single parent almost always sought a new husband. Many who remarried for this reason passionately believed that they were doing the right thing, not necessarily for themselves, but for their children, whom they could not envision growing up without a father.

Did the amount of support a woman received from her network of friends and family affect her views about remarriage? Were wid-ows who received little or no help more likely to turn to a new mar-riage for sustenance? I was surprised to discover that the amount of support women received from friends and family actually had a neg-ligible impact upon remarriage plans. I did find, however, that *whom* they received help from was important. Widows who obtained less help from their parents and more help from their married friends were more likely to remarry. Also, a widow involved with a network of married friends, in the absence of other important sources of sup-port, would be more likely to view marriage as a solution to her un-comfortable feelings. Recall from chapter 6 that married friends were typically full of advice about finding a husband. It is perhaps not surprising that a widow whose major source of support is her married friends would seek remarriage. A new relationship may promise renewal.

The Effects of Remarriage on Recovery

To discover the effects of remarriage on widows' mental and physical health, their feelings about themselves, and their happiness and sat-isfaction, I compared those who did remarry to those—similar in age, education, and family circumstances—who did not. Women who remarried relatively early in their widowhood, within the first two years, did not recover more quickly or thoroughly than those who remained single. They were not any happier than single widows and certainly did not feel more in control of their lives. Nor did their sense of self-esteem increase. Surprisingly, their feelings of grief were not even substantially reduced. Symptoms that are often a product of grief—anxiety, bodily complaints, and health—did not improve as a result of their new status. The remarried women, however, experienced a substantial lightening of depression and used less medication and alcohol to allay sad feelings. They also reported less economic stress. Finally, despite the fact that many women who sought out a new husband were motivated by concerns for their children, I found no evidence that parental stresses and strains were reduced by remarriage.

The cultural myth that remarriage is the best antidote to the problems of widowhood is simply not true. The evidence does not even demonstrate a uniform improvement in the lives of those who remarried. All my data underscore the reality of remarriage for widows. It simply is no panacea. Yet, like so many of my findings, there are few absolutes. Some of the women who chose to remarry did very well indeed, but some felt that they were worse off than they were before. Kitty's practical marriage relieved her economic burdens but did little to help her recovery. Again and again, I was more impressed by the variety rather than the uniformity among widows' lives. The pathways to recovery and growth are indeed many.

The best way to see the effects of remarriage on recovery is to read how it affected the lives of two people. I have chosen to share the stories of two successful second marriages: one by a sixty-one-year-old widow and one by an eighty-year-old widower. Both had experienced their losses intensely; both had relatively good first marriages; and both made a successful go of their second. Beyond these similarities, these two call attention to the vast differences between men and women.

A Hasty Marriage

Barbara, a sixty-one-year-old widow, is the mother of two grown children in their thirties. A highly energetic and charming woman, she bounced into my office dressed in a high-fashion gray suit without adornment. The absence of embellishment made a clear statement about her underlying sadness. Barbara had been surrounded by family and friends right after Jim's death, but that emotional support had waned with time, and she had become very lonely. Five months after the death, she decided to move in with a gentleman friend whom she subsequently married.

Barbara told me her story: "Jim retired early, but I continued to work because I loved my job as a social worker, helping people less fortunate than me put their lives back together. Jim's illness was prolonged and difficult, however, and when I made the decision to do most of his caretaking and nursing, I finally had to give up my job. That was about two years before his death. I often wish that I had retired when Jim did, because that would have allowed us more time together. I still have terrible regrets about that.

"The day after Jim's funeral, I went to pieces. I couldn't stop crying, although I knew I should keep busy. I made all sorts of lists of things that needed to be done, but I never did them. I was a wreck. If it weren't for Sandra, my oldest daughter, I don't think I could have gotten through that terrible time.

"Several months after Jim died, I went to a club we used to go to weekly to dance. It was our favorite place, and we had lots of good friends there. I wasn't sure if I would feel comfortable going back, but I felt that I had to go and tell everyone that Jim had died. It was a sad evening for all of us, but I'm glad I went. Our friends from the club were all very kind and understanding.

"That night I met Bob, the man who was to become my husband. I'd known him slightly from the club, but I'd never paid much attention to him. Bob was one of those guys whom our friends labeled an eternal bachelor. They warned me not to become involved with him, telling me, 'Bob has a stable full of lady friends.' I didn't worry about that, though. Besides, although I was interested, I didn't feel ready to become too friendly with him yet.

"Several weeks later I decided to take a vacation and sort myself out; so I went to the Caribbean. All that sun and peace felt good, and it gave me time to think about the future and what I wanted out of life. I decided that my life was in God's hands and that he was working in mysterious ways. How true that was. After I came home, Bob and I began dating, and we really hit it off. Several months later, we started living together.

"At times I still think of going back to work, but Bob is a full-time job. We're very compatible and like the same kind of music and the same kinds of activities. I don't know why Bob suddenly came into my life, but there must have been a reason for it. Sometimes I feel that God sent him to me as a reward for caring for my husband so long and so much."

Despite her happy and satisfying relationship with Bob, Barbara had not put her past life behind her. She still felt grief and unresolved regrets about her marriage and the early paths in life that she and Jim had taken. When I suggested that grieving was a way of letting go of someone, she said, "I don't want to let go of Jim. If I could have my way, I'd be with both of them."

During our second interview, Barbara was much more subdued, saying that she had become very depressed after our talk: "I felt upset when I left here, and I cried a lot. I couldn't even stop when Bob came home from work. Our talk helped me realize how much I really miss my Jim and all the times we shared together.

"There are family problems too. My mother is still causing me a lot of grief. Although I was brought up in a very religious home, for the last twenty years I haven't gone to church. That doesn't mean that God isn't important to me. I still maintain a close and personal relationship with Him, and I know He understands the decisions I've made about my life, but my mother is very judgmental. She calls my situation with Bob 'living in sin' and keeps pushing me to get married.

"But I'm not sure I'm ready. I need to get some sort of sign or hear a voice first. I know it's really my inner voice, but I'm still waiting. If I got married again, it would somehow finalize Jim's death. Maybe I just haven't grieved long enough. I remember Lora, a friend of mine who grieved for her husband for two full years. Look at me, I met Bob after only two and a half months. A friend of mine said recently that I really hadn't gone through any grieving period and that perhaps I really didn't love my husband. That hurt.

"I'm also getting some bad vibes from Bob's sister. Though she hasn't said it to my face, she's done everything else to imply that she thinks Bob and I moved in together too quickly. But I *know* it was the right thing to do. Everything has been better with Bob than it was with Jim. Even the sex is better. I'm enjoying my life much more since I met Bob, yet Jim is still my baby. I still love him. I wish I didn't have to make these comparisons, but I can't seem to help myself."

As Barbara continued talking, I was reminded of the fact that, without wishing to, almost all remarried widows constantly, and often painfully, contrast their former and current husband: "Jim used to center his whole life around me, but Bob is better for me because he's more balanced. We are much more evenly matched and we like to do the same things. Jim never really wanted to share certain activities that were important to me; he never was an outdoor person. Hiking, camping, getting close to nature were always very important to me. Jim never fulfilled that part of me, but Bob does. Nevertheless, I really loved Jim dearly. We were very close, and our sex life was pretty good until the very end of his life. We didn't argue much; we didn't struggle; and we never had a separation, like so many other couples I know.

"I feel a little guilty when I compare Jim to Bob, but I can't seem to help myself. Even Bob tells me that it's not fair for me to keep saying how much better I get along with him. Sometimes I still feel very resentful that Jim was taken away from me. I just keep asking myself why. But all the pain taught me something. I've learned to grab hold of the moment. Bob is due to retire in a year, but lately he's been saying that maybe he won't. Well, as far as I'm concerned, he's going to retire whether he wants to or not. There's no point in postponing things until tomorrow because we don't know how many tomorrows we have left. I wish I had known that before Jim died.

"I've learned that it's important to do what I really want to do with my life. Before, I could never have lived with someone without marrying him, but now I've decided that I really don't care what other people think. Appearances just aren't that important. I lost Jim, who was very important to me, after three years of hell nursing him. I had to break out of that box and feel free again. I was bogged down and I needed some sort of release. Now, I'm living my life the way I want to, and I feel liberated in ways I never felt before."

A year later when I had my follow-up interview with Barbara, she had some news for me. She literally bounced into my office, breathless, looking well-tanned, and dressed in vivid colors, a sharp contrast to one year ago, when she was all grays unrelieved by jewelry or color. She signaled very clearly that her sadness was over. In spite of her vitality and general sense of well-being, however, she was still facing certain issues about her first husband.

"I married Bob six months ago. Things are really going well, and our marriage grows stronger all the time. In spite of that, I've realized that I'm not over crying for Jim. I really didn't give myself enough time to mourn him. Though I'm happy, there are times when I wish I'd waited a bit longer before I remarried, because I could have spared Bob all this grief.

"Sometimes, when I compare Jim and Bob's habits, attitudes, and personal quirks, I find that I prefer Jim's way of doing certain things. It's taken me a little time to get used to Bob's ways. For example, when we went on our first vacation last year, the first day I hated him because he was there and Jim wasn't. I know that was irrational, but I did feel better after a couple of days.

"I had a dream about Bob that sort of sums up the way he makes me feel. Bob and I were in a raging flood. Though it looked like we were about to be swept away, I knew he would find a way to save us.

Sure enough, he ripped off the door of our house and said, 'Climb on.' I told him I wasn't strong enough to hold on, but Bob threw me on top of the door and then climbed on top of me to hold me. I felt very secure.

"It's nice to have somebody you can depend on, but sometimes I think Bob wants me to be too dependent on him. Sometimes he gets upset if I come home even ten minutes late. I guess I'm willing to give up a bit of my independence, because it's important to Bob that he feel protective. He's a bit insecure, but he gives me security, so I think it's important that I let some things go for him. I've even given up some of my friends for Bob, but I don't have any complaints."

Remarriage has worked out for Barbara, but rushing into it has given her some painful moments. Her search for a separate identity after Jim's death is clearly incomplete, as is her mourning process. Barbara admits this: "If I had it all to do over again, I would have waited longer before marrying Bob. I still feel some grief, and I think it's a burden on Bob, even though he says it isn't."

The following story about a widower who also "rushed into" a new marriage demonstrates better than anything I could say the vast differences between men and women when they are faced with the multiplicity of challenges caused by the death of a spouse.

Loss and Renewal

Andrew is an eighty-year-old retired judge who had a very eminent and successful career. His wife, Martha, died six months ago.

"I was married for fifty-two years to a beautiful, brilliant woman who lived with me in the same house for over forty years. Although I retired many years ago, after Martha's death I kept up my heavy schedule, traveling around the country speaking in front of civic groups and boards of directors, and at universities and other national organizations. Even at my age, I'm very busy, maybe too busy. I'm on the phone all day, making arrangements, and writing my memoirs. I had a large group of friends when Martha was alive because she knew a lot of people and used to run our social life. Now I don't have many close friends. Our only child, Catherine, lives in New Orleans.

"Martha was ill for a very long time, and I kept her at home until the very end. During the last three years of her illness, I dedicated myself totally to her care. Her death was the hardest thing I've ever faced. She was my best friend and my best critic. Whenever I'd have to give a talk, I would practice in front of her first, and every time I came home, she'd ask me how it went. Now when I come home, there's no one to talk to.

"Right after her death, it seemed as if I went into a trance. Martha was so much a part of my life. Now it's almost six months, and I'm still tortured by memories of her, particularly when I'm around the house and come across some of her personal things. All of her clothes are still in the house, as are her mementos. I keep them there to remind myself of how lucky I was to have had a woman like that. Martha was my best friend, but I find myself thinking lately that maybe I neglected her because I gave so much of my time to others. I'm sorry now that I didn't stay at home more often to spend time with her.

"Losing her has made me realize that there are still parts of myself that I don't understand, and lately I've begun to see a lot of things more clearly. I've even started going to church and Bible class, something I haven't done since I was a child. I know I can't change the past, but maybe I can let go of my frantic schedule even though I'm over eighty and retired. For the first time in my life, I feel comfortable with myself, even when I'm not working so hard. I'm also beginning to feel a little less sad—able to look at Martha's things without coming apart. More often than not, I feel lucky to have gotten as much as I did from her over the fifty-two years that we knew one another."

Andrew has begun to examine his life and its meaning. This "internal conversation" may be the beginning of a transformation that could lead to substantial personal growth.

A week later, Andrew talked more about his fifty-two years with his wife: "It wasn't a perfect marriage. I feel now that I should have taken more interest in things that she was interested in, but we never really had any conflict about this, or about other things in our marriage. Our sex life could have been better too.

"I've made some definite changes since her death. I'm more able to appreciate and take pleasure in other people and their interests. I regret that I never did much self-examination in the past, but I think I'm finally beginning to do a little of that. I'm much more interested in religion, and I've begun to think about the hereafter. I'm convinced that, when it's my time to go, I'm really going to see all the people I've met in life."

When I saw Andrew a year later, he looked much younger than I remembered him, and his sports coat and tie were more colorful than the grays that had predominated his dress a year ago. The reasons for these changes soon become clear: "Since we last talked, my life has changed completely. I'm married now to a woman named Claudia, whom I met about nine months ago. Although she recently turned sixty-one, she's small and trim and looks like she's forty. Not only is she attractive, she's brilliant. I'm deliriously happy, and I've changed totally. I got rid of all my clothes and went out and bought all new ones. I sold my house and all the old furniture and moved into a new home with Claudia. I even bought a new car.

"I've given up my past life as well. I don't travel or give speeches anymore, but I do volunteer work at a hospice, so I still feel as if I'm doing other people some good. My health is excellent, and I haven't even had a head cold since I remarried. I go to church and Bible class on Sunday, and every day Claudia and I read the Bible for an hour in the morning. I feel that Martha is aware of what I'm doing and would approve of it.

"My marriage to Martha was perfect; my new marriage is also

perfect. I no longer blame Martha for our poor sex life. In fact, I never held a grudge against her for that, because everything else was so perfect. I don't think about her anymore, and I've put away all the things that might remind me of her.

"Claudia takes total care of me. She calls me three or four times a day from her office to see whether I'm OK, and she watches what I eat. I used to be concerned about being successful, but now I realize that what's really important to me is to be helpful to others. Aside from continuing my hospice work, I started to teach a Bible class every Sunday to teenagers in our church. It's hard work! I'd forgotten how up-and-down kids' emotional lives are at that age, but I'm enjoying it tremendously. I've learned that I'm not really much more important than anyone else, and I guess it was my wife who used to make me feel that way. When I realized that she really was gone, I began to see that I'm just like everyone else."

Andrew has been literally reborn over the past year. The symbolic actions of throwing away his clothes, selling his furniture, and entering into a new relationship "naked" says much about the meaning of remarriage for men. In his need to let go of his previous marriage, he has even forgotten its flaws, claiming now that it was "perfect." Contrast this attitude with Martha's sense that she is still married to two husbands. Martha's self-evaluation and search for a new identity continued throughout her new marriage. In Andrew's case, however, the growth process that began after his wife's death has completely stopped. Since meeting Claudia, looking inward no longer appeals to him.

Martha and Andrew dramatize many of the similarities and some of the differences between widows and widowers. Both had relatively satisfying first marriages and experienced the loss of their spouse profoundly. Both are also clearly satisfied with their new marriages.

Despite these similarities, there are vast differences in their attitudes. Remarriage is clearly more difficult for a woman than for a man. There are psychological issues that seem to distinguish the sexes. Most significant is the almost universal feeling of disloyalty that plagues widows. They can't seem to stop themselves from comparing their previous marriage with the current one. This is much less of a problem for men, who handle their feelings by literally forgetting about the past, as we saw Andrew so poignantly do. Upon remarrying, men rarely seem to struggle with feelings of grief or a sense that perhaps they have moved too fast. Unlike widows, they aren't haunted by a feeling that remarriage will make the reality of their spouse's death irrevocable. In a sense, they seem to *need* the symbolic death of their deceased spouse in order to get on with their lives, and men are much more efficient at this task than the typical widow.

For most women, however, the inner life comprises a much more cherished and salient part of themselves. Many widows experience the need to explore their inner feelings and thoughts. Even those parts of themselves that are vague, confusing, and painful are cherished and examined, and often become a source of growth.

Men certainly start on the growth process, but for many remarriage stops their self-exploration dead in its tracks. When they seek out new relationships, widowers are much less likely to nurture their inner life and the pleasures and benefits that it can bring them.

Why do men and women react so differently? I believe that the key is how each gender interprets aloneness. Men have only limited resources when it comes to dealing with solitude. Most mid- to late-life men have built their emotional lives almost exclusively around their wives. When their spouse dies, they don't have many meaningful alternative sources of emotional support and intimacy. Being a widower overstrains their impoverished resources, and they tend to see remarriage—replacement of the old wife with a new wife—as the only way out of their loneliness. While widows are able to find support from family and friends, widowers are strikingly less able to do so. For men, finding a new wife becomes the only solution they can imagine.

None of this means, however, that the terrible pain of loneliness is less of a problem for widows. They just seem to have a wider range of strategies for surviving grief. Discovering unused and long-forgotten parts of themselves, developing new relationships with both men and women, as well as strengthening those with old friends and family are strategies widows use to diminish their loneliness. The next chapter examines in detail the differences between widows and widowers.

Chapter 12

The Other Side of the Coin:
How Widowers Cope

Although this book is primarily about widows, over the course of seven years I listened to the stories of over a hundred widowers. Even so, I felt that a full understanding of what it means to be a widower in today's society eluded me. Men's reactions to their loss were not always as easy to decode as those of women. Some sharp contrasts did emerge, however. Unlike widows, who often use bereavement as a springboard for looking inward and reevaluating their lives, widowers seem more likely to focus their attention outward. Remarriage seemed to be the most common pathway to a widower's salvation.

This chapter cannot provide a full view of the widower's experience, but it does offer a comparison with the widow's journey so that she may better understand her own path.

People associate two seemingly contradictory myths with widowerhood. The first, embraced especially by widows, is that widowers have "an easier time of it." This belief is most likely based upon the simple fact that a higher proportion of widowers do remarry. To many widows, these frequent and early remarriages seem to indicate that widowers recover from their grief more rapidly. Also, since women live an average of seven years longer than men, it seems that widowers have a wider choice of partners. A lack of available men is not the reason why so many widows do not remarry. It is their greater satisfaction with being single.

There are health care professionals who subscribe to an alternative view—that men suffer from more physical and emotional problems than do women. Some studies provide evidence that widowers do, in fact, have greater difficulty than widows. Widowers may be more vulnerable to the loss because of their male proclivity to hide rather than express emotions, including grief and sadness. Coupled with the almost universal tendency of men not to maintain ties with kith and kin and their unwillingness or inability to share their feelings, widowers possess fewer coping strategies. They don't have as many people to call on for help and through most of their married life have relied on their wife as their sole confidant. While a number of studies have found that men have more problems after the death of a spouse than women and may be at risk for increased mortality and morbidity, we have to remember that many studies paint an equally grim picture of recovery for widows.

I used identical standards for both men and women, comparing levels of anxiety; depression; somatic symptoms; substance abuse; feelings of stigmatization; intensity of grief, anger, and guilt; feelings of well-being or satisfaction with life; health; self-esteem; and sense of control over the world they live in. I compared widows and widowers soon after the death of a spouse, and then looked at their responses one year later. I found that both genders showed similar patterns of recovery by the end of the first year, so I concluded that the impact of losing a spouse is similar in intensity for both.

Contrary to the general view, men do *not* have an easier time, nor do they have a considerably worse time. There are, however, important and dramatic differences between how men and women react to the death of a spouse.

Men experience grief differently. They are much more reserved about discussing unwanted or unwelcome thoughts about their wives. They are much less likely to be angry with the medical establishment about the care their wives received. Though most widows describe experiencing the "presence" of their husbands during the first six months of widowhood, only one-quarter of the widowers reported this experience.

Devastating feelings of loneliness at the loss of a spouse are common to both men and women. Although the intensity of such feelings does not differ, men and women picture this loneliness and what they are missing differently. For women, loneliness is not being thought of, not being held, and feeling unprotected. For men, in contrast, the feeling of loneliness can be summed up in one devastating sentence: Being lost without a compass.

When I met Bob, he was sixty years old and recently retired from his civil service career. After thirty-six years of marriage, his wife Mary had died that past July. Four months later he had remarried.

As Bob sat down for our first interview, the first thing he said was, "I married my next door neighbor. Lisa's husband died one and a half months before Mary's passing." His voice was clear and proud, and I could tell how contented he was with this second marriage. He also told me how supportive his children had been: "I have five children, all married and all living within an hour's drive. They were wonderful during Mary's illness and have been quite attentive to me since her death."

When I asked Bob about his life before Mary died, he told me how happy they had been together: "Our marriage was an ideal one, and we were completely compatible. We were totally devoted to one another and to our children. We never once went to bed mad."

The two of them had done quite a bit of talking before Mary passed away, though she had been more willing to talk than Bob: "Many times I tried to bury my head and not see what was happening, but Mary never hid it from herself. I know, however, that she tried to protect me from pain. Only once did she talk directly about her terror of dying. I know her strong religious faith helped her immensely. Mary stayed at home throughout her illness. We enjoyed life right up to the very end and left nothing unfinished between us."

Bob knew Mary had worried about how he would manage after

she was gone: "I think I'm a dependent person who never strongly cultivated a great many personal interests or friends. Mary used to tell me of her concern about my not having any outside interests. When she was dying, we talked a lot about her worries that I wouldn't be able to take care of myself. She spent time trying to teach me how to cook. My mother spent the last three months living with us and helping out, but I know what Mary told her: 'Help take care of him but don't move in. After all, Bob isn't a baby; he needs to learn how to manage for himself.'"

My interviews with Bob elicited strong, at times overwhelming feelings from him. When he first mentioned his wife to me, he remembered her sitting alone in the dark living room. He broke down a couple of times before he was finally able to tell me about that. On several occasions he wept and went through a half dozen Kleenexes in the office. Other times he seemed almost jovial and obviously very pleased with the turn that his life has taken—his unexpected, happy marriage to Lisa.

"After Mary died, I felt lost. I didn't know how to live without her. The hardest thing I had to deal with was the terrible loneliness. It felt like a big, black silence.

"Then one day I was working in the yard, and my next door neighbor Lisa was cutting her lawn. Suddenly I thought about my tickets to the community theater and asked her to go with me. From that point on, our relationship steadily deepened. I would never have gone to the theater or to the movies alone, because I hate being by myself. Lisa literally just dropped into my life. I doubt I could have taken an active role in finding someone on my own."

It was interesting that Bob saw his meeting with Lisa as something accidental, almost magical. To him, it "just happened," a sentiment that no doubt went a long way toward defusing any guilt he may have felt about remarrying so quickly after Mary's death.

When I asked him how his marriage to Lisa was unfolding, he said, "It has gone well except for some problems with sex. I had no sex life with Mary during the last year of her illness, and even before that I had occasional problems with impotency because of the medicine I take for my hypertension. I sometimes wonder, though, if my performance in bed has something to do with feeling that I'm with another man's wife. I knew Lisa's husband for twenty-seven years. The four of us were all very close. Mary and Lisa used to share a lot of confidences together, and I know that Lisa had problems with her husband."

Bob was clearly dealing with his grief and was well on the way to recovery. He had a new lease on life, and a new wife who made him happy. I was curious, however, about what had helped him get through the dark time of Mary's illness and the months following her death. "My belief in God is very important to me," Bob told me. "It sustained me through the worst part of Mary's illness and the time after she died. My parents were religious, and Mary's father was a minister. I've always firmly believed in God. Why else could it be that Lisa and I, living next door to one another, are able to share a life together? I have always believed that, ultimately, we don't really control our destinies, that there is Someone who has a clearer picture of the design behind my life than I do."

When I asked Bob about the most important lesson he'd learned from his grief, he summed it up in one word—brevity: "We're only here briefly, so we should enjoy life, leave our mark, be a good citizen, and be helpful to others. I've lost my wife of thirty-seven years, and I'm retired now and obviously in the last phases of my life. I know that it's time for me to be honest with myself—if there is anything in my life that I really want to do, now is the time for me to get it done."

When I saw Bob once again a year later, he had changed very little. He was still living in the same house with his new wife, and the marriage had gone extremely well. His physical health was good.

When I asked him about the progress of his marriage, he said, "Lisa and I are very close to one another. There are no conflicts, no problems in the relationship. It's funny, though. Remember last year when you asked me if I was having any interesting dreams, and I told you I couldn't remember any? Well last week I had a dream where I was getting instructions from *both* of my wives. Hah! I guess that's just like me, being led and taken care of by women, except now there are two of them, Mary *and* Lisa. I don't mind though."

This dream and Bob's response to it didn't surprise me. If anything, Bob seemed even more of a dependent person than he had been before. Since his marriage to Lisa, he does virtually nothing alone; in fact, there were a couple of questions that he couldn't fill out on the study questionnaire because he had to wait for his wife to help him.

Bob, like so many of the widowers studied, experienced extremely painful and, from their perspective, unbearable feelings of being utterly alone. Like Bob, many widowers maintain that they "fall" into another relationship without "lifting a finger." This rationale helps them to fend off feelings of disloyalty to the previous spouse and the good marriage they shared. Relying on another woman to help them pick up the pieces of their lives, they need not look inward and don't have to take the initiative to make changes in their lives.

On the Road to Recovery

Although men and women may end up adjusting equally well to the loss of their spouse, their paths through bereavement are different. Men code their problems differently from the way women do when facing the same loss. They view their marriage with different eyes. Memories of the relationship have a distinctive male flavor. When widowers begin to move beyond devastating feelings of grief and start to put their lives back together, they handle common tasks entirely differently. Consider, for example, how widowers and widows deal with disposing of the spouse's belongings. Many women begin this process later and take much longer, doing it piece by piece. Typically, widowers rid themselves completely of their spouse's belongings early in the mourning process, almost as if they could magically make their loss disappear by making the objects associated with their spouse vanish.

When talking to both woman and men about their marriages, I was struck by how much more willing widows were to discuss feelings of marital loneliness than were widowers, and their high level of distress at this. Half of the women I studied had been lonely at some time during their marriage. In contrast, only one in twelve men reported being lonely.

Most men and women described their marriages as positive and satisfying. Two out of three men and two out of three women positively evaluated their marriages. Surprisingly, 40 percent of the men felt that their marriage had placed restrictions on their self-development, compared to 20 percent of the women. The men felt that had it not been for their marriage, they could have accomplished more in their careers, traveled more, and been more adventurous. Despite this feeling of being stunted, unlike women, men did not use this as a springboard for exploration and growth.

Widows, on the other hand, were more likely to report regrets about their lives in general. Two-thirds of the women interviewed had some major regrets about unaccomplished goals and unfulfilled desires, whereas only 25 percent of the men reported such feelings. Finally, and probably not too surprisingly, despite their regrets and the loneliness that was part and parcel of their married life, women were twice as likely to idealize their spouses. For many of the women I studied, now in their sixties, marriage was the culmination of their lives. Even when dissatisfied, they participated in the cultural myth and needed to view their spouses as possessing stellar qualities—even if they really knew better.

The Inner Life of Widowers

The inner lives of men and women, as they struggle with the loss of a spouse, show pronounced differences. Many women use their struggles with grief as a launching pad for change and for looking inward. They often try to understand where they have come from and where their lives are going. Four times as many women reexamined their purpose in life, and twice as many addressed directly painful regrets about their past lives. They struggled to find some way of understanding where they had been and, now that they were widowed, what new meaning could they give to their existence. Twice as many women viewed their husband's death as an opportunity to learn about themselves and their lives. The consequence of this grappling with who they were and who they wished to become is clear: Women grew in response to their loss at double the rate of men.

For men, on the other hand, the death of a wife is more likely to set off thoughts about their own mortality and vulnerability. Ron, a fifty-nine-year-old widower illustrates this pattern.

Preoccupation with Death

During his first interview, Ron told me about his fears: "After Ruth died, all I could think about was my own death. It's not that the way Ruth handled her death wasn't reassuring. She was very courageous and often said that life offered us no guarantees. I often wonder, though, if I can be like her when the time comes. Could I step back and get the absolute most out of dying, as she did? As painful as her illness was for us, during the last several months we both lived very intensely.

"Before Ruth died I was very naive about death. Now I realize I could die tomorrow. That thought never occurred to me before her illness. I've come to realize that if it's true that none of us lives forever, it's foolish to waste time with relationships that aren't working well. Why be sad, why be hassled? If something's not going well, do something about it. In the last eight months my priorities have been to focus on the things I can enjoy about life."

Even a year after Ruth's death, Ron continued to be nervous and afraid: "I'm still very aware of death and aware of its consequences," he told me, "especially of leaving all the people I love alone. Yester-day I hurt my knee bowling and began to worry about whether I had bone cancer. These thoughts usually pass, but sometimes they are more persistent. I had bronchitis a while ago and got so worried about cancer that I went to my doctor to have it checked out. I'm aware of all my aches and pains—my sore feet, my sore back. I feel as if I've aged five years in the last year."

The death of Ron's wife upset his stable and comfortable view of existence. For him, the resultant anxiety became focused on his health. We don't know why men so frequently funnel their unease into threats to their survival, but this is clearly a distinction between men's and women's responses to the death of a spouse.

What are the strategies widowers use to deal with their loss and the challenges they face as a single person? How do they differ from wid-ows? Men seem to have fewer strategies and more limited resources. They throw themselves into their work and into new relationships, keeping constantly on the move to avoid having to stop and look at themselves.

One of the striking differences between widowers and widows is that the women find it easier to turn to friends and family for help. Widows and widowers of the same age had the same amount of con-tact with family and friends, but men received much less emotional support and were much less likely to believe that they could count on family and friends for help, for guidance, or for providing support and comfort in their search for a new or changed life-style. The men got help for day-to-day tasks, such as cleaning the house, cooking, and health care. But most widowers simply could not ask for certain kinds of help, and, sadly, friends and family often appeared unable to reach out to the widower. I also discovered that men are much less likely to seek out professional help and that widowers are less likely to benefit from support groups than women. In fact, many men I in-terviewed described finding help with the problems of widowerhood as their main dilemma.

· · ·

Larry's story is a good example of the limited resources and coping strategies demonstrated by many widowers.

A Desperate Race
with Loneliness

Larry is a slight, bespectacled fifty-six-year-old widower whose wife, Ellen, died four months ago. He has lived in the same house for the last twenty-one years. Married somewhat late in life, Larry has only one child, named Anna, age sixteen. An MBA from Yale provided Larry with a good but unexciting middle-management position in a biotech firm, but Larry is not disappointed in his career: "Comfort and free time for myself and my daughter have always been more important to me than climbing the corporate ladder."

I asked Larry how he felt about his wife's death. "At first, after Ellen died, I did a lot of crying. I don't need to do that anymore. Looking back, what helped me get through those awful first months was the way that Ellen dealt with everything. The way she went was her last gift to me. It helped me experience the intensity of my life with greater vividness. After Ellen's death, I got in touch with just how much of me was actually tied up with her. I have a recurring dream about her where we are having an argument and she decides to leave me and closes the door behind her. Of course her death made me angry, and maybe this is the anger I'm supposed to be feeling because she died and left me.

"I went back to work about three weeks after Ellen's funeral. I sleep pretty well, and I don't need pills. I never had any use for drugs. I do a lot of swimming for exercise. Overall, except for being lonely, I think I've coped pretty well."

Larry talked about Ellen's final illness: "Ellen complained of breast soreness and an examination revealed a very serious, advanced cancer. We knew she was going to die, and I took care of her at home throughout her illness. Ellen was a unique person. Even on her deathbed she was supporting and comforting me. After she died, my friends and family were wonderful to me. My aunt and mother-in-law stayed for a couple of weeks, and many of the mothers of my daughter's friends were also helpful. I got rid of Ellen's clothes within the first week, except for a drawer full of things I wanted to save for my daughter."

Larry is typical of most widowers: Family and friends do reach out to them. During the first month of their bereavement they "allow" others to help with the tasks of dealing with their immediate problems. However, they rarely reach out to their friends for emotional support and almost never talk about their feelings.

Three months after Ellen died, Larry started dating Susan, a divorced neighbor he and Ellen had known for years. In a short time, he began to see her almost every day. When his daughter's school term ended, he felt like he had to get away for a while, and the three of them went to Hawaii together. "In Hawaii I felt much better and could forget all the pain," Larry told me. "After three weeks, when I came back home, I continued to do well." Larry sounded a little defensive, however, when he followed that statement with the words "I'm not hiding things from myself."

Two months later Larry reported that Susan had been on vacation for the past three weeks. He was completely at loose ends without her: "The time Susan has been gone has been terrible for me. I was surprised by the pain. Even though Anna is at home, I've been extremely lonely. I spend a lot of the day and night thinking about my past with Ellen, and I've begun to wonder if my relationship with Susan doesn't interfere with my really saying good-bye to Ellen. Even if this is true, however, I don't want to stop seeing Susan. I just can't stand being alone."

During his time by himself, Larry had begun comparing Ellen to Susan: "Ellen and I were close friends, and there was a great deal of respect and understanding that had evolved over the twenty years we spent together. Susan is different from Ellen in many ways. She's more independent and she has a separate career, which Ellen was never interested in. My wife and I were quite interdependent, but, you know, I feel much more independent now. Ellen was hard on me. She would blame me for catching a cold, whereas Susan tends to be oversupportive and perhaps overnurturing. I don't mind that. I do feel cared for."

A year later Susan had moved in with Larry: "We are talking about setting a time for getting married; yet, at the same time, things are not going perfectly between the two of us. I am still grieving for Ellen, probably even more than I did last year. These feelings get in the way of Susan's and my life together. In spite of all this, I love Susan and really would like to marry her. I know it's a different kind of love than what I felt for Ellen. I also know that I still have a lot of grieving to do.

"One of my problems is that I'm having trouble giving Susan the same status I gave Ellen. Somehow I still consider Ellen my wife. Maybe remarrying would really give me a sense that Ellen is dead and no longer married to me. Perhaps it would make Susan her equal, yet I don't know if that's really possible. Ellen feels much more special to me—irreplaceable. She and I shared so much and understood each other so well. We were so comfortable together. If we got mad, we could explode at each other and tell each other we were acting like jackasses. I can't quite do that with Susan because our relationship doesn't feel as secure. When Susan and I fight, we pull away from each other.

"Ellen was my special friend. I still feel scarred and burdened, but I need Susan. What can I do? Ellen was a unique, special person, and we worked well as a team. Susan and I are more alike, but she doesn't fill in the gaps that are missing in me. When I think about marriage it hurts; it hurts me to think that Ellen won't be my wife anymore. I still can't commit myself fully to Susan. When I married Ellen, she was my total focus. That's not the case with Susan, because now my main focus is my daughter, Anna."

Larry vacillated, never quite sure what to do. Finally, six months later, he married Susan. When I asked him what influenced his final decision, he said, "It was easier for me to do than face the terrible void of loneliness!"

Larry illustrates how some widowers have very limited and re-strictive strategies for coping with grief. Though friends and family helped him immediately after the funeral, he did not turn to them later when he needed comfort and support. Instead, he developed a precipitous and less-than-satisfactory new relationship. The work of grieving and the chance to develop a new self more appropriate to his life changes were almost completely neglected.

Lest we all too hastily conclude that all widowers are alike in their desperate search to find someone, anyone, to relieve the twin dilemmas of loneliness and the dread of death, let's listen to Bill, a successful widower who coped, developed, and grew without the prop of remarriage.

Resolution and Integration

Bill was a sixty-seven-year-old jolly, bulbous-nosed widower who al-ways spoke right from the heart. He impressed me as enormously honest and very sensitive. Bill was very cooperative, had a good sense of humor, and has genuine access to his emotions. Bertha, his wife of thirty-eight years, had died four and a half months before. Bill's three sons live nearby, and he sees each of them and his grandchil-dren about once a week. After having nursed his wife for over a year during her final illness, and now retired from his engineering job, Bill has time on his hands.

When asked what his days were like now, he said, "I go out a couple of evenings a month to a hospice bereavement group. It's been extremely helpful. I do a lot of my own cooking and I watch TV. On the weekends, my sons usually come over.

"Before Bertha died, she and I were totally open with each other. We talked about everything you could imagine talking about, about her prognosis, about how much longer she was going to live, and about the funeral arrangements. Nothing whatsoever was left unsaid."

When I asked Bill what his marriage was like before Bertha became ill, I was somewhat surprised at his answer: "I often thought she was cuckoo. Bertha was always irrationally jealous. She had a sharp tongue and was very critical and often unpredictable. Let me give you some examples. I insisted that we move closer to my work because the commute was becoming very hard for me. She didn't want to, but finally we did. She warned me, however, that if we moved, she would never have any of the people I worked with over to the house. She stuck to that, and we never entertained any of my work friends.

"Another time she set fire to my workbench. Over the past five years, she did simmer down, but she continued to be irrationally jealous, not only of other women but of anyone I liked or befriended. Several times I seriously thought of separating from her. I even called a lawyer once, but I never followed through. The best years of our marriage were the last five, and the worst were the first ten. I do think I married the wrong person. We didn't have a lot in common. Bertha never liked classical music or opera. She was very bright, the valedictorian of her high school class, yet after we were married she never read a book."

When I asked him if he felt lonely, Bill told me that he didn't mind being alone: "I did have one attack of lonesomeness one weekend when no one came to visit me and I suddenly realized I had nothing to do. I couldn't get up the steam to go see anyone either. I guess I was feeling sorry for myself, but I soon snapped out of that. My life is really different now. I was very intimate with Bertha and shared everything with her. Now, there's no one really to be intimate with. I have one woman friend named Carol with whom I share a good deal over the telephone, but she doesn't confide much in me. She's the wife of an old friend, and I guess she acts mainly as a sounding board for me. I have no male buddies I can really talk to, and I've never been a joiner. Sometimes I feel as if I'm just sitting around waiting for something to happen. I do plan to do more volunteer work in the future.

"The hardest thing about being alone is the frustration at not being able to share things. Bertha knew all about me and our past. Now when I read something about someone we both knew and look around to tell her about it, I realize there's no one to tell it to. It's as though my past is in a parking orbit."

When I asked Bill if he ever thought about remarrying, he expressed reservations: "I don't want to take on the responsibility again. I'm scared of going through another loss with a new wife. But don't get me wrong. Although I'm not planning on remarrying, I'm still interested in women. This time around, I'm ready to find a younger woman, perhaps someone who is forty or forty-five. I don't want any 'old bags,' although I'm probably one myself."

When I asked Bill if he had any regrets, he answered with a confident no: "I have no guilt about anything I did during Bertha's illness—I did everything that was humanly possible—nor do I have any regrets about my life. I was always lucky to be in the right place at the right time. I started life in the tenements and yet retired with a comfortable income and a feeling of a job well done. I always seemed to make the right choices in life. I don't even regret my marriage. At best, it was tolerable. Bertha and I had major problems, and I often think that I married the wrong woman; yet we were always able to communicate with one another.

A year later, Bill was still feeling good about himself and seemed almost fully recovered: "Things have gone well for me," he said. "I just returned from a cruise to Alaska. My health has been fairly good and I'm definitely over my grieving. I still think often about Bertha, but there's no tug. Remembering her is never painful.

"My life now is pretty good. I go where I want; I do what I want; and, more important, I don't do things I don't want to do. I'm not lonely. My social life with my hospice group and my family feels quite sufficient. When I come home from visits, I'm often quite happy to be alone. I haven't dated and have begun to believe I'll never become involved with another woman. Sometimes I worry whether I'd even be able to sexually perform. That's one issue that I haven't put to rest as yet. I don't think it upsets me, but I think about dating; so it must be something I need work on.

"I still think about death a lot. I don't believe I'm afraid of it, but it comes to mind any time I do even simple things that involve long-range plans, such as subscribing to magazines or making investments. I don't make any real estate or long-term investments any longer. I'm not interested in amassing much money. I already have a lot of money to spend and I want to spend it faster than before.

"I worry sometimes about the fact that no one calls me every day. Sometimes I wonder what would happen if I were to die in the house and no one were to find me for a while. I also worry about the decay and the garbage in the house. Lately I've been toying with the idea of buying one of these alarms that you wear on you so that you can automatically call the police station if something were to happen."

When I asked Bill to sum up how he'd changed over the past year, he said, "I'm more carefree and more merry. I joke more than ever before and I have no ax to grind, no wife and no job to worry about. When I realize that I can do as I please, it's liberating! In the past I always used to struggle to save money for some kind of eventuality. Now I don't worry about my estate at all. If anything, I'm always looking for things to buy. I feel unburdened. When death comes, it comes."

Bill's grieving process is one of the better examples of a person who's coped well. He has managed to integrate a less-than-satisfactory marriage into his life and to overcome any lingering feelings of regret. He's done that by looking within and by being very honest with himself.

To address the misconceptions that began this chapter, there is no convincing scientific evidence that men are likely to suffer from the loss of a spouse any more than women do. There are, however, countless differences between the genders in how they address the problems of bereavement. The coping strategies of widowers are more constricted and operate within a narrower band. They rely less often upon the support of friends, families, or professionals for help with their recovery, and when they do, the results are often less successful. The most outstanding difference between widows and widowers is that for most men the loss of a spouse does not become a launching pad for growth and development.

Epilogue

Widowhood in the Twenty-first Century: A Look at the Future

This book is a snapshot of women at a particular point in their history, and in ours. Of course grief at the loss of a spouse is to be expected; loss is part of the human condition. However, the challenges faced by widows will change as we enter a new century. The experiences of the baby-boom woman will reflect the dramatic and at times cataclysmic alterations in the status and role of women. Our daughters will confront a wholly different widowhood.

How you are as a widow is in large measure shaped and influenced by the attitudes and beliefs of those around you: family, friends, professionals, and the media. How you experience the loss, what you do about it, your pattern of recovery, and who you become are embedded in the world around you. Collectively they reflect the current culture. As I have tried to demonstrate, society's beliefs about widows and widowhood often reflect myths that do not mirror the real experiences of widows. These misconceptions and half-truths can interfere with recovery and with personal development.

Most of this book has been about the widows' challenges that go beyond grief: how to enter the single state, how to deal with family and friends, what to do with the unresolved feelings and regrets left over from marriage, how to face the challenge of developing a new self-image based on an "I" rather than a "we," exploring questions of existence: personal meaning and confrontation with death and with the past.

The majority of women described in this book were born at a time when the role, status, and expectations for them were radically different from what they are today. Many women, despite their history, managed to make the leap into the contemporary world, but only a few could wholly escape their early experiences.

Women in the twenty-first century will enter widowhood with different life experiences and will confront a wholly different reality. We know that both men and women will live somewhat longer, but, more important, they will be healthier and more vigorous through their seventh and possibly their eighth decade. They will face a society peopled by many more of their age-mates. Since it is not expected that the differential life span between men and women will change, widows in the twenty-first century will live in a setting where there will be many more people like themselves.

Family life is changing before our very eyes. More and more families will include children and grandparents from serial marriages. The "family" will be composed of children from a first and second marriage, with offspring from all four parents.

The sharp distinction between single and married friends so often characteristic of the helping network of today's widows will disappear, since the evolving independence of the woman, married or not, will be the norm. So the context for widows will be quite different.

Perhaps more important will be the psychological state of women who confront the loss of a spouse. The increasing empowerment and the development of women as separate persons beyond their marriages will more and more be the norm. Many will become widows having held major positions in life and having fully realized their potential.

Women in the twenty-first century will not be burdened by a view of marriage characteristic of the mid- and late-life widows whose stories comprise this book. Regrets for not having developed themselves will be rare, as will the total reliance of the self-image on marriage. It is likely that the idealization and dependency characteristic of many widows will be a rarity.

As society begins to catch up with women's experiences, the view of widows as "less than whole" will disappear. Many women will live twenty years after the loss of their husbands. They will begin this time having experienced a fuller and more independent existence all their lives. So creating a new way of being after the loss of a spouse will not be the same kind of challenge it is today. It will be more acceptable to be a woman alone, and as the social expectations change, so will the joys and challenges our daughters will face. Perhaps the experiences described and the stories told in this book will give parents the strength to prepare a better way for their daughters and sons, and children a new understanding of the generation that gave them life. Redevelopment, new lives after the loss, will be the norm. That women can grow as a result of crises will not be considered strange but a natural part of the life cycle.

Technical Appendices

The book's findings are based on two samples that totaled 700 widows and widowers. Questionnaires, clinical interviews, and observations of groups were used to generate data. This appendix is divided into five sections: I. Main Findings, II. Samples, III. Measures, IV. Analysis and Detailed Findings, and V. Locating Support Groups.

FIGURE 1.1

Changes in Symptoms of Grief

Soon after the Death Compared to Those of One Year Later

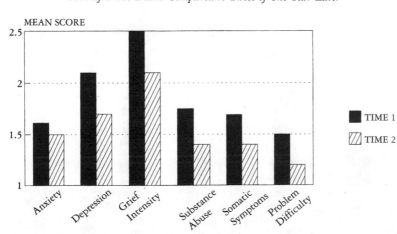

Time 1 = Soon after the loss; Time 2 = One year later

FIGURE 1-2

Adjustment

Soon after the Death Compared to That of One Year Later

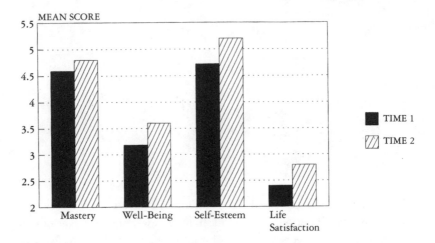

Time 1 = Soon after the loss; Time 2 = one year later

FIGURE 1-3

Stress Associated with Widowhood

Changes Soon after the Death Compared to Those of One Year Later

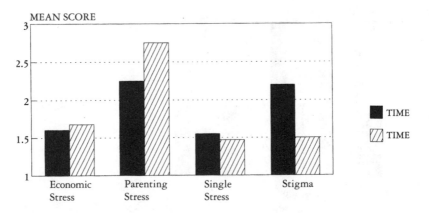

Time 1 = Soon after the death; Time 2 = one year later

FIGURE 2-1

Comparisons:

Four Grief Patterns and Nonwidows, Time 1 and Time 2

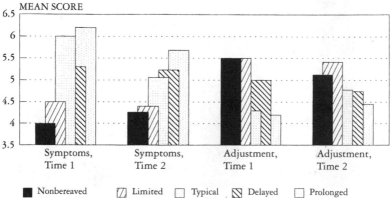

■ Nonbereaved   ▨ Limited   ☐ Typical   ▨ Delayed   ☐ Prolonged

Symptoms = Depression + Anxiety + Substance Abuse + Somatic + Health
Adjustment = Mastery + Self-Esteem + Well-Being
Combined Z Scores Used to Summarize

FIGURE 6-1

Who Provides Help to Widows

Type of Help and Source of Help*

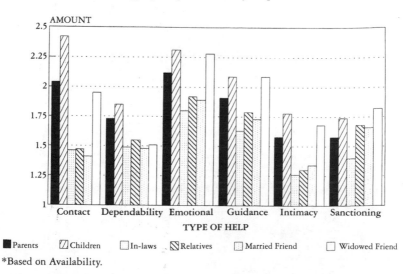

■ Parents   ▨ Children   ☐ In-laws   ▨ Relatives   ☐ Married Friend   ☐ Widowed Friend

*Based on Availability.

FIGURE 9-1

Existential Explorations and Growth

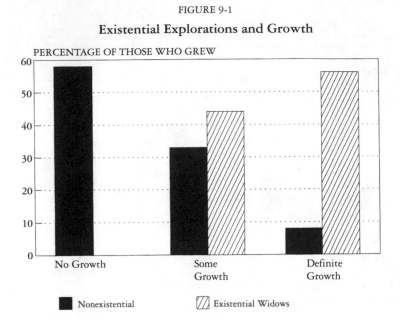

PERCENTAGE OF THOSE WHO GREW

■ Nonexistential   ▨ Existential Widows

FIGURE 9-2

Profile of Widows Who Engaged in Existential Exploration*

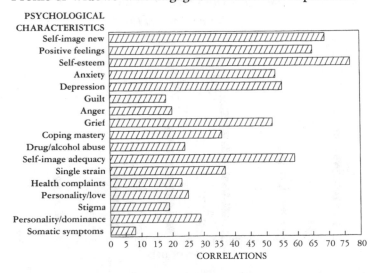

▨ Existential

*Time 1 scores

FIGURE 12-1

Comparisons: Widows and Widowers

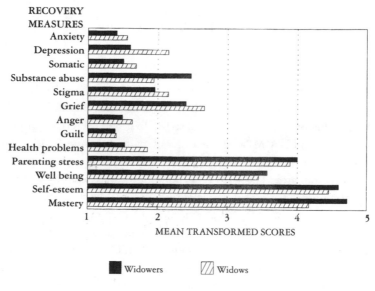

**RECOVERY
MEASURES**
Anxiety
Depression
Somatic
Substance abuse
Stigma
Grief
Anger
Guilt
Health problems
Parenting stress
Well being
Self-esteem
Mastery

MEAN TRANSFORMED SCORES

■ Widowers   ▨ Widows

FIGURE 12-2

Comparisons: Widows and Widowers*

Amount and Source of Support

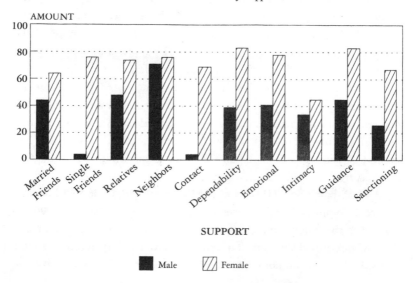

AMOUNT

Married Friends, Single Friends, Relatives, Neighbors, Contact, Dependability, Emotional, Intimacy, Guidance, Sanctioning

SUPPORT

■ Male   ▨ Female

*Age and Social Class Matched.

I. MAIN FINDINGS

II. SAMPLES

Sample 1

Widows/widowers were recruited by using lists of the recently bereaved that were provided by two self-help organizations, THEOS (They Help Each Other Spiritually), a national self-help group (SHG) for widows and widowers, and NAIM (after the name of a village where Jesus performed a miracle for the sake of a widow), an organization based in the Chicago metropolitan area. The widowers and widows were assessed at three different points in time: at the time of their spouse's death (Time 1), one year later (Time 2), and 6.5 years after the initial assessment (Time 3).

The THEOS sample was recruited from mailing lists provided by seventy-one chapters across the country. THEOS members come from a variety of sources: widows and widowers who seek them out, those brought by group members, and others who are identified as bereaved persons from obituaries and professional referrals that are targeted by the groups for recruitment. One thousand four hundred seventy-eight Time 1 questionnaires were mailed to THEOS members and to nonmembers (those who had declined the invitation to participate in the self-help groups). Of this number, 721 completed and returned the first questionnaire. A year later, the Time 2 questionnaire was sent to the 721 widows and widowers who had responded. This time 502 individuals completed it.

NAIM is sponsored by the Catholic Archdiocese of Chicago. The research team I worked with on this project attended NAIM's informational conferences and described the research to attendees. Afterward, a questionnaire was mailed to each of those conference attendees. A total of 145 people (49 percent) responded to the Time 1 questionnaire, and 96 of these returned the Time 2 questionnaire.

A total, based on THEOS and NAIM combined, of 866 widows and widowers completed and returned the initial questionnaires; 596 responded to the follow-up a year later; and 190 to the final questionnaire. Those who returned the Time 2 questionnaire were compared to the Time 1 respondents who did not return the Time 2 questionnaire on the basis of demographic and status variables as well as several psychological indices. Included in this analysis was employment status, socioeconomic status, length of membership (if SHG members), educational level, economic distress, marital status, living arrangements—alone or not, religious affiliation, number of years married, age, and length of bereavement. No significant differences were found (based on chi square analysis) in any of these demographic and status characteristics. These Time 2 widows were also compared (using two-tailed t tests) on several mental health indices: depression, anxiety, somatic symptoms, and substance abuse. *No significant differences were found between those who returned the questionnaire and those who did not.*

Of the 596 respondents who returned their questionnaire at Time 2, 517 were women; 16 percent were under age forty; 24 percent were in their forties; 40 percent were in their fifties; and 20 percent were sixty or over. Four hundred and thirty-seven were or became members of a SHG; 159 did not. Their educational background was as follows: 8 percent had not completed high school; 53 percent were high school graduates; 16 percent had some college; 17 percent were college graduates; and 6 percent had gone beyond college to either graduate school or professional schools. Ninety-three percent had children, of whom slightly more than half (54 percent) were still living at home. Approximately three-quarters of the men and half of the women were working prior to the spouse's death. After the spouse's death, employment status increased for the women by 14 percent, so that 63 percent of them were working within the first year of widowhood.

The demographic characteristics of the widows sampled, by age, were found to be as follows:

Employment. Before the death of their spouse, 42 percent of the youngest widows (those twenty-eight to thirty-nine) were working full or part time. Among the forty to forty-nine-year-olds, 55 percent worked; among the fifty to sixty-year-olds, 60 percent; and of those over sixty, 48 percent. For some age groups there was a substantial increase in employment following the death of the spouse. The breakdown of those who were working after the death is as follows: 54 percent of the youngest group of widows, 72 percent of those between forty and forty-nine, 74 percent of those between fifty and sixty, and 42 percent of those over sixty (a small drop from prebereavement).

Contact with the Family. Thirty-nine percent of the youngest group of widows had more contact with the family after death; 15 percent had less. Nineteen percent of the forty to forty-nine-year-olds had more, and 26 percent, less. For the fifty to sixty-year-olds, 19 percent had more contact, and 26 percent had less. For those over sixty, 25 percent had more, and 25 percent had less.

Dating. Dating, as might be anticipated, is highly age linked. Only 26 percent of the youngest widows report never dating; but 54 percent of those age forty to forty-nine do not date; 74 percent of those age fifty to sixty, and 73 percent of those over sixty.

Standard of Living (on a five-point scale ranging from much higher to much lower). When asked to compare their current standard of living with the standard of living prior to their spouse's death, 27 percent of the youngest widows reported lower and 23 percent higher; for those forty to forty-nine, 37 percent reported lower and 50 percent higher; for those fifty to sixty, 38 percent reported lower and 10 percent higher; and for those over sixty, 35 percent lower and 12 percent higher.

Remarriage. There is a substantial relationship between age and the widows' predictions about remarrying. Seventy-six percent of the youngest widows believe they will remarry; 50 percent of those between the ages of forty to forty-nine; 35 percent between fifty and sixty; and 10 percent of all widows over sixty.

Family Composition. All but one of the youngest widows have a pre-adolescent or adolescent child living in the household. In marked contrast, only four of the widows over age sixty have an adolescent child living in the household.

Self-Help Membership. When SHG members (N = 437) were compared to those who chose not to affiliate themselves with self-help groups (N = 159), it was found that both groups were similar with respect to gender distributions, mean age, sex, education, work status, religious affiliation, living arrangements, current standards of living, and self-reported levels of grief.

Representative of the Widows Studied. How did my sample correspond to widows and widowers in the United States? When compared to the spousally bereaved population shown by the 1980 census, the sample I interviewed was younger, of a higher socioeconomic class, and more likely to be female. The sample is also skewed by the greater participation in some type of psychotherapy for problems associated with bereavement. Twenty percent of the individuals I studied sought professional psychotherapeutic assistance as compared to an estimated 4 percent of the overall number of widows in a national probability sample taken by one research team (Veroff, Kulka, and Down, 1981).

The characteristics of the sample I used can be further documented by comparing it to the spousally bereaved drawn from a longitudinal study based on a probability sample (Pearlin and Lieberman, 1981). The two samples were compared on symptoms of depression, anxiety, and somatization; level of self-esteem; and ability to successfully cope. The sample of individuals who participated in my study were younger, better educated, more likely to be Protestant, more recently widowed/widowered, more likely to be female and less likely to be remarried than those of the spousal loss sample drawn from the Pearlin and Lieberman study. The spousally bereaved in my study sample were also significantly more distressed than the spousally bereaved drawn from the normative sample. They showed higher levels of anxiety, depression, and somatic symptoms. They also showed lower self-esteem and lower mastery scores.

How poorly was the sample of widows examined in this book functioning? To provide a context for looking at the scores used to index recovery, my study sample was compared with a demographically matched *nonspousally bereaved* sample from the Lieberman and Pearlin study. As anticipated, death of a spouse has profound effects on the social-psychological functioning of the survivor. On all measures (symptoms of depression, anxiety, and somatization; level of self-esteem; and coping mastery) the *nonbereaved normative sample* was functioning significantly better (using the t statistic $p < .05$) than the widows/widowers sample used in my study.

Sample 2

A consecutive sample (N = 78) of all surviving spouses of individuals who had died of cancer in the previous four to ten months at two medical centers were targeted for a random clinical trial of psychotherapy. Twenty of the seventy-eight individuals were randomly selected as controls and asked to complete two batteries of questionnaires, the first within the next week and the second a year later. All twenty agreed.

Of the remaining fifty-eight who agreed to participate in the study, forty-seven agreed to be seen in two to three in-depth interviews, at which time they were invited to participate in a bereavement therapy group. The interview was loosely structured and designed to investigate a broad range of areas pertaining to bereavement: past and current life situation, events surrounding the spouse's death, adjustment to widowhood, the history and quality of the marriage, personal autonomy, coping modes, emotional symptoms, social adaptation, dreams, death awareness, regrets, isolation, loneliness, and meaning in life. The interviews were audiotaped and later rated by trained judges.

Of the forty-seven individuals who were interviewed, thirty-six agreed to participate in the bereavement therapy groups and eleven declined. Of the eleven who declined, three had scheduling conflicts that made attendance impossible, and two had serious psychiatric problems. Two others were Hispanic, and declined the group because they spoke limited English. The remaining four who declined, all male, felt that "a group would be irrelevant," that they were too busy, or that they were "coping very well and did not need support."

Comparability of the group participators (E) and the controls (C)— who received no treatment—at Time 1 were tested on the four areas of measurement (fifteen indices) by a series of t tests. Mean score trends were observed only for two indices: somatic symptoms ($p < .10$) and guilt ($p < .10$). E's were more somatic and guilty. One-way Anovas were used to test the possible differences in effects of the four psychotherapy groups on outcomes; no significant differences were found.

III. MEASURES

Measures of "Recovery"

My colleagues and I chose three conceptually relevant areas to quantify adaptation levels of the study's participants: mental health, positive states, and role functioning. *Mental health* measures reflect indices typically used by researchers to assess the effects of spousal bereavement. Based on an individual's self-evaluation, Chart 1A describes the measures of depression, anxiety, and somatic symptoms experienced. These measures reflect the degree to which the respondent perceived health problems as interfering with his or her normal life tasks. It also shows the amount (and frequency) of alcohol and/or psychotropic medication that the respondent utilized to alleviate negative emotional states.

Positive states measured include self-esteem, coping mastery (a variant of locus of control), and positive and negative well-being and life satisfaction. The positive states listed in Chart 1B are not simply polar opposites of distress measured by the mental health scales. A person suffering from high levels of mental distress can still have positive status scores.

Role functioning (Chart 1C) provides us with a behavioral assessment of how well an individual is adapting to his or her new life following the death. Each study participant was asked to evaluate how well he or she is performing in certain major role areas, such as the economic area, the parental area, and in the newly acquired "single role." Strain in single role measures the performance and difficulty of being single again.

The three categories discussed above may each reflect areas of "recovery" at different points in time from the loss. Depression, anxiety, and the use of alcohol and psychotropic medication may be the earliest behaviors to disappear as grief diminishes. It may take an individual somewhat longer to return to prebereavement levels of the positive states, particularly well-being and self-esteem. Role measures may be the most resistant to "recovery" because the social context in which they are imbedded may be permanently skewed after the loss of the spouse.

CHART 1—RECOVERY MEASURES

1A. MENTAL HEALTH

Depression, Anxiety, and Somatization. Three Hopkins-Symptom Checklist scales drawn from a random sample of 2,300 adults. (Pearlin, Lieberman, Menaghan & Mullan, 1981) (Lieberman, M.A., and Videka-Sherman, 1986). Reliabilities alpha: Depression (.87), Anxiety (.82), Somatization (.74).

Frequency of Using Psychotropic Medication and Alcohol for Tension Reduction. Five-item scale assessing the frequency of using psychotropic medication and alcohol for tension reduction and mood improvement.

Health. Respondents were asked to judge their health by comparing it to that of people their own age and to rate how much their health problems interfered with their functioning.

1B. POSITIVE PSYCHOLOGICAL STATES

Psychological Well-Being. The Bradburn Affect Balance Scale (Bradburn, 1974), a widely used measure, provides two independent dimensions of affective state—positive and negative well-being. Reliability, alpha .91 and .92.

Coping Mastery. A seven-item scale based upon confirmatory factor analysis of a random sample of 2,300 adults (Pearlin et al., 1981). However, we found low reliability among the spousally bereaved (alpha = .53).

Self-Esteem. Rosenberg (1965) a well-established eleven item, Gutman scaled questionnaire.

Life Satisfaction. Four-point scale, ranges from very satisfied to not at all.

1C. ROLE FUNCTIONING.

Economic Distress. Perceived difficulty in living on present income and comparison of current living standard to status prior to the death of the spouse.

Single-Role Strain. A seven-item scale (ranging from never to very often) composed of the following: feeling out of place, having fun, fear of going out, having people to talk to, sharing experiences, fear of not being interesting and not having the kind of sex life one would prefer (alpha = .86).

Quality of Parenting. The scale is based upon confirmatory factor analyses of the Pearlin-Lieberman normative study (Mullen, 1981) (alpha = .84).

Parental Strain. Two general dimensions—worries and problems.

Measures of Grief

Grief was measured by indexing levels and intensity of grieving, evaluating an individual's self-assessment of his or her level of grieving (three-point scale), and recording the frequency of the intrusive thoughts about the lost spouse (four-point scale). Widows who reported that they experienced no grief and did not think about their dead spouse were classified as belonging to the low-grief group. Those who experienced some grief and occasionally thought about their dead spouse were classified as the mild-grief group. Those who experienced some grief and reported that they frequently thought about their dead spouse were placed in the moderate-grief group, and those who indicated a great deal of grief and were frequently preoccupied with the dead spouse were classified as showing intense grief. At baseline, *12 percent reported little or no grief; 30 percent reported mild grief; 43 percent moderate grief; and 15 percent intense grief.*

How well did this phenomenological measure mirror grief assessed by more typical reaction measures? Zero-order correlations showed that for mental health, grief intensity was correlated with depression (r = .52), anxiety (r = .34), somatic symptoms (r = .23), abuse of alcohol/drugs (r = .27) and health (r = .12). For positive states, grief intensity was negatively related to coping mastery (r = −.23), self-esteem (r = −.17), well-being (r = −.42), and life satisfaction (r = −.44). In the role area, grief intensity was correlated with single strain (r = .35), parental strain (r = .20), and economic strain (r = .08). Grief intensity was not associated with economic distress. Nor was there a significant relationship between grief intensity and age or social class.

Grief Patterns. Scores on grief intensity at baseline and one year later (Time 2) were used to develop four grief types. *Typical,* or normative, grief was defined as those widows/widowers who at baseline showed high levels of grief (moderate to intense) but at Time 2 demonstrated little or very mild grief (21 percent). These widows and widowers showed the prototypical "healthy" pattern of grief described in the loss literature. We also defined three atypical grief patterns: Widows/widowers who showed little or no grief both at Time 1 and Time 2 were labeled *limited grievers* (25 percent); *delayed grievers* reported little or no grief at baseline but one year later demonstrated moderate to intense grief (11 percent); and last, there was a group of widows/widowers who showed moderate to intense grief both at Time 1 and Time 2 and were designated as *prolonged grievers* (43 percent).

Validity of These Phenomenologically Defined Grief Patterns. How well did the phenomenologic measure of grief patterns mirror reaction measures typically used to index grief? Analyses of variances were used to compared baseline recovery scores. All were found to be statistically significant ($p < .05$). For all scales, widows/widowers who showed limited grief at Time 1 scored highest in measures of coping, mastery, self-esteem, and well-being, and had the lowest scores on various measures of distress. The typical and prolonged grief types had the most negative symptoms, the lowest coping mastery, and substantially lower well-being. Those classified as the delayed-grief group, widows/widowers who early on in bereavement did not show patterns of grieving but did a year or two after the death of their spouse, demonstrated a baseline score similar to that of the limited grief group.

Target Problem

At baseline, the subjects were asked to describe, in their own words, the main problem they were experiencing as a widowed person and to rate how much this problem impacted on their lives (on a scale of one to nine, with one representing "not at all" and nine representing "could not be worse"). The open-ended responses were coded into seven categories.

1. *Loneliness*—being alone when the last child leaves, worrying about growing old alone, finding companionship
2. *Mourning reactions*—missing one's spouse, depression, guilt, anger, grief
3. *Problems of being the head of the household*—making decisions; maintaining the home, garden, and the car; managing finances; keeping up the family business
4. *Parenting*—maintaining family togetherness, worrying about the kids
5. *Problems of being single*—feeling like a fifth wheel in social situations; coping with anxiety about being single, remarrying, and sexuality; finding opposite-sex companionship

6. *Interpersonal friction*—problems with relatives; with friends
7. *Existential concerns*—developing a sense of self, new goals, and an appropriate life-style; finding meaning in life

Relationship to the Spouse

Dependency. In this category widows rated themselves on how much they had relied on their deceased spouse (completely, quite a bit, somewhat, or not at all) for help in raising the children, companionship, day-to-day household decisions, transportation, managing money, arranging social get-togethers with friends and family, and discussing personal problems (alpha = .71).

Guilt. Subjects were asked to respond (1) "not at all," (2) "somewhat," or (3) "very much" to the following types of statements: You felt God was punishing you by taking your spouse. You felt guilty about the way you treated your spouse when he or she was alive. In some way you felt responsible for the death. You felt that your relationship was incomplete. You felt that God had abandoned you. You felt guilty because there was something you said or didn't say to your spouse (alpha = .70).

Anger. Since your spouse died have you felt upset with: the unfairness of it all, your spouse for dying, doctors and nurses who cared for your spouse, the funeral home, someone connected with the death, your spouse because of the financial situation the death brought about, God for allowing the death, God for abandoning you (alpha = .72).

In addition, raters were asked to evaluate the recordings of the clinical interviews for Sample 2 subjects. Upon listening to the recordings, they were asked to make three judgments about the marital relationship: (1) the degree, on a three-point scale, to which the bereaved spouse *idealized their spouse;* (2) whether the interview presented evidence that the respondent believed himself/herself *stunted by the marriage;* and (3) to make an overall judgment about the *quality of the marital relationship* based on a five-point scale ranging from most positive to most unsatisfactory. (At Time 1, 42 percent of the respondents had idealized their dead spouse; 30 percent felt stunted by their marriages; and 66 percent were rated as having had positive marriages. Idealization was correlated .27 with quality of

marriage and .34 with stunting. Quality of marriage and stunting correlated on a .44 level.)

Ratings of an individual's autonomy during the tenure of the marriage were based upon a variety of areas—work, independent friends, and
the like. Raters also made a judgment about a widow or widower's overall
level of psychological autonomy. Approximately half of the respondents
(48 percent) were rated as showing overall psychological autonomy.

Attitudes

Stigma. To quantify perceptions of society's negative reactions to the
widow and widower, we used a factor–analytically derived scale (Lieberman and Videka-Sherman, 1986) based upon twelve items, such as automatically assuming widows have low moral standards, treating bereaved
people differently from other people, thinking it is disrespectful to the
dead for widows to have fun (Reliability; alpha = .68).

Other attitudes toward and beliefs about society's reactions to widows were based on eight questions that were factor analyzed to a simple
two-dimensional structure.

Negative Stereotypes. These include statements such as "Most people
assume that widows are always mourning"; "People feel that it is disrespectful to the dead for widows to have fun"; "Married friends regard widows as a threat to their marriage"; "People assume widows have low moral
standards."

**The Belief That One's Widowhood Makes Others Uncomfortable
or Anxious.** This is covered by statements such as "People treat you
differently when they find out you are a widow"; "Married people feel
uncomfortable around widows"; "Relatives feel uncomfortable around
widows"; "There is a lack of public knowledge about the problems of
widows."

Attitudes and beliefs about mourning. A factor analysis of these beliefs yielded two dimensions: Social stances toward mourning: "Widows
need to take their minds off their problems"; "Widows should keep busy";

"Widows need to stop thinking about their spouses all the time"; "Widows should be as independent as possible." These items reflect a view of mourning as something that should be kept at bay. Social aspects of mourning: "Widows need to share their grief"; "Widows should be with other widowed people"; "Widows need to begin a new social life."

Views about Marital Life. In order to ascertain widows'/widowers' views on marriage, they were asked to respond to the following four statements: "I feel sorry for some of my married friends who have little freedom"; "Married people are happier than single people"; "Widows can have a full life without remarrying"; "I feel more independent now that I am widowed."

The intercorrelations among these four items is low and did not yield a single dimension.

Social Supports

This term was defined on the basis of who provides the support, how much is given, and the type of support provided. Types of social support provided were in the areas of *intimacy*—freedom to talk about important personal problems; *emotional support*—ability to depend on various people for support and comfort when the individual was feeling down; *guidance and information*—availability of others to talk about the issues with which subjects were being confronted as widows; *dependability*—ability to count on people for help in emergency situations; and *sanction,* support for one's life-style and behavior as a widow. In each area, the widows were asked to indicate how much each of the following people provided support: parents, in-laws, children, relatives, married friends, and single widowed friends. A five-point scale was used for each source: 0 = source not available, 1 = never, 2 = occasionally, 3 = frequently, 4 = very often. Thus, for each respondent we had a 6×6 matrix—six types of support and six sources of support.

Network Characteristics. These were defined as the following: (1) *density* of the network (the number of people defined as close friends who knew one another; (2) *heterogeneity-homogeneity* of the network (the proportion of widows subjects had among their close friends); (3) *network stability* (the ratio of old friends to new friends made since the death of the spouse); (4) *size* of network (the number of close friends); and (5) *changes in the amount of contact* a widow/widower had with family: more, about the same, less.

Concurrent Stress

This was defined as a measure of role strain and role stress reported by the widow in the major role areas: economic, parenting, and the newly acquired role of singleness (see Chart 1C).

Existential Exploration

There is little precedent in research or satisfactory standardized methods of testing for this kind of rating. The people participating in Sample 1 were asked about problems they were encountering as a consequence of their spouse's death at three points in time: directly after the death, one year after, and seven years after. (See Target Problem analysis.) In Sample 2, several intensive interviews were used for assessing "involvement in existential explorations" (Yalom and Lieberman, 1991).

Global ratings on a review of all the data were generated on each respondent from Time 1 and Time 2 research interviews as well as from observations of the group therapy meetings. These global ratings were made independently of the questionnaire data. All respondents were rated as to whether or not they were actively exploring existential issues in life: Were they honest, authentic, self-deceptive? Were they consciously dealing with such issues as finitude; the inevitability of death; life's brevity and, hence, preciousness; the fragility, capriciousness, and contingency of being; one's personal responsibility for one's life and one's choices; and one's isolation (not social isolation or loneliness but the unbridgeable isolation inherent in existence). They were also asked about the meaning of life: Does life, in general have meaning? Does my life in particular fit into this meaningful schema? These judgments were based on a clinical gestalt rather than on the presence or absence of any single item.

In addition, two independent raters who listened to the tapes of Time 1 and Time 2 interviews made independent ratings of whether each widow or widower was involved in an exploration of the following three issues: (1) Were the respondents more aware of the presence and inevitability of personal death? (2) Were they struggling with the question of the meaning of life? (3) Did they have regrets about choices made in life?

Awareness of Death. Judges evaluated awareness of death on a three-point scale. The rating of high awareness was given when a respondent thought often about death, was pervasively concerned about health matters, or was preoccupied with death in his or her dreams. These individuals often reported a powerful new awareness of life's transience, making statements such as: "I realize that everything that's present right now can suddenly stop being. I know this is very obvious but somehow it's something I never experienced before. Death can really happen"; "I see it happening to others, to my husband, to my friends"; "My husband's death has made it very clear to me that I was born to die, that death is inevitable"; "My time will be up eventually. This is obvious. Who doesn't know it? But somehow I'm aware of this in a way that I never really was before."

Purpose in Life. Respondents were asked if they thought that life had a meaning or purpose? If individuals were evaluated as currently struggling with the question, the raters were asked to make a further judgment as to whether this struggle was linked to bereavement. For example, one widower responded: "I know that the purpose of life isn't to be successful economically and, since my wife died, I've gotten out of the rat race. Yet this still seems like an invalid question to me somehow. It's not inherent in life; we just impose that question on the world. Still, I have lots of questions about what I should be doing in the future and whether I should be using my education; and I have guilt about dropping out of the rat race." This patient's concerns were rated as *not* linked to bereavement because they antedated the death of his wife by many years.

A widow whom raters did judge as currently struggling with life meaning in a manner that was linked to bereavement responded: "I feel no sense of purpose. The world and my life feel empty. Previously I'd gotten my purpose from being a wife and companion, and now I don't have anything in my life. I'm not making progress and I'm not sure what I want to accomplish. I'm just standing in neutral, marking time. A long time ago I used to have goals—to make my husband happy—and now I don't have any goals at all."

Regrets. Evaluators scored subjects' regrets about the choices they had made in their past lives on a scale of (1) "no regrets" to (5) "major regrets." The scales were anchored as follows: (1) No regrets—the person is totally and completely satisfied with every aspect of life and has no regrets for any choice or direction either taken or not taken. The individual has no regrets about the relationship with the spouse, nor regrets about anything he or she might have done differently in the relationship or in life. (5) Major regrets—the person is experiencing a great lack of fulfillment in life. The respondent expresses regrets for such things as not pursuing a career and not having gotten to know his or her spouse better before marriage in order to have made a more informed and different choice of a mate. Also included are regrets for having married the wrong man or woman, for having stayed married rather than having had the courage to leave the marriage, for not having expected and demanded more from oneself, and for living one's whole life for spouse or children—in other words, regrets for having given so much of one's self with so little expectation (or receipt) of return.

Comparison of Global Ratings and Ratings of Component Parts. Based on the global ratings, 37 percent of those interviewed were engaged in existential explorations. The ratings of independent judges indicated that "definite" heightened death awareness was present in 22 percent; "some" was present in 48 percent; and "no evidence" of personal death awareness in 30 percent. Thirty-four percent were rated as currently struggling with issues of life meaning; 64 percent showed signs of regrets.

The ratings were combined into a single score, ranging from a low of 3 (showing no existential awareness on any of the three component scales), to 6 (showing existential awareness on all three scales). The mean score for those rated as nonexistential was 4.47; for the existentially aware, 5.10, which yielded a t of 1.81, p = .08 (r = .34; p = .04).

Growth

In Sample 1, responses to open-ended questions such as "What have you learned since your spouse died?" were rated by two independent judges for evidence of growth. In Sample 2, these judgments were based on the Time 1 and Time 2 clinical interviews. Two independent raters listened to audiotapes of the Time 1 interviews and rated each subject on a four point scale: 1 = no growth; 2 = slight; 3 = some; 4 = much growth. The raters were also asked to listen to both Time 1 and Time 2 interviews and to rate whether the subjects had continued to grow, started to grow, stopped growing (evidence from Time 1 interview suggested growth that was not found in the Time 2 interview), or showed no growth.

The growth scale (1 through 4) was anchored by: (1) none—no signs of personal growth; i.e., the person is very much the same; to (4) much—definite signs of personal growth. The person is obviously stretching (doing new things, taking educational courses, struggling to find his or her own identity and roots); is more aware of being an "I" rather than a "we"; has developed new interests, visited new places, and is willing to explore new relationships. A respondent rated at 4 may be more self-sufficient, taking care of his or her own finances, cars, and house maintenance. The subject may also be taking better care of his or her physical health (for example, following an exercise regimen, walking more, or taking swimming lessons). He or she may be engaged in new or renewed forms of creative expression like painting or writing.

Self-Concept and Personality

The self-sort questionnaire and interview (Lieberman and Tobin, 1983) consist of forty-eight interpersonal statements (Leary, 1957). The items are: I enjoy being in charge of things. I am a good leader. I am somewhat of a dominating or bossy person. People think well of me. I believe that I am an important person. I frequently give advice to others. I am a self-respecting person. I am an independent and self-confident person. I am proud and self-satisfied. I am able to take care of myself. I am a competitive person. I can be a cold and unfeeling person. I am firm but fair in my relations with other people. I can reproach people when necessary. I am short-tempered and impatient with mistakes other people make. I am frank and honest with people. I am critical of other people. I frequently get angry with other people. When necessary, I can complain about things that bother me. I will argue back when I feel I am right about something. I am frequently disappointed by other people. I am touchy and easily hurt by others. It is hard for me to trust anyone. At times, I can be rebellious or feel bitter about something. I am able to criticize or find fault with myself. I am easily embarrassed. I am rather timid and shy. I can be obedient when necessary. Usually I give in without too much of a fuss. Frequently I feel weak or helpless. I am grateful for what other people do for me. I am often helped by other people. I hardly ever talk back. I am a trusting person. I prefer to let other people make decisions for me. I will believe anyone. I am a cooperative person. I want everyone to like me. I agree with what everyone says. I am a friendly person. I am an affectionate and understanding person. I love everyone. I am considerate of others. I am somewhat tender and soft-hearted. I am too lenient with other people. Generally, I can be counted on to help others. I often take care of other people.

Respondents were asked to evaluate statements in one of two ways, either "This is like me now," or "This is not like me now." For statements that currently described them, they were asked to indicate whether these descriptions reflected new self-images. If the interviewer asked them to designate a time period, they responded "new within the last year." Similarly, subjects were asked to look at items they had designated as currently "not like myself" and to indicate which of these characteristics *used to be* like them. Finally, the respondent was asked to provide examples from his or her current life that supported the current self-image. These open-ended responses were coded on an eleven-point scale assessing the quality of support (evidence) for self-image (Rosner, 1968).

Personality Traits. Personality traits were measured using the self-sort patterned after Leary's model of personality, which relies upon two basic dimensions: dominance-submission and affiliation-withdrawal. Scores on the dimensions are generated by a formula based on a weighted circumplex model.

Self-image, Stability, and Change. Scores were based on the ratio of characteristics chosen as (1) presently like myself or (2) items currently like myself that are new to me (within the past year), and on the ratio of characteristics that are currently unlike the self but used to be part of one's self-image. Adequacy of self-image was based upon an eleven-point scale rated by judges whose job was to assess the quality of evidence offered by the respondent in response to the examples a subject provided from his or her current life supporting each statement about self-image chosen. The eleven-point scale ranges from responses that provide current experiences supporting the self-image, to characteristics of the self-image based upon past experiences (the recent as well as the distant past), to responses indicating distortion or mythology created to support an inaccurate current self-image. Previous research (Lieberman and Tobin, 1983) found that adequacy of support for one's self-image—based on high scores of accurate and current experiences for supporting the current self-image—had a direct relationship to future adaptations to stress. The more adequate and realistic the self-image, the better the person could withstand high levels of stress and adapt successfully.

IV. ANALYSIS AND DETAILED FINDINGS

Grief Patterns

Analysis. To test the relationship between the four grief types (limited, typical, delayed, prolonged) and recovery, three multivariate analyses of covariance were computed (one for each area of recovery: mental health, positive states, and role functioning). Because the widows differed in the number of months since their loss at the Time 1 assessment, and the period of time since the loss can affect recovery, months since the death were entered into the analysis as a covariate.

The first analysis, controlling for months widowed, examined mental health measures (depression, anxiety, somatic symptoms, health, and amount and frequency of drug and alcohol abuse). Time 1 scores on these measures were used as covariants (mo. widowed, $F = .75$; NS interactions, $F = 1.12$; NS grief types $F = 1.75$, $p = .05$). The second analysis examined emotional states indexed by self-esteem, the Bradburn well-being index, coping mastery and life satisfaction (mo. widowed, $F = .34$; NS interactions, $F = 1.09$; NS grief types, $F = 1.84$, $p = .03$). The third analysis used measures of role performance indexed by levels of economic distress, the strains of parenthood, and the stresses of being single (mo. widowed, $F = 1.07$; NS interactions, $F = 1.04$; NS grief types, $F = .40$ NS).

In two of the three categories, mental health and positive emotional states, significant differences were found among people exhibiting the four grief patterns. None of the interactions of the control variable (months since the death) were significant, which suggests that length of widowhood at baseline did not skew the findings. An examination of the five mental health components indicates, in order of significance levels, that each of the four grief groups is very different in its respective level of depression, anxiety, and substance abuse. In all instances, the limited grievers are the least anxious and depressed, and utilize less psychotropic medication or alcohol to regulate mood change. In all cases, those classified as prolonged grievers show the highest level of anxiety, depression, and next to the highest level of substance abuse. The typical grief pattern shows the next best level of adaptation, whereas delayed grievers generally show poorer performance, particularly in their use of alcohol and psychotropic medication.

In terms of positive emotional states, the best recovery measured by the positive states indices is shown by the limited grievers; the lowest by the prolonged grievers. This comparison pattern repeats when evaluating negative effects, self-esteem, coping mastery, and life satisfaction. The patterns among the remaining groups (the typical and the delayed) are somewhat more complex. When evaluated for positive feelings, the delayed group is somewhat higher than the typical. Their positions are reversed on negative emotional states, and they are about equal in terms of self-esteem and life satisfaction. With regard to coping mastery, the delayed group shows better scores.

Long-term Follow-up. How did the various grief types fare in long-term recovery seven years after the loss? One hundred and ninety widows were available for the analysis of grief patterns and long-term recovery. Multivariate analysis of covariance with the dependent variables at both baseline and Time 2, as well as age and length of bereavement as covariates, were calculated. For mental health, the overall F was 1.37, p = .18. None of the univariate tests were statistically significant. For positive states, the overall F was .73, p = 69, and, again, none of the univariates approached statistical significance. Role measures, however, did reveal an overall F of 2.16, p = .05. The univariate test indicated that economic distress was significant.

It is not surprising that the linkage between different patterns of grieving and adaptation are manifested during the first several years of bereavement nor that the effects lessen considerably seven or more years after the loss of a spouse. The mean scores for each of the grief types, however, do suggest that the relative position of the groups was similar at all three measurement times. Multivariate analyses of covariance, based only on Time 3 scores, controlling for age and length of widowhood, supports the observations on the mean scores for the various grief patterns. These analyses reveal that, at Time 3, there was an overall (F = 3.75, p = .001 for mental health; F = 2.35, p = .02 for positive states; and for role, F = 2.33, p = .03.

Replication of the Grief Findings. The results from the previous analysis were tested on a new sampler, sample 2. Identical measures were used. The findings in this replication sample were similar to those reported in the larger sample: The best adapted were the limited grievers. At baseline both the typical and prolonged are similar; however, one year later the typical grievers demonstrated recovery, whereas the prolonged remained symptomatic.

Gender

Because of unequal sample sizes between the genders, comparisons were made using a sample of widows matched to the age, number of months widowed, SES (social-economic status), and household composition (number of children living at home) of the widowers. T tests and Manovas were used to examine the differences between widows and widowers at each point in time. In terms of mental health, widows showed significantly higher depression scores and health problems at both Time 1 and Time 2. No differences were found in any of the positive-state indicators. Widows displayed higher scores on economic distress at baseline, but there were no differences at Time 2. Widows also experienced higher parental distress at Time 2. Grief intensity was significantly higher among widows at all points in the measures.

When the widow/widower's relationship to the deceased spouse was examined, a substantial and significant difference in anger was revealed, with widows, on average, scoring higher. A separate analysis of Sample 2, however, with its more detailed measure of the marital relationship, found that there were few differences between the sexes. No significant differences were observed in idealization of the dead spouse, in the quality of the marital relationship, or in stunting. The only real difference between the genders was that women reported significantly higher amounts of loneliness during the marriage: 10 percent for men versus 48 percent for women.

The largest difference among widows and widowers was found in the characteristics of their social support systems and social networks. In all areas of social measurement—such as being able to count on others when you need help or emotional support when you are down—widowers were significantly and substantially lower.

Significant differences were also found in how men and women approached the existential issues. Sixty-eight percent of the widows entertained regrets about their past life, compared to 25 percent of the widowers. Forty-one percent of the women versus 10 percent of the men engaged in a purposeful life exploration. Another major distinction between men and women was their involvement in heterosexual relations: 80 percent of the men as compared to 20 percent of the women soon after the death of their spouse.

Social Supports

Amount of Support. About three-fourths of the widows we studied had at least one adult child (age twenty-one or older), and one-half had a living parent or parents. To calculate the amount of support provided by adult children and parents, the sample results were divided into four kinds of "availability" groups. The widows in Group 1 (4.2 percent) reported having no parents or adult children. Group 2 widows (18.3 percent) had an available parent or parents, but no adult children. Group 3 (42.5 percent) had at least one adult child but no available parents. Among this group of widows, 58 percent had no other children at home, while 42 percent had at least one or more children living in the household. Group 4 widows (35 percent) had both adult children and living parents. Forty-five percent of this group had no children living within the household, and 55 percent had at least one child at home.

The amount of support provided by adult children substantially exceeded the amount of support provided by parents. The amount of support provided by parents was examined under two different conditions. When the widow had no adult children, parents provided significantly greater amounts of all six types of support. This finding holds up in an analysis, taking the age of the widow into consideration.

Parental Availability and Recovery. Widows without living parent(s) were, on average, ten years older than widows with living parent(s). To determine the adaptational effects of availability, we utilized a multivariate analysis of covariance (age and months widowed), since age and length of bereavement can affect scores on the outcome variables. The results were classified into three groups: (1) those widows who had no living parents, (2) those whose parents were available but from whom the total amount of support received was low (below the population's mean), and (3) those who reported considerable support from parents (above the mean). The total amount of support received was the sum of all six types of support provided by the parents.

The support available to the women in each of these three groups had a direct and significant affect upon their recovery. The mean recovery scores (adjusted for the two covariates) indicate that the poorest adaptation was found among the widows who had living parents but did not receive much support from them. The highest level of adaptation was shown by the widows who had living parents who provided considerable support. Widows who did not have living parents were actually doing quite well, much better than those who had living parents who did not provide support.

Impact of Parent-Child Support on the Course of Bereavement. When both a parent(s) and adult children are available, what kind of support do they provide and what effects does it have upon a widow's recovery? Widows who had at least one living parent and one or more adult children were selected for this analysis. Four regression equations were computed, one for each of the four dimensions of recovery (grief intensity, mental health indices, positive emotional states, and role functioning). An unrotated first principal component was used to represent mental health, mourning, positive feelings, and role strain. The age of the widows and the months they had been widowed were entered first in the regression equation; at the second step, the six types of support provided by children and parents were entered as a group.

The age of the widow was found to be associated with mental distress, positive feelings, and single strain, whereas the months she had been widowed contributed appreciably to variations in mourning. Support from children and parents, when both were available, contributed to successful adaptation. An examination of the various types of social support provided suggests that parents most often offer emotional support. This type of support appears to have the most impact on the success of a widow's adaptation, both at baseline and one year later. Frequent contact seems to be the most beneficial type of support that adult children can provide. For three of the four outcome measures—mental health, positive feelings, and single strain—the amount of support provided by children is a substantial predictor of adaptation, whereas parents play the most important role in the fourth area—mourning and grief. There is a relationship between the two types of support and mental health, positive feelings, and single strain. Only in the area of mourning do parents (but not children) appear to be critical to a widow's adjustment.

Attitudes of Others

Regression equations were used to calculate the relationship between the attitude dimensions (stigma, negative image of widows, belief that widows are uncomfortable to be around, mourning attitudes) and the four major outcome measures: mental health, positive states, mourning, and role strain/stress. To control for the effects of age and length of widowhood, these two variables were entered at the first step, and the attitude and belief parameters at step two.

There is a significant relationship between the beliefs and attitudes held by the widow and the course of her bereavement at baseline and one year later. Widows who believe society holds a negative image of widows showed significantly poorer scores in mental health measures and had lower positive feelings, more intense mourning reactions, and more problems reported in the single role. The same can be said for the widows who believe others feel discomfort or anxiety around widows.

Marriage and Remarriage

Characteristics of the Marital Relationship. At Time 1, 42 percent of the respondents had idealized their dead spouse; 30 percent felt they had been stunted by their marriages; and 66 percent were rated as having had positive marriages. Idealization was correlated .27 with quality of marriage and −.34 with stunting; quality of marriage and stunting correlated at a −.44 level. Approximately half of the respondents (48 percent) were rated as showing overall psychological autonomy. The least stunted were the limited grievers; the most stunted, the prolonged. The typical (those who experienced intense grief initially but by the end of one year showed considerably less intense grief) were at midpoint.

Of equal interest is the absence of statistically significant findings on the quality of the marriage. It would be an oversimplification to conclude that the quality of the marriage in general terms is linked to patterns of grieving. It appears that what is significant to widows are particular aspects of the marriage—the sense of anger and guilt they have and their belief that their marriage prevented them from being fully "my own person."

Predictions of Remarriage.   Widows were asked, at baseline, about their remarriage expectations. An analysis (Anova with a covariate of age) found that there was a significant association between a widow's predictions about remarriage and her subsequent remarriage. As might be anticipated, there was also a strong relationship between age and prediction of remarriage and actual remarriage.

An analysis was also computed to determine other predictors of remarriage: the widow's level of anger toward her previous spouse, her economic distress, the intensity of her baseline grief, her feelings of guilt toward her previous spouse, amount of dependency on the deceased spouse, cause of her spouse's death (sudden, not sudden, suicide), the degree of stigma she felt in the widowhood role, and her attitude toward marriage. A significant discriminant analysis (X^2 of 124.7, df 7, P = .000) that distinguished between widows who thought they would remarry and those who did not (73 percent correct prediction) was found. The main variables in the discriminant analysis were youth, more anger, less grief, how recently widowed, and their attitudes toward marriage—factors all linked with beliefs that they would subsequently remarry. A similar discriminant analysis examining their social support network and sources of support found a χ^2 of 7.3, df 3, p = .06. Widows who received less help from their parents and more support from their married friends were more certain that they would remarry.

A third linear discriminant analysis examining economic distress, single strain, parental distress, anxiety, coping mastery, depression, negative well-being, use of drugs or alcohol to alter mood, positive well-being and self-esteem revealed a significant discriminant analysis χ^2 of 63.5, p = .000. The higher the strain of being single and the greater economic distress, the more likely predictions of remarriage were made.

Widows and Attitudes Toward Marriage. At Time 1, widows were asked a series of questions regarding their views toward marriage and their married friends:

- Forty-one percent agreed with the statement "I feel sorry for some of my married friends who have little freedom to do as they please."
- Seventy-three percent agreed that "married people are happier than unmarried people."
- Seventy-two percent believed that "widows can have a full life without remarrying."
- Seventy-four percent felt that "widows are more independent."
- Forty-one percent said, "I feel sorry for my married friends."
- Seventy-three percent agreed that "full happiness comes from being married."
- Seventy-three percent said "you can have a full life without marrying."

Attitudes Toward Marriage and Recovery. Regression equations between the attitude questions about remarriage and the four major outcome measures (mental health, positive states, mourning, and role strain/stress) were calculated. To control for the effects of age and length of widowhood, these two variables were entered at the first step, and the attitude and belief parameters at step two. Three of the four attitude scales assessing widows' views of marriage found that those who viewed married people as happier have poorer outcomes. On the other hand, those who believed they could have a full life without marriage and who see themselves as more independent than they did before they became widowed, do better.

Impact of Remarriage. This analysis compared a group of widows who actually remarried to an unmarried group of widows who were matched for age, length of widowhood at Time 1, and social class. T tests were used examining Time 1, Time 2, and Time 3 scores on coping mastery, depression, economic distress, anxiety, grief intensity, guilt, dependency, anger, well-being, parental strain, use of alcohol or pills for mood alteration, self-esteem, life satisfaction, single strain, and somatic symptoms. No significant differences were found in this analysis. After remarriage, only two significant differences were noted: Those who remarried had less depression than those of the matched paired controls and used less alcohol and pills to alter moods. A similar analysis using long-term data (seven years) again indicated only one variable: Anger toward the previous spouse was significantly different among those who remarried and those who didn't. Those who remarried were less angry. These analyses did not suggest any major effect upon the functioning of the widow, whether she remarried or not.

Age and Adaptation

A number of analyses were carried out to examine the effects of age on the course of widowhood.

Reaction to the Loss Soon After the Death. To determine whether there were differences in the immediate reactions to the loss based on age, a multivariate analysis of variance designed with two factors, age and length of bereavement, was tested. When no significant interaction effects (age × bereavement length) were found, multivariate analyses of covariance in a one-factor design with length of bereavement as a covariate were used to assess the effects of age on the four adaptation domains. To examine effects over time, multivariate analyses of covariance with baseline measures as the covariates were used. The overall significance level for the effects of age on mental health is .11; none of the univariate tests reached an acceptable level of statistical significance. Positive states are significant at an overall level of $p = .000$ ($F = 2.79$). Univariate tests indicate that both positive and negative feelings, coping mastery, and life satisfaction are significant contributors to this overall F. An examination of the means adjusted for number of months widowed indicates that there is a linear relationship between age and positive feelings, with the youngest widows having the highest positive feelings. There is also a linear relationship between negative feelings: The youngest widows have the most negative feelings; the oldest, the least. Coping mastery and life satisfaction are highest among the very old.

Mourning reactions (grief) show a significant effect for age (F = 7.2, p = .000) Grief is linearly related to age: The youngest show the lowest grief; the oldest, the highest. Role strain (parental strain and stress, single strain, and economic stress) is significantly affected by age (F = 10.6, p = .000). Three of the four role measures contribute to this overall significance; only single strain did not show a statistically significant univariate test. There is a linear relationship between age and both parental stress and strain. The youngest have the highest stress and strain; the oldest, the least. The oldest widows scored lowest on economic strain. Only small adjusted mean differences were observed for the other three age groups.

The relationship between age and the type of problems widows experience soon after the death were tested. A chi square between the four age groups and the seven problem areas yielded a χ^2 of 48.3, p = .001. The youngest widows reported the least amount of loneliness and the greatest amount of interpersonal friction. The youngest and those under fifty reported the highest number of parenting problems. In contrast, the two oldest groups of widows and particularly the elderly reported more problems with mourning reactions, head of household problems, and issues of the single role. Existential concerns were higher among mid-life widows. Both the youngest and the very oldest widows were less likely to be involved in exploring existential issues.

Age Difference One Year Later (Time 2).   There were no overall effects of age on mental health (F = 1.26, p = .22) or on positive states (F = 1.07, p = .38). Grief intensity was significantly different at Time 2 (F = .18, p = .006). The adjusted grief intensity score for Time 2 was higher for the elderly widows and lowest for the younger widows. Role strain was significantly differentiated by age (F = 3.8, p = .000), with univariate significance for parental strain, single strain, and economic distress. Similar to the findings of Time 1, the youngest had the most parental strain, and the oldest, the least. Single strain was lowest for the elderly group, as was economic distress.

Recovery Over Time (Time 3).   To test for recovery difference and age in the long-term follow-up, analyses were computed for Time 3 scores.

For the mental health measures F = 1.56, p = .09, the adjusted mean scores (adjusted for Time 1 and Time 2 mental health scores) showed that the oldest group of widows was doing the worst, and the youngest, the best. No statistically significant differences were found for positive states (F = 1.2) nor for the role measures (F = 1.27). Intensity of grief, significant both at Time 1 and at Time 2, remained significant at the long-term follow-up, with an F = 2.01, p = .10. Again the elderly widows showed higher grief than did their younger counterparts.

Family Life Stage and Reactions to Widowhood. The designation of family stage closely corresponds to, but is not identical with, either the widow's or the children's age. For the youngest widows (those under forty), 92 percent were nonlaunchers, 6 percent transitions, and 2 percent empty nest. Of widows between the ages of forty to fifty, 44 percent were nonlaunchers; 42 percent were in transition; and 14 percent were empty nest. For widows between fifty and sixty, 11 percent were nonlaunchers; 34 percent were in transition; and 55 percent were empty nest. For widows over sixty, 1 percent were nonlaunchers; 20 percent were in transition; and 79 percent were empty nest. For families where the age of the youngest or only child was under eighteen, 57 percent were nonlaunchers, 39 percent transitional families, and 5 percent empty nest. In contrast, families where the age of the youngest or only child was over eighteen were 7 percent nonlaunchers, 21 percent transition, and 72 percent empty nest.

Analyses identical to those conducted for age groupings were computed. The findings indicate that the presence of young children in the household does not support the hypotheses that family composition burdens a woman's adjustment to widowhood in the categories of mental health, positive states, or mourning. Widows with young children, however, do experience significantly more problems in the parental role.

Social Supports and Age

The systematic age-linked variations of availability of adult children and parent(s) pose a problem for the analysis of age, social support, and adaptation. In addition the availability of other widows in a widow's social network varied. Fifty-six percent of the youngest widows had no other widows in their network, compared to 35 percent for the forty- to forty-nine-year-old group, 24 percent for the fifty- to sixty-year-old group, and 16 percent for those over sixty. Given these distributions of social supports from parents and children, the analysis of social supports and life stage was computed using only the relatives, in-laws, single friends, married friends, and amount and type of social support.

At baseline all of the multivariate analyses for both source and type of support showed highly significant differences across age groups. For each type of support there was a direct linear relationship between the age of the widow and the amount of support provided by in-laws, relatives, single widowed friends, and married widow friends. The youngest widows reported the most, and the oldest, the least. Status at Time 2 was similar: In the covariance design (Time 1 social support scores entered as covariants) age remained a significant effect. The univariate shows statistical significance for all four categories of people, with the youngest widows receiving the most support.

The examination of the types of support provided (contact, dependability, emotional, intimacy, guidance, and sanctioning) yielded similar results. For all six types of support at Time 1, the youngest widows received the most, and the oldest, the least. At Time 2, in which Time 1 types of supports were entered in as covariates, age still remained a significant factor.

Age, Social Support, and Recovery. Evidence that variations in both source and type of support played a role in recovery is shown in the following analyses. For heuristic purposes, in order to calculate the regression equations between social supports, age, and recovery, the various measures used to index each recovery dimension were entered into a principle component factor analysis and the first principle component was used as an index of recovery. Regression equations, one series computed for the young widows and another series for the oldest widows, revealed that for both age groups, significant linkages between adaptation and both source and type of support were found.

MENTAL HEALTH For the young widows, the multiple R was .44, with $F = 2.42$, $P = .04$ for sources of support; .41 multiple R, $F = 2.07$, $P = .06$ for type of support. The comparable figures for the oldest widows were multiple R = .32, F = 2.2, P = .05 for source and the multiple R of .37 for type, with an F = 3.04, p = .008.

POSITIVE FEELING. For the younger widow, the multiple R was .45 for source, with F = 2.51, P = .03; for type of support, the multiple R = .44, F = 2.46, p = .03. For the elderly widows, source R = .30, with F = 1.86, P = .09, and for type of support, R was .31, F = 2.11, p = .05.

GRIEF. The multiple R was .35, with an F = 1.36, NS for the younger widows; type of support yielded a multiple R of .48, F = 2.99, p = .01. For the elderly widows the multiple R for source was .30, F = 1.86, p = .09, and for type of support, multiple R was .33, F = 2.51, and p = .02.

ROLE STRAIN. Single-role strain for younger widows on source of support, show a multiple R of .41, F = 1.93, p = .09; for type of support, the multiple R was .53, F = 3.88, P = .001. Among the elderly, the multiple R was .39 for source of support, with F = 3.56, p = .002, for type of support the multiple R was .38, with F = 3.32, p = .004.

Age and Widow's Relationship to Her Spouse. We asked whether there was a relationship between the age at which a woman was widowed and her views of the marital relationship? To arrive at this relationship, we calculated a two-factor multivariate analysis of variance using age and length of widowhood. Though the interaction between age and length of bereavement was not significant, age is highly significant with an overall F of 2.75, p = .003. An inspection of the means reveals that there is a systematic relationship between age and anger toward the spouse. Young widows have the highest amount of anger and those over sixty the lowest. A similar pattern was found for levels of guilt.

Risk Factors

Five hypotheses were explored to test the relationship between grief patterns and: (1) psychological characteristics of the widow's relationship to the dead spouse, (2) concurrent stress, (3) social context, (4) social network structure, and (5) sources and types of support. These hypotheses were explored using a multivariate analysis of variance for each of the domains representing the hypotheses.

To aid in the analyses of the differences among the four grief patterns, four planned-contrast analyses were computed using the multivariate analysis of variance.

Hypothesis 1. Overall, the three measures used to index the relationship to the deceased spouse are significantly associated with patterns of grieving ($F = 3.92$, $p = .001$). The widows showing the limited grief pattern had the lowest dependency, guilt, and anger. In sharp contrast, the prolonged grievers demonstrated the highest dependency, guilt, and anger toward their deceased spouse. The other grief patterns showed less consistent characteristics. The delayed grief group was most similar to the limited grievers, except for their reported higher dependency during the marriage, whereas the typical group (those widows who had intense grief at Time 1 but who had recovered significantly one year later) was similar to the prolonged and delayed grievers at baseline. Although the typical grievers demonstrated relatively high anger and guilt, in contrast to the prolonged grievers, they were lower in dependency during the marriage.

Hypothesis 2. There was a substantial relationship between concurrent stress and grief patterns ($F = 2.81$, $p = .001$). The prolonged experienced considerably more single strain and parental distress than did the other three grief patterns, limited, typical, and delayed.

Hypothesis 3. Social context indexed by the widow's age, social class, work status, education, and living arrangements as well as children in the home did not show overall significant differences among the five grief patterns ($F = .94$, NS).

Hypothesis 4. Social Network characteristics were overall significant ($F = 1.64$, $p = .05$). The univariate analyses suggest that the major contribution to the difference was the number of new friends made since the loss. The limited and delayed grievers show the highest number of new friends, the prolonged, the lowest. None of the other network characteristics show univariate significance. The contrast analyses in this area revealed that the typical made significantly more new friends than did the prolonged grievers and had social networks characterized by more heterogeneity. Comparisons between the limited and delayed found that the delayed had a social network of close friends larger than that of the limited and, in fact, to all other grief patterns.

Hypothesis 5. Differences were found in type and amount of social support ($F = 1.80$, $p = .01$). Those classified as limited, typical, and delayed grievers reported more intimacy, sanctioning, guidance, and emotional support than did the prolonged grievers. The contrast analyses did not reveal significant differences among the limited, typical, or delayed grievers.

Sources of support were similarly significantly different among the grief types: Generally, the prolonged and delayed received more overall support from the children than did the limited or typical. In contrast, the limited grievers were highest in receipt of support from single widowed friends, and the prolonged group, the lowest in this area. Contrast analyses revealed that there were significant differences between the limited grievers and delayed grievers in sources of social support as well as significant differences between the typical grievers and the prolonged. This analysis suggests that it is not only the amount and type of social support received but the source of the support that appears to make a difference in the pattern of grieving.

Did each of the areas explored independently contribute to poor recovery. Data reduction of the dependent variables was achieved by computing principal components for each of the areas previously used to test the risk hypotheses. These seven summary indices were entered in a regression with grief types as the dependent variable. (Anovas using the seven summary measures yielded the expected statistical significance distinguishing among the grief patterns.) A simple regression equation revealed that two of the seven composite scores contributed to the recovery; ($F = 6.01$, $p = .000$; Multiple $R = .26$. The relationship to the spouse (Beta $= .18$, $F = 4.1$, $p = .000$) and one principal component of social supports, children (Beta $= .18$, $F = 4.1$, $p = .000$).

Ambivalence toward the deceased spouse, a finding that echoes classical loss theory, increases risk of poor recovery. The reliance for support on children and relatives with less attention to friends appears also to *increase* risk: All the other support dimensions operate in the opposite direction— the more support the less the risk.

Psychotherapy

A series of analyses was conducted to test the impact of psychotherapy on recovery. In Sample 1 we found that during the course of study over 20 percent (129/549) of the widows sought psychotherapy. Most, 14 percent, entered within a year of the loss.

Perceptions of Psychotherapy. The widows were asked to indicate their reasons for seeking psychotherapy and to rate the helpfulness of "therapeutic experiences." Seventy-one percent said they entered therapy because they needed to be able to speak with someone about what was troubling them; 47 percent hoped to find a better perspective on the experience of widowhood; 27 percent hoped to receive approval of the way they were leading their life; 25 percent wanted to be understood; 20 percent wished to gain hope; 18 percent hoped to receive helpful advice; 17 percent wanted to be comforted; and 11 percent needed help in making decisions. The length of treatment was as follows: 5 percent had one session; 42 percent attended two to five; 26 percent had between six and twenty sessions; and 28 percent attended more than twenty sessions. The majority of the widows saw psychotherapy as helpful: "very helpful"—54 percent, "moderate"—40 percent, "not helpful"—5 percent, "made worse"—2 percent).

Characteristics of Widows Entering Psychotherapy. Comparisons were made between widows who relied solely on family and friends for help, those who sought out the help of professionals such as physicians and clergy, and those who entered psychotherapy. At Time 1, each widow was asked to indicate the single most important person from whom they had sought help for their most pressing problem. Sixty-five percent used family and friends only; 21 percent sought help from physicians and clergy; and 14 percent sought help from a psychotherapist for their most pressing problem.

We compared the three types of help-seeking groups on Time 1 measures of anxiety, depression, somatization, and substance abuse; self-esteem; coping mastery; well-being; role strains (economic, parental, and single); dependency, anger, and guilt; the characteristics of their social network; the amount and type of support received as well as changes in the frequency and quality of contact with family members; and, lastly, the nature of their relationship to the deceased spouse. All of these conditions were examined using a multivariate contrast analysis of variance. A significant difference was found between the type of helping setting used (psychotherapist, other professionals, or only family/friends): $F = 3.85$, $p = .000$. The results of this inquiry indicated that widows who sought psychotherapy were beset by higher parental strain, had turned to many more people for help, were more dependent upon their husband and manifested more anger and feelings of guilt toward their husband and the circumstances of his loss.

There were significant differences among the help resources utilized and the type of problem ($\chi = 32.6$, DF = 12, $p = .001$). The strains of assuming the role of head of the household was not the most common problem among the widows who sought professional help. Widows who did seek out psychotherapy usually saw parenting as their central problem and reported more interpersonal conflicts and existential concerns in general. Those who sought out other professionals for support and counsel most often reported problems in adjusting to the single role.

Psychotherapy Effects. The effects of psychotherapy on recovery relied on a multivariate analysis of covariance two-factor design (psychotherapy versus support groups), co-varying the Time 1 scores and age as well as number of months widowed. No significant effects of psychotherapy were found (Lieberman and Videka-Sherman, 1986).

The Unique Contribution of Psychotherapy. Although we could find no overall effects of psychotherapy, the next analysis asked if there were widows who did seek out therapy for whom it worked and for whom there were measurable effects? The purpose of this part of the study was to identify spousally bereaved who were at risk and to determine if their seeking out and utilizing psychotherapy was associated with recovery when compared to high-risk widows who utilized other help-providing settings. To accomplish this, we contrasted widows who were high in guilt and anger with those who were rated relatively low in these qualities. A composite score was generated by adding guilt and anger scores, and for the purposes of analysis, the sample was divided into thirds.

To examine this question, four multivariate analyses of covariance (mental health, positive states, grief intensity, and role measures) in two-factor design (anger/guilt and psychotherapy) with Time 1 outcome measures, months widowed, and age as covariates were calculated. The mental health dimension was significant ($F = 2.03$, $p = .03$), and the two variables that contributed most to the overall significance were depression and somatic symptoms. For positive state, the overall F was 1.33, $p = .24$. One measure—well-being—showed a univariate significant P. In regard to role measures, the F was 1.71 with an overall p of .11. Statistically significant effects were found for grief intensity, $F = 4.95$, $p = .008$.

When we examined the mean scores, we found that the major "improvement" in positive outcomes occurred in the mental health measures and in the grief dimension. The mean scores were adjusted for length of widowhood and age. The Time 1 measures suggest that widows who experienced higher levels of anger and guilt associated with the death of their spouse and who sought psychotherapy for these reasons were more likely to have fewer depressive and somatic symptoms. Their grief was also somewhat reduced over the course of one year.

A subsample was selected to compare widows who participated in psychotherapy and widows who only attended self-help groups (psychotherapy, n = 71; only SHGs, n = 290). Despite the overall positive impact of the self-help group, when compared to matched controls of nonparticipants and psychotherapy participants, widows who experienced high levels of guilt and anger were more likely to show improvement in one-on-one psychotherapy than in self-help groups.

The next study to measure the effects of therapy took advantage of a randomized clinical trial. We used Sample 2 to test the effects of brief group psychotherapy. The question we asked was: "How effective was this intervention and did widow and widowers 'at risk' show more improvement from this type of treatment?" (Lieberman and Yalom, 1992).

Therapy Intervention. Each experimental subject participated in one of four psychotherapy groups. Each of the groups was led by the same experienced male/female co-therapy team. The task of the leaders consisted primarily of norm setting, process review, introductions of topics for discussion, and occasional here-and-now interventions. The major themes discussed tended to be similar from group to group. A common topic was the theme of change—the transition from being a "we" to becoming an "I." There was much discussion of the fear and the difficulty of learning to live as a single person. Many shared their deep loneliness and their sense of no longer being special to another person. But there were also group members who experienced a sense of liberation, of exhilaration with their new freedom. Many feared that if they were to change, to grow, to develop a new relationship, and to enjoy their life, they would betray their relationship with the dead spouse. Members discussed the tyranny of the "shoulds," the social expectations confronting them.

There was considerable discussion of existential issues, of the new awareness of the fragility, brevity, and preciousness of life. Some members shared an increased appreciation of the randomness and contingency of the world. Most were more aware of personal finitude and the value of living one's life in the immediate present rather than postponing life into the future. Many members, especially widows, were much troubled by a sense of meaninglessness in life. The content and processes of the groups are described in detail in Yalom and Vinogradov (1988).

Methods for Classifying At-risk Subjects. Risk has been defined in previous bereavement studies on the basis of impoverished social resources (e.g., SES), limited psychological resources (e.g. coping strategies), or presence of psychiatric illness. The latter criterion was used in the present study. Since our sampling frame was a normative one and not recruited on the basis of psychopathology, we utilized the Mellinger-Balter (1983) method for classification developed on a random probability sample of 3,000 households. Their methods were replicated by Lieberman, Bliwise, and Pearlin on a different random sample of 2,300 adults aged eighteen to sixty-five. Using the Mellinger-Balter algorithm, we found that 44 percent of our experimental subjects and 47 percent of the controls were classified "at risk," that is, showing "some" or "high" signs of psychiatric disorder.

Comparability of the therapy participants (E) and the randomized no-treatment controls (c) at Time 1. We evaluated the four areas of recovery measures (fifteen indices) by a series of t tests. Mean score trends were only observed for two indices: somatic symptoms $p < .10$ and guilt $p < .10$. E's were more somatic and guilt-ridden.

Since the widows and widowers were assigned to one of four treatment groups (the therapists were the same in all four) before examining the effects of psychotherapy, we needed to determine if there were differences in characteristics of the spousally bereaved among the groups. One-way Anovas were used to test the possible differences in effects of the four psychotherapy groups on recovery. No significant differences were found. Thus the remainder of the analysis examined the experimental group as one treatment.

A two-factor (treatment and psychopathology) multivariate analysis of covariance was used to test the major hypothesis: that brief group psychotherapy during the early stages of bereavement would facilitate good social and psychological adjustment to the stresses and strains associated with spousal bereavement (a test of the main effects). The two-factor design permitted us to determine whether brief therapy would be of maximal benefit to the "high-risk" subjects. Four outcome areas were examined. Two reflected traditional psychotherapy outcomes (mental health and mourning), and two were associated with psychological and social areas known to be affected by spousal bereavement (positive psychological states and role functioning).

Comparisons based on the two-factor (treatment and pathology) multivariate analysis of covariance revealed that two areas of evaluation—positive psychological states and role functioning—approached overall (multivariate) statistical significance ($F = 2.62$ for role; $F = 1.41$ for positive psychological states). Univariate tests for these two outcome areas indicated that the self-esteem of group participants increased significantly more than that of the controls ($F = 4.24$, $p < .05$). In addition, there was a decrease in single strain ($F = 5.37$, $p < .05$). In comparison, no differences were detected in the overall tests for mental health ($F = 0.62$) or for mourning ($F = 0.16$). No statistically significant treatment-pathology interaction was observed, indicating that improvement was no greater for the individuals designated as "at risk" who attended therapy than for the "at-risk" controls who did not.

At the end of a year, both the experimental and control samples showed less depression, less anxiety, fewer somatic symptoms; less abuse of alcohol and psychotropic medications; greater well-being; higher self-esteem; a heightened sense of mastery or internal locus of control; less grief; and fewer feelings of being stigmatized for being a widow or widower. We also found overall improvement in health, single strain, guilt, and anger. This overall improvement makes it more difficult statistically to determine the unique contribution of therapeutic intervention. Particularly powerful effects associated with therapeutic intervention would be necessary to achieve statistical as well as clinically significant results.

Support Groups

What was the impact of support-group participation on a widow's or widower's recovery? (Lieberman and Videka-Sherman, 1986.) The spousally bereaved from Sample 1 were used for these analyses. Unlike the test of therapy effects, where a randomized control group was available, the analysis of support-group effects was based on statistical controls. Not having recourse to random assignment, we chose an analytic strategy that could provide some estimation of certain biases inherent in the sample studied. Individually, each strategy represents a flawed substitute for random assignment, but collectively the variety of control conditions makes it possible to evaluate self-help–group effectiveness. To the degree that each strategy provides results in the same direction, the more conclusive is the evidence that support groups do affect widows' psychosocial functioning. For some of the analytic strategies, we drew upon a random sample of widows and nonwidows, matched in age and socioeconomic class with the support-group sample. (See previous discussion of Pearlin and Lieberman study, 1986).

Analysis 1 compared changes in the support-group sample over time to changes in a nontreatment control group. Here the question we explored was whether the passage of time in the ordinary course of widowhood may, in and of itself, alleviate some of the distress and flawed psychosocial functions. Analysis 2 compared changes in support-group participants to changes in those who had access to the self-help group but chose not to participate. Analysis 3 compared those who participated in support groups, as well as those who did not participate, to a subsample of participants and nonparticipants who also sought help from a psychotherapist for problems associated with being widowed. Such a comparison provided some approximation to alternate treatment designs.

Analysis 4 focused on the effects of participation in support groups alone. We compared the hierarchical definitions of support-group membership groups, based upon group involvement and extragroup friendship patterns. Measures of involvement were based on a combined score based on widows' roles in and commitments to the support group. We also compared the type and intensity of their relationships outside the group to those of other participants. Measures of commitment included an index of cohesiveness, intention of remaining in the group, leadership roles occupied, and the level of proselytizing. Social linkage was assessed by the amount of support given to and received from other participants between group meetings, frequency of contact, and number of close friendships formed.

Four groups were defined and classified: (1) Nonmembers (N = 100)—Defined as individuals who had attended two or fewer support-group meetings or those who had not attended any. Both subgroups considered themselves to be nonmembers. (2) Meeting attendees only (N = 133)—This group attended meetings regularly but reported that none of their close friends were members of a support group, nor did they give or receive support from other support-group members outside the monthly meeting. This group usually attended monthly meetings on a regular basis but had not developed linkages with other members that went beyond the meeting boundaries. (3) Members with some social linkages in the group (N = 117)—This group both attended meetings and satisfied one or two of the following social linkage indicators: at least one of their best friends was also a support-group member; they gave support to other members outside the monthly meeting; they received support from other group members outside the group meeting. (4) Members with high social linkages within the group (N = 126)—This group attended meetings regularly and satisfied all three of the social linkage indicators.

Nonmembers (group 1) were compared to all participants (groups 2, 3, and 4). Those who attended meetings only (group 2) were compared to those who reported at least some social exchange in the group (groups 3 and 4). And finally, those with some social exchange (group 3) were compared to those who had high social exchange (group 4). This is an approximation of a specification of treatment design in which the active ingredient that comprises the actual treatment is examined rather than assuming that all participants in the treatment were exposed to identical in-fluences.

Residual scores (with effects of age, sex, education, current marital status, and number of years widowed removed) were computed for de-pression, anxiety, somatic symptoms, mastery, and self-esteem at Time 1 and at Time 2. In addition, residual scores for Time 1 well-being and Time 2 psychotropic medication were computed. Differences in change of the residual mental health scores between the support-group membership groups and the nonnative sample were tested. In this multivariate analy-sis of covariance procedure, the residual Time 2 mental health scores were used as outcome criteria; the residual Time 1 mental health scores were used as covariates controlling for initial mental health differences; and each of the four support-group involvement groups (nonmembers, those who attend meetings only, members with some exchange, and members with high exchange) was compared to the normative widows for differen-tial change. Multivariate statistical tests were conducted since the depen-dent variables were related conceptually as well as empirically (correlations averaged around .40). This analysis controlled for demo-graphic differences in the samples and allowed us to test the question: "Was change in mental health for each of the support-group involvement groups similar to changes experienced by a typical sample of widows?"

The statistically significant multivariate test (Multivariate F = 15.18, p = .00) indicates that the progress of the five groups was different. First of all, we made some simple contrasts by comparing each of the sup-port-group involvement groups to the normative sample. Effects of age, sex, education, current marital status, and the number of years one had been widowed were statistically removed from Time 1 and Time 2 mental health indexes. Analysis of covariance was then conducted with residual mental heath indexes as covariates, using residual Time 2 mental health as criteria variables. Entries were adjusted Time 2 means. Three simple con-trasts between each support group and the normative sample were tested. Each of the four support-group sample groups was statistically different from the normative sample on multivariate tests of these samples.

On all indices except depression, the normative sample showed dete-rioration over time, while the mental health status of all four groups in the support-group sample report improved over this one-year period. The trend was reversed for depression. The normative sample evidenced less depression over time when compared to the support-group sample.

Comparison of Mental Health Intervention and Support-Group Participation. Analyses 2 and 3 used a two-way multivariate analysis of covariance. The two factors in the design were support-group participation and professional mental health intervention. Time 1 mental health indices were used as covariates in the design. Time 2 mental health indices were used as outcome measures. The two-factor design tested whether those who sought professional mental health assistance underwent changes different from those who did not seek professional help. It also examined whether changes in support-group participants were different from those of nonparticipants and whether there were synergistic effects produced by participation in self-help groups and by obtaining professional help.

The nonsignificant interaction effect indicates that there are no differential mental health changes based on combined use of self-help and professional psychotherapy. This study also yields no evidence that there are synergistic or antagonistic effects between the two helping modalities.

Comparisons were made between those in our sample who had entered psychotherapy for problems associated with the loss of a spouse and those who had not. Psychotherapy did not result in a main effect. There was, however, a multivariate main effect for support-group participation (p = .03). Since the four involvement groups are hierarchically related, that is, each category builds by adding criteria for involvement with the support group, orthogonal Helemert contrasts were used to test for specific effects of levels of support-group participation. These contrasts tested the following relationships: Nonmembers were compared to all three member groups combined to test whether any level of support-group participation led to different outcomes. Those who attended meetings only were compared to both levels of members with high social exchange (support-group participants who established relationships on the outside with group members and who called on one another for support). This comparison tested whether social linkages made in the support group were an active therapeutic mechanism over and above the simple attendance at meetings. Finally, the members with some social exchange were compared with the high-exchange members, testing whether greater numbers of social linkages were associated with more positive mental health outcomes.

Members who had made social linkages in the group showed higher positive change on six of the eight mental health measures than that of members who only attended the meetings without interacting socially with other group members. Specifically, those who made social linkages in support group became less depressed and anxious, used less psychotropic medication, felt increased well-being and self-esteem, and reported greater overall improvement than did to widowed people who only attended group meetings but did not befriend other members.

Nonmembers differed from support-group members on two of the eight univariate comparisons. Nonmembers remained slightly more depressed and used more psychotropic medication than support-group participants combined. Members with some social linkages and members with many such linkages showed no statistically significant differences in mental health change. Those for whom the group became important experienced it as a setting in which they were willing to undertake structured roles of leadership and in which they experienced a sense of camaraderie.

The results indicate that involved participants derived the most positive mental health benefits from the group. Those who attended meetings for the same length of time but did not form such linkages to others in the group did not show positive changes.

Existential Exploration

Existential Exploration and Outcomes. The first analysis was of the effects of existential exploration on recovery. We used Sample 2 for this exploration. Only two of the thirteen recovery measures reached statistical significance, an occurrence that does not differ from random chance for multiple tests, particularly for those with relatively high intercorrelations. Next we tested the relationship between existential exploration and growth. Thirty-seven percent of the sample showed clear-cut evidence of growth. There was a substantial relationship between heightened existential awareness and growth: $\chi^2 = 9.80$, p = 0.02.

Profiles of the Existentially Involved. What was the association between heightened existential awareness and the widows' reactions to the loss? To explore this question a series of Time 1 characteristics were examined: (1) symptoms of grief, (2) intensity of mourning, (3) ease or difficulty of assuming the single role, (4) degree to which widows perceive themselves as stigmatized, and (5) intensity and characteristics of loneliness. We also explored several personality characteristics that are assumed to be stable and to have existed previous to the particular crisis of bereavement: (6) personality traits, (7) personal effectiveness, and (8) the content and structure of the self-image. We also asked whether it was possible for certain characteristics of the person's prior history to have had a bearing on his or her willingness or ability to engage in the existential task. Hence we investigated: (9) the nature of the prior marital relationship and (10) the perceived autonomy of the person in that relationship. In addition we examined the current circumstances facing the bereaved person by looking at his/her (11) loneliness, (12) social supports, and (13) the importance of religious belief systems in dealing with major life crises.

Heightened existential awareness occurred significantly more often in women than in men (χ^2 = 7.88, p = .05). Those who engaged in the existential task were, at Time 1, more likely to show more pronounced symptoms of grieving (anxiety and depression) while at the same time possessing higher personal effectance scores (self-esteem and well-being). Ambivalence toward the dead spouse was lower (anger, guilt). Both the existentially and nonexistentially aware subjects revised their self-image to about the same extent; however, the existentially aware respondents did this by grafting on new elements of the self rather than by rejecting the old ones.

The existentially aware widows and widowers were much more likely to: (1) perceive their overall relationship with their spouse as being more positive but also personally stunting; (2) report more loneliness in that relationship, in contrast to the nonexistentially aware, who were more likely to idealize their spouses; and (3) report more loneliness (both before and after their bereavement) than their nonexistentially aware counterparts, even though the social activity and family relationships of both groups were similar. Although existentially aware subjects had the same degree of pairing as nonexistentially aware subjects, they did not use the pairing to evade the work of bereavement.

To further understand the effects of existential explorations and growth, Sample 1 was used. Growth in Sample 1 was based on a simple coding of open-ended responses to the question "What have you learned since your husband died?" Analysis explored the determinants of growth in this sample. Large sample size (compared to that of Sample 2) permitted the use of multivariate statistics and logistic regressions. The first logistic regression used all the variables that assessed recovery and, in addition, included the widow's age and the three measures of guilt, anger, and dependence. A single-factor logistic regression revealed an overall χ^2 improvement of 30.6, with 16 and 157 df, p = .01. An inspection of the univariate p's revealed only two significant factors: widows who did not grow were four times as likely to have been dependent upon their husbands and five times as likely to have been depressed at baseline.

A second discriminate analysis examining social and contextual variables revealed no significant differences between those who grew and those who did not. Individual χ^2 examining work status, patterns of relationships to family and friends since widowhood, and the structural characteristics of the widows' social network all proved not to be significant.

The large sample size permitted a subanalysis of the type of growth, and related inner changes were focused on self characteristics. Of the 59 percent of the widows who grew, growth was primarily characterized by interpersonal changes in 36 percent.

Self-Revisions and Widowhood

Correlations were calculated between self-concept revisions using three scores: the amount of new, old, and total self-change. These variables were correlated with the outcome measures. Those individuals who had revised their self-image, based on both old and new patterns, had statistically significantly less grief at both Time 1 and Time 2 (average correlation r = 0.30). They also had lower scores on symptoms of grief, but the directions were different for those whose self-concept revisions were based on new self-constructs. These individuals showed significantly fewer symptoms (r = 0.32) when compared to those whose change was based upon the revision of self by rejecting old elements of the personality.

The changing of the self as a positive characteristic among the spousally bereaved was further evidenced by finding a relationship between changes in the self-image and involvement by the widows/widowers in existential explorations. This finding provides further evidence that, for the spousally bereaved, revisions of the self-image play a positive role in adaptation to one's new state in life.

Appendix V
Finding a Support Group

Most areas of the country do have accessible support/self-help groups serving widows and widowers. The best place to locate a group is to call a local self-help clearinghouse. The following is a current list of such organizations.

Self-Help Clearinghouses and Information Helplines in the United States

Arizona	East Valley area (602) 231-0868
Arkansas	northeast area (501) 932-5555 (info on groups only)
California	San Diego (619) 275-0607; San Francisco (415) 921-4044; Sacramento (916) 368-3100; Davis (916) 756-8181
Connecticut	(203) 789-7645
Illinois	(312) 368-9070; Champaign County (217) 352-0099
Iowa	(800) 952-4777; in Iowa (515) 576-5870
Kansas	(800) 445-0116; in Kansas (316) 689-3843
Massachusetts	(413) 545-2313
Michigan	(800) 777-5556; in Michigan (517) 484-7373

Missouri	Kansas City (816) 472-HELP; St. Louis (314) 773-1399
Nebraska	(402) 476-9668
New Hampshire	(800) 852-3388 (info on groups only)
New Jersey	(800) FOR-MASH; in New Jersey (201) 625-9565
New York	New York City (212) 586-5770; Westchester (914) 949-0788, ext. 237
North Carolina	Mecklenberg area (704) 331-9500; admin., call (704) 377-2055
Ohio	Dayton area (513) 225-3004; Toledo area (419) 475-4449
Oregon	Portland area (503) 222-5555 (info on groups only)
Pennsylvania	Pittsburgh area (412) 261-5363; Scranton area (717) 961-1234
South Carolina	Midlands area (803) 791-9227
Tennessee	Knoxville area (615) 584-6736; Memphis area (901) 323-0633
Texas	(512) 454-3706
Utah	Salt Lake City (801) 978-3333 (info on groups only)
Greater Washington, DC	(703) 941-LINK

Self-Help Clearinghouses in Canada

Calgary	(403) 262-1117
Nova Scotia	(902) 466-2011
Toronto	(416) 487-4355
Prince Edward Island	(902) 628-1648
Vancouver	(604) 876-6086
Winnipeg	(204) 589-5500 or 633-5955

Other Countries with National Self-Help Clearinghouses

Argentina	1-582-8680
Germany	30-891-4019
Israel	03-2999389
Poland	22-314551

Other helpful addresses

AARP
Widows Programs and Information
601 E Street
Washington, DC 20049
202-434-2260

If you are comfortable with computers, the Internet contains much useful information for widows and widowers. In addition, there are support and discussion groups on-line. It is hard to know how effective these are, but some widows who use the Internet do report that they found it helpful.

Widows and widowers discuss issues ranging from early grief feelings to daily living and family topics. These are not organized support groups. They are discussion groups where people of all ages and stages of grief, from all over the United States and Canada, exchange ideas, experiences, jokes, and just friendship.

The purpose of this list is to allow discussions between widowed persons in order to provide mutual support, friendship, and information. To subscribe, send e-mail to majordomo@fortnet.org. Include only the following in the text of your message: SUBSCRIBE WIDOW. That's all there is to it. Once you have subscribed and received a confirmation of success, all e-mail to the list should be addressed to widow@fortnet.org

Then, if you choose to subscribe, please send a note saying hello so that others may welcome you. They ask that only those who have lost a spouse subscribe to this mailing list. Because subscribers range from those newly widowed to those with many years of coping experience, discussions here will cover a variety of subjects:

aspects and manifestations of grief
coping with the paperwork

dealing with family members and friends
snappy answers to stupid remarks
books on grief
information on support groups in various locations
national support organizations
creating a life after death
personal exchanges among newfound friends

Rivendell Resources, a nonprofit foundation based in Ann Arbor, Michigan, sponsors a collection of resources of value to those who are experiencing loss and grief: http://argus-inc.com, and griefnet@rivendell.org

GriefNet is a system that can connect you with a variety of resources related to death, dying, bereavement, and major emotional and physical losses. It offers retrievable information in this gopher/web server and has interactive communication facilities—discussion groups—all for bereaved persons and those working with the bereaved, both professional and laypersons. GriefNet is a product of Rivendell Resources.

Notes

Chapter 1

P. 11 HUNDREDS OF YEARS OLD. . .: ⟩

Burton, Robert. *The Anatomy of Melancholy,* edited by A. R. Skilleto. London: G. Bell, 1896.

Rush, Benjamin. *Medical Inquiries and Observations.* 3rd ed. Philadelphia: Hopkins & Earl, 1809.

P. 11 WIDOWHOOD AND MENTAL ILLNESS. . .:

Bowlby, J. *Attachment and Loss. Vol. 3, Loss: Sadness and Depression.* London: Hogarth Press, 1980.

Freud, S. *Mourning and Melancholia.* In *The Standard Edition of the Complete Original Works of Sigmund Freud,* edited and translated by J. Strachey, vol. 14, pp. 152–70. London: Hogarth Press, 1957. (Original work published 1917.)

Osterweis, M.; Solomon, F.; and Green, M., eds. *Bereavement: Reactions, Consequences, Care.* Washington, DC: National Academy Press, 1984.

Parkes, C. M.; Weiss, R. S. *Recovery from Bereavement.* New York: Basic Books, 1983.

Pollock, G. "Mourning and Adaptation." *International Journal of Psychoanalysis* 42:341–61.

P. 12 SEEK PSYCHIATRIC HELP. . . :

Veroff, J.; Kulka, R. A.; and Dowan, E. *The Inner American: A Self-Portrait from 1957–1976.* New York: Basic Books, 1981.

P. 12 RECENT NATIONWIDE STUDY. . . : Author's analysis of the ECA data, using DSMIII diagnosis based on DIS instrument. For a description of the ECA study, see Robins, L. N., and Regier, D. A. *Psychiatric Disorders in America.* New York: The Free Press, 1991.

P. 21 WOMEN SCIENTISTS. . . :

Lopata, Helena Z. "Becoming and Being a Widow: Reconstruction of the Self and Support Systems." *Journal of Geriatric Psychiatry* 19, no. 2, (1986): 203–14.

Lopata, Helena Z. "The Support Systems of American Urban Widows." In *Handbook of Bereavement: Theory, Research, and Intervention,* edited by Margaret S. Stroebe, Wolfgang Stroebe, Robert O. Hansson. New York: Cambridge University Press, 1993, pp. 381–96.

Lopata, Helena Z. "Widows: Social Integration and Activity." In *Activity and Aging: Staying Involved in Later Life.* Sage Focus editions, Vol. 161.; John Robert Kelly, Newbury Park, CA: Sage Publications, Inc., 1993, pp. 99–105.

Wortman, Camille B., and Silver, Roxane C. "The Myths of Coping with Loss." *Journal of Consulting & Clinical Psychology* 57, no. 3 (June 1989): 349–57.

Wortman, Camille B., and Silver, Roxane C. "Successful Mastery of Bereavement and Widowhood: A Life-course Perspective." In *Successful Aging: Perspectives from the Behavioral Sciences,* edited by Paul B. Baltes and Margret M. Baltes. New York: Cambridge University Press, 1990, pp. 225–64.

Wortman, Camille B.; Silver, Roxane C; Kessler, Ronald C. "The meaning of loss and adjustment to bereavement." In *Handbook of Bereavement: Theory, Research, and Intervention,* edited by Margaret S. Stroebe, Wolfgang Stroebe, and Robert O. Hansson. New York: Cambridge University Press, 1993, pp. 349–66.

Chapter 2

P. 24 ALL WIDOWS MUST FOLLOW. . . :
> Bowlby, J. *Attachment and Loss.* Vol. 3, *Loss: Sadness and Depression.* London: Hogarth, 1980/81.
> Glick, I. O.; Weiss, R. S., and Parkes, C. M. *The First Year of Bereavement.* New York: Wiley, 1974.

P. 25 WOMEN WHO REPORT LITTLE OR NO GRIEF. . . : Delayed grief, a concept implying long periods of absent grief after which grief symptoms emerge, is a controversial idea with no professional consensus:
> Osterweis, M.; Solomon, F.; and Green, M., eds. *Bereavement: Reactions, Consequences, Care.* Washington, DC: National Academy Press, 1984.

Chapter 3

P. 41 CULTURAL ATTITUDES TOWARDS WIDOWHOOD. . . : For a review of research in this area, see
> Osterweis, M.; Solomon, F.; and Green, M., eds. *Bereavement: Reactions, Consequences, Care.* Washington, DC: National Academy Press, 1984, pp. 199–212.

Chapter 4

P. 59 WHAT MAKES THE DIFFERENCE. . . : Three general hypotheses have guided the search for risk factors:
Commencing with the seminal work of Freud [Freud, S. (1957) "Mourning and melancholia." In *The Standard Edition of the Complete Original Works of Sigmund Freud,* edited and translated by J. Strachey, vol. 14, pp. 152–70). London: Hogarth Press, 1957. (Original work published 1917.)] and echoed by the classical studies of Bowlby (Bowlby, J. *Attachment and Loss:* Vol. 3, *Loss: Sadness and Depression.* London: Hogarth Press, 1980) and Lindemann (Lindemann, C. "The Symptomatology and Management of Acute Grief." *American Journal of Psychiatry* 101(1944): 141–49), risk was viewed as linked to a process: the vicissitudes of mourning or the inability to mourn. The role of ambivalence in mourning and melancholia has led investigators to identify the nature and quality of the

lost relationship as playing a key role in the vicissitudes of grief and mourning. Particularly highlighted has been the role of ambivalence and dependency in the marriage (Raphael, B. "Preventative Intervention with the Recently Bereaved." *Archives of General Psychiatry* 34(1977): 1450–54; Raphael, B. *The anatomy of bereavement.* New York: Basic Books, 1983; Parkes, C. M., and Weiss, R. S. *Recovery from Bereavement.* New York: Basic Books, 1983).

Other investigators have focused on the widow's social envelope as a source of risk, exploring such factors as age or life-cycle status, social class, economic resources, family composition, and the like. Highlighted in the past twenty years has been the focus on the widow's social networks, the resources provided by family and friends, and other social supports. Madison, D. C., and Walker, W. L. "Factors Affecting the Outcome of Conjugal Bereavement." *British Journal of Psychiatry* 113, (1967): 1057–67; Madison, D. C.; Viola, A.; and Walker, W. L. "Further Studies in Bereavement." *Australian and New Zealand Journal of Psychiatry* 3 (1969): 63–66; Gallagher, Dolores E.; Breckenridge, James N.; Thompson, Larry W.; and Peterson, James A. "Effects of Bereavement on Indicators of Mental Health in Elderly Widows and Widowers." *Journal of Gerontology* 38, no. 5 (September 1983): 565–71; Heyman, Dorothy K. and Gianturco, Daniel T. "Long-term Adaptation by the Elderly to Bereavement." *Journal of Gerontology* 28 (July 1973): 359–62; Henderson, S.; Byrne D.; and Duncan-Jones, P. *Neurosis and the Social Environment.* New York: Academic Press, 1981, have pointed to the role of social supports and social network characteristics in adaptation.

Some investigators have examined the widow's social envelope through the lens of stress, e.g., the presence of life stresses in the current life circumstances. See the review by Wortman, C. B., and Silver, R. C. "Successful Mastery of Bereavement and Widowhood: A Life-course Perspective." In *Successful Aging: Perspectives from the Behavioral Sciences,* edited by P. B. Baltes and M. M. Baltes, New York: Cambridge University Press, 1990, pp. 225–64.

Still others look to preexistent psychopathology and/or enduring "personality" characteristics as a likely framework for explaining the vast variations in response to the loss of a spouse: Strobe, W., and Strobe, M. *Bereavement and Health.* New York: Cambridge University Press, 1987.

P. 59 RELATIONSHIP TO HER SPOUSE. . . : Parkes and Weiss (1983) found
that ambivalence toward their spouse was associated with higher anxiety
and depression. Parkes, (Parkes, C. M. "Risk Factors in Bereavement,"
Psychiatric Annals 20 (1990): 308–13) Sanders, (Sanders, C. M. "Risk Factors in Bereavement Outcomes." *Journal of Social Issues* 44 (1988): 97–112)
and Sable (Sable, P. "Attachment, Anxiety, and Loss of a Husband." *American Journal of Orthopsychiatry* 59 no. 4 (1989): 550–56), experienced considerably more difficulty in recovering.

Chapter 5

P. 79 IS YOUR DESTINY FIXED. . . : The empirical support for age differences
is mixed. Madison, D. C., and Walker, W. L. ("Factors Affecting the Outcome of Conjugal Bereavement." *British Journal of Psychiatry* 113 (1967):
1057–67.) report that there was no close relationship between health de-
terioration and age at bereavement. In contrast, Madison, D. C.; Viola, A.;
and Walker, W. L. "Further Studies in Bereavement." *Australian and New
Zealand Journal of Psychiatry* 3 (1969): 63–66.) found that widows and
widowers under forty were at greater risk for psychopathological reactions
than were older widows and widowers. Zisook et al. (1987) found that
younger widows show more severe and protracted reactions.

P. 82 MAIN DIFFICULTIES. . . : A comparison of the young to the older widows revealed that, for loneliness, 26 percent young and 32 percent old saw
this as a major problem; for mourning, 7 percent versus 13 percent; for
head of household, 20 percent versus 20 percent; for parenting, 32 percent
versus 2 percent; for becoming single, 9 percent versus 23 percent; for interpersonal problems, 3 percent versus 3 percent; and for existential, 3
percent versus 7 percent.

P. 90 GET MORE HELP AND SUPPORT. . . : Several kinds of comparisons were
calculated for source of support and for who provided the help as well as
who provided the help by type of help. Since the availability of parents or
adult children obviously is in part a function of the widow's age, I compared friends for the young and older women. For contact, young had 1.8
times more help from friends; depend on, 2.5 times; emotional, 2.3 times;
guidance, 2 times; intimacy, 6 times; and sanctioning, 2.6 times more

help than widows over sixty. Similar ratios in favor of the young widow obtained when I summed across all sources of help.

Chapter 6

P. 95 WHO PROVIDES THE HELP? . . . : Five characteristics of the widows' social networks were examined:

Network Size: Only 2 percent indicated they had no close friends; 12 percent described a small network (one or two friends); 31 percent indicated they counted on three or four people as close friends; and the remainder, 55 percent, indicated large networks, over five friends.

Changes in Social Supports: In response to the question about changes in frequency of contact with family or friends subsequent to the death of their husband, 24 percent indicated they were seeing their family less; 53 percent the same as before the death; and 23 percent stated that they were seeing the family more since the death of their husband. They perceived more changes in contact with their friends; 61 percent were seeing their friends less after the death of their spouse; 30 percent at the same level of contact; and only 9 percent indicated that they had more contact.

Network Stability: Fifteen percent of the widows studied had reconstituted, subsequent to the death of their husband, a new social network composed of all new close friends. Another 26 percent had reconstituted their social network so that most of their close friends were now new friends (defined in terms of over 50 percent of their close friends being new friends); 33 percent of the sample's social network was composed of friends, most of whom were old friends, but contained a mixture of old and new; 27 percent had stable social networks, all close friends were those who were friends prior to the death of the spouse.

Network Density: Sixty-four percent of the widows' network of close friends could be described as loose, while the remaining 36 percent were in social networks of close friends that were dense (all or most of their close friends knew one another).

Homogeneity: Twenty-nine percent had no widows in their close social network; 47 percent had a few; and 24 percent had close social networks composed of most, if not all, widows.

Social Isolation: Only 2 percent did not have a confidant, defined as someone who was a close friend, although if we define confidant function-ally—people one can talk with about personal problems—slightly over one quarter (26 percent) reported no one. When asked about people they can count on for emotional support, "no one" responses drop to 7 percent.

P. 96 MOTHER ESPECIALLY CAN OFFER UNIQUE HELP. . . :
See Bankoff, E. A. "Peer support for Widows." In *Stress, Social Support and Women,* edited by S. E. Hobfoll. Washington, DC: Hemisphere, 1986, pp. 207–22.

P. 106 THE BOOKSTORES ARE. . . : Recent examples of such books are:
> Ainley, Rosa, ed. *Death of a Mother: Daughters' Stories.* London: HarperCollins, 1994.
> Boston, Sarah, and Rachel Trezise. *Merely Mortal: Coping with Dying, Death and Bereavement.* London: Methuen, in association with Channel Four Television Company, 1987, 1988.
> Campbell, Scott, and Phyllis Silverman. *Widower.* 1st ed. New York: Prentice Hall Press, 1987.
> Carroll, David. *Living with Dying: A Loving Guide for Family and Close Friends.* 1st pbk. ed. New York: Paragon House, 1991.
> Chance, Sue. *Stronger Than Death.* 1st ed. New York: Norton, 1992.
> Corr, Charles A., Clyde M. Nabe, and Donna M. Corr. *Death and Dying, Life and Living.* Pacific Grove, Calif.: Brooks/Cole, 1994.
> DiGiulio, Robert C. *Beyond Widowhood: From Bereavement to Emergence and Hope.* New York: Free Press; London: Collier Macmillan, 1989.
> Donnelley, Nina Herrmann. *I Never Know What to Say.* New York: Ballantine Books, 1987.
> Fitzgerald, Helen. *The Mourning Handbook: A Complete Guide for the Bereaved.* New York: Simon & Schuster, 1994.
> Hoard, G. Richard. *Alone Among the Living.* Athens: University of Georgia Press, 1994.
> Kaplan, Louise J. *No Voice Is Ever Wholly Lost.* New York: Simon & Schuster, 1995.
> Kast, Verena. *A Time to Mourn: Growing Through the Grief Process.* Translated from the German by Diana Dachler and Fiona Cairns. 1st ed. Einsiedeln: Daimon Verlag, 1988.

Levine, Aaron. *To Comfort the Bereaved: A Guide for Mourners and Those Who Visit Them.* Northvale, N.J.: J. Aronson, 1994.

Miller, Jack. *Healing Our Losses: A Journal for Working Through Your Grief.* San Jose, Calif.: Resource Publications, 1993.

Neeld, Elizabeth Harper. *Seven Choices: Taking the Steps to New Life After Losing Someone You Love.* 1st ed. New York: C. N. Potter, 1990.

Osterweis, Marian, and Jessica Townsend. *Understanding Bereavement Reactions in Adults and Children: A Booklet for Lay People.* Rockville, Md.: U.S. Dept. of Health and Human Services, Public Health Service, Alcohol, Drug Abuse, and Mental Health Administration, National Institute of Mental Health, 1988.

Rando, Therese A. *Grieving: How to Go on Living When Someone You Love Dies.* Lexington, Mass.: Lexington Books, 1988.

Rudman, Masha Kabakow. *Books to Help Children Cope with Separation and Loss: An Annotated Bibliography.* 4th ed. New Providence, N.J.: R. R. Bowker, 1993.

Silverman, William B. *When Mourning Comes: A Book of Comfort for the Grieving.* Northvale, N.J.: J. Aronson, 1990.

Staudacher, Carol. *Men and Grief: A Guide for Men Surviving the Death of a Loved One.* Oakland, Calif.: New Harbinger Publications, 1991.

Truman, Jill. *Letter to My Husband: Notes About Mourning and Recovery.* London: Hodder and Stoughton, 1988.

P. 107 NEGOTIATING THE CHALLENGES OF WIDOWHOOD IS NOT A STATIC PROCESS. . . : During the initial experience of grieving and adjusting to loss, a dense homogeneous network of individuals who have known one another for a long period of time is the optimal structure for providing emotional support and reducing initial loneliness [Walker, K. N.; MacBride, A.; and Vachon, M. L. S. "Social Support Networks and the Crises of Bereavement." *Social Science and Medicine* 11 (1977): 35–41]. Later, as a widow begins to reorganize her life as a single person, new adjustments may be needed, particularly if a widow seeks to adopt a new life-style or seeks a changed identity as someone other than a wife. During this period of role change, new social contacts may be important to help resolve problems associated with role transitions. In this case, a network of less dense ties is more capable of providing the information and opportunities to facilitate role transitions. Granovetter (1973) argues that a network of "weak ties" is more likely than a dense, cohesive network to provide the information, mobility, and opportunity necessary to facilitate role transition. For example, weak, diffuse ties were found to be more helpful in facilitating job seeking than were homogeneous, dense networks (Granovetter, Mark, and Roland Soong. "Threshold Models of Diffusion and Collective Behavior." *Journal of Mathematical Sociology* 9, no. 3 [1983]: 165–79).

Chapter 7

P. 111 OF COURSE MENTAL HEALTH EXPERTS. . . : Most studies that rely on unselected samples show serious recruitment problems that make the interpretation of the results highly questionable (sample retention is considerably better in the studies that selected high-risk people than in studies based on unselected populations). Only one study, targeted to unselected spousally bereaved, the present one, had a retention rate of above 75 percent. Many had retention rates of 35 to 40 percent. The adequacy of the samples was further compromised by the sampling frames used: Some, like our own, specified a target population; others used self-selected samples recruited through newspaper advertisements. Consider, for example, the oft-quoted random assignment study by Barrett (Barrett, C. J. "Effectiveness of Widows' Groups in Facilitating Change." *Journal of Consulting and Clinical Psychology* 46 [1978]: 20–31). This study's low sample retention rate was further compromised because the widows recruited averaged *five years bereavement prior to intervention.* Implication of that study's findings for addressing the issues of prevention is limited.

P. 114 WHAT DO WE KNOW ABOUT THE EFFECTS OF PSYCHOTHERAPY? . . . : Mental health professionals have experimented with three different strategies for evaluating the effectiveness of psychological intervention for the spousally bereaved: (1) testing the effectiveness of treatment for the *bereaved who seek psychotherapy* (Horowitz, M. J.; Marmor, C.; Weiss, D. S.; DeWitt, K. N.; Rosenbaum, R. "Brief Psychotherapy of Bereavement Reactions." *Archives of General Psychiatry* 41 (1984): 438–48); (2) identifying a *high-risk subsample* from the general bereaved population (Raphael, B. "Preventative Intervention with the Recently Bereaved." *Archives of Gen-*

eral Psychiatry 34 (1977): 1450–54); (3) offering *all bereaved spouses* a preventive, therapeutic intervention.

There is some evidence supporting the effectiveness of both brief dynamic individual therapy and self-help bereavement groups for widows and widowers who seek help. There is evidence that brief individual crisis therapy used preventively for a preselected high-risk population (defined as those possessing limited social or psychological resources) was able to decrease physical-health symptoms and visits to physicians but leaves unanswered the question of psychological and social functioning. Lieberman and Videka-Sherman (1986) found that the Self-Help Groups were more effective than psychotherapy in a nonpatient population. A recent study (Liebermann and Yalom, 1991) that compared brief, expertly provided, "preventive" group psychotherapy based on a model developed specifically to address the problems of bereavement with a random control group failed to provide clear-cut evidence of therapeutic effectiveness beyond the "normal" recovery.

P. 114 THE WIDOWS VIEWED THEIR EXPERIENCES POSITIVELY. . . : Information was developed on widows' evaluation of psychotherapy and their perceptions of helpful processes: When asked to rate the frequency and helpfulness of "therapeutic experiences," 71 percent rated being able to say what was troubling me, 47 percent, perspective; 27 percent, approval of the way leading life; 25 percent, understood; 20 percent, hope; 18 percent, advice; 17 percent, comforted; and 11 percent, help in decisions. Length of treatment: 5 percent—1 session, 42 percent—2 to 5, 26 percent—6 to 20, 28 percent > 20 sessions. The majority of the widows saw psychotherapy as very helpful or helpful, and only a few reported being disappointed (very helpful, 54 percent; moderate, 40 percent; not, 5 percent; worse, 2 percent).

P. 114 KINDS OF CONTROL GROUPS. . . : Untreated controls are essential in the evaluation of bereavement outcome because almost all Ss improved with the passage of time. This requirement is perhaps best illustrated by one of the most methodologically sophisticated studies of a "high-risk" population (Marmer, C. R., H. J. Horowitz, D. S. Weiss, N. R. Wilner, and N. B. Kalreider. "A Controlled Trial Brief Psychotherapy and Mutual-Help Group Treatment of Conjugal Bereavement." *American Journal of Psychiatry* 145, no. 2 [1988]: 203–12). The author's definition of risk was based upon a careful and theoretically relevant model, and their intervention was based upon a sophisticated posttraumatic stress model. They found that those treated in individual psychotherapy for bereavement improved, but so did those treated in support groups. Without access to a nontreatment control, it is difficult to determine whether either treatment made a difference.

Chapter 8

P. 123 "DO SUPPORT GROUPS WORK?" . . . :
> Lieberman, M. A. "Bereavement Self-Help Groups: A Review of Conceptual and Methodological Issues." In *Bereavement: A Sourcebook of Research and Intervention,* edited by M. S. Strobe and R. O. Hanson. New York: Cambridge University Press, 1992.

P. 124 WHAT ARE SUPPORT GROUPS. . . : See the following for extensive discussions of support/self-help groups:
> Donovan, Joe. *The Self-help Directory: A Sourcebook for Self-help in the United States and Canada.* Joe Donovan. New York: Facts on File, 1994.
> Lieberman, M. A. "Healing Groups." In *Wiley Encyclopedia of Psychology,* edited by R. J. Corsini. New York: Wiley Press, 1984.
> Lieberman, M. A. "Understanding How Groups Work: A Study of Homogenous Peer Group Failure." *International Journal of Group Psychotherapy* 10 (January 1990): 31–52.
> Lieberman, M. A., and Borman, L. *Self-Help Groups for Coping with Crises: Origins, Members, Processes and Impact.* San Francisco: Jossey-Bass, 1979.
> Katz, A. H. *Self-Help in America: A Social Movement Perspective.* New York: Twayne, 1993.
> Katz, A. H., and Bender, E. I. *Helping One Another: Self-help Groups in a Changing World.* Oakland, Calif.: Third Party Publishing Co., 1990.
> Riessman, F. *Redefining Self-help: Policy and Practice.* San Francisco: Jossey-Bass, 1995.
> Surgeon General Workshop on Self-Help and Public Health. Los Angeles, Calif., U.S. Dept. of Health and Human Services, Pub-

lic Health Service, Health Resources and Services Administration, Bureau of Maternal and Child Health and Resources Development, 1987.

P. 124 8 MILLION PEOPLE. . . :

Lieberman, M. A., and Snowden, L. "Problems in Assessing Prevalence and Membership Characteristics of Self-Help Group Participants." *The Journal of Applied Behavioral Science* 29, no. 2 (June 1993), 164–78.

Lieberman, M. A., and Videka-Sherman, L. "The Impact of Self-help Groups on the Mental Health of Widows and Widowers. *Journal of Orthopsychiatry* 56, no. 3 (July 1986): 435–49.

P. 128 HERE IS WHY SUPPORT GROUPS WORK. . . :

Lieberman, M. A. "Comparative Analyses of Change Mechanisms in Groups." *International Journal of Group Psychotherapy* no. 35, 2 (1985): 155–74.

Chapter 9

P. 137 CAN TRAGEDY PRODUCE GROWTH? . . . : See Yalom, I. *Existential Therapy.* New York: Basic Books, 1980, for an overview of existential issues.

P. 138 "GROWTH SCALES. . . :

Yalom, I. D., and Lieberman, M. A. "Bereavement and Heightened Existential Involvement." *Psychiatry* no. 54 (Nov. 1991): 334–45.

P. 148 CONFRONTATION WITH DEATH. . . :

Becker, E. *Escape from Evil.* New York: Free Press, 1975.

P. 148 LIFE REVIEW. . . : See the following

Butler, R. N. "The Life Review: An Interpretation of Reminiscence in the Aged." *Psychiatry* 26 (1963): 63–76.

Fishman, Sarah. "Relationships Among an Older Adult's Life Review, Ego Integrity, and Death Anxiety." Special Issue: 1991 IPA Research Awards in Psychogeriatrics: Winning Papers and Selected Outstanding Submissions. *International Psychogeriatrics* 4 (1992): 267–77.

Haight, Barbara K., and Webster, Jeffrey Dean, eds. *The Art and Science of Reminiscing: Theory, Research, Methods, and Applications.* Philadelphia: Taylor & Francis, 1995.

Lieberman, M. A., and Tobin, S. Chapter 11 of "The Function of Reminiscence." *The Experience of Old Age: Stress, Coping, and Survival.* New York: Basic Books, 1983.

P. 149 THE SEARCH FOR PERSONAL MEANING. . . . :

Frankl, V. *What Is Meant by Meaning. Journal of Existentialism* 7 (1966): 21–28.

Russell, B. *A Free Man's Worship.* Portland, Me.: T. B. Moser, 1927.

Chapter 10

P. 156 MANY WOMEN EXPERIENCE THIS. . . . :

Pearlin, L. I., and Lieberman, M. A. *"Social Sources of Emotional Distress."* in *Research in Community and Mental Health* edited by R. Simmons. Greenwich, Conn.: JAI Press, 1979.

Pearlin, L.; Lieberman, M.; Mennaghan, B.; and Mullan, J. "The Stress Process." *Journal of Health and Social Behavior* 22 (1981): 337–56.

P. 158 OUR VIEW OF WHO WE ARE. . . . :

Lieberman, M. A. "Perspectives on Changes in the Self. The Impact of Life Events and LGAT." Chapter in *Self Change: Social Psychology of Self-Initiated Externally Impaired Changes,* edited by Fisher, J. D.; Chinseley, J. M.; Klar Y.; and Nadler, A. New York: Springer-Verlag, 1992.

Lieberman, M. A., and Tobin, S. 1983. *The Experience of Old Age: Stress, Coping and Survival.* New York: Basic Books (chapter 10, pp. 238–61).

Markus, H., and Wurf, E. "The Dynamic Self Concept: A Social Psychological Perspective." *Annual Review of Psychology* 38 (1987): 299–337.

Mead, G. H. *Mind, Self & Society.* Chicago: University of Chicago Press, 1934.

Rosenberg, M. *Conceiving the Self.* New York: Basic Books, 1979.

P. 158 NUMEROUS STUDIES. . . :

Block, J. *Lives Through Time.* Berkeley, Calif.: Bancroft Books, 1971.

Lieberman, M. A., and Tobin, S. 1983. *The Experience of Old Age: Stress, Coping and Survival.* New York: Basic Books, 1983.

Thurnher, M. "Turning Points and Development Change: Subjective and Objective Assessments." *American Journal of Orthopsychiatry* 53 (1983): 52–60. P178 shortened survival

P. 161 JACK BLOCH. . . :

Block, J. *Lives Through Time.* Berkeley, Calif.: Bancroft Books, 1971.

P. 161 WERE LESS PSYCHOLOGICALLY HEALTHY. . . :

Lieberman, M. A. "Perspectives on Changes in the Self. The Impact of Life Events and LGAT." Chapter in *Self Change: Social Psychology of Self-Initiated Externally Impaired Changes,* edited by Fisher J. D.; Chinseley, J. M.; Klar Y.; and Nadler, A. New York: Springer-Verlag, 1992, pp. 43–62.

Chapter 11

P. 170 GO FAR BEYOND DEMOGRAPHICS. . . :

Knodel, John, and Katherine Lynch. "The Decline of Remarriage: Evidence from German Village Populations in the Eighteenth and Nineteenth Centuries." *Journal of Family History* 10, no. 1 (Spring 1985): 34–59.

Cleveland, William P., and Gianturco, Daniel T. "Remarriage Probability after Widowhood: A Retrospective Method." *Journal of Gerontology* 31, no. 1 (January 1976): 99–103.

P. 177 THE EFFECTS OF REMARRIAGE. . . :

Gentry, Margaret, and Shulman, Arthur D. "Remarriage as a Coping Response for Widowhood." *Psychology & Aging* 3, no. 2 (June 1988): 191–96.

Helsing, K. J.; Szklo, M.; and Comstock, G. "Causes of Death in a Widowed Population." *American Journal of Epidemiology* 114 (1981): 41–52, report that mortality rates for widowers but not widows were reduced by remarriage.

Chapter 12

P. 190 CONTRARY TO THE GENERAL VIEW. . . : The findings are variable; some studies report that women have poorer outcomes:

Carey, R. G. Weathering Widowhood: Problems and Adjustment of the Widowed During the First Year. *Omega* 10 (1979): 163–74.

Lopata, H. *Widowhood in an American City.* Cambridge, Mass.: Schenkman Press, 1973.

Others found that widowers suffered more:

Bowling, Ann. "Mortality after Bereavement: A Review of the Literature on Survival Periods and Factors Affecting Survival." *Social Science & Medicine* 24, no. 2 (1987): 117–24.

Helsing, K. J.; Szklo, M.; and Comstock, G. "Causes of Death in a Widowed Population." *American Journal of Epidemiology* 114 (1981): 41–52.

Jacobs, Selby, and Ostfeld, Adrian. "An Epidemiological Review of the Mortality of Bereavement." *Psychosomatic Medicine* 39, no. 5 (September–October 1977): 344–57.

Li, Guohua. "The Interaction Effect of Bereavement and Sex on the Risk of Suicide in the Elderly: An Historical Cohort Study." *Social Science & Medicine* 40, no. 6 (March 1995): 825–28.

Siegal, J. M., and Kuykendall, D. H. "Loss, Widowhood and Psychological Stress Among the Elderly." *Journal of Consulting and Clinical Psychology* no. 58, (1990): 519–24.

Strobe, M., Strobe, W. 1983. "Who Suffers More? Sex Differences in Health Risks of the Widowed." *Psychological Bulletin* 93 (1983): 297–301.

Still other studies report no differences in outcomes:

Clayton, P. J. "Mortality and Morbidity in the First Year of Bereavement." *Archives of General Psychiatry* 30 (1974): 747–50.

Heyman, D. K., and Gianturco, D. T. "Long-term Adaptation by the Elderly in Bereavement." *Journal of Gerontology* 28 (1973): 359–62.

McCrae, R. R., and Costa, P. T. "Psychological Resilience among Widowed Men and Women." In *Handbook of Bereavement,* edited by M. Strobe, W. Strobe, and R. O. Hansson. New York: Cambridge University Press, 1993.

P. 190 MEN EXPERIENCE GRIEF DIFFERENTLY. . . :

Brabant, Sarah; Forsyth, Craig J.; and Melancon, Catherine. "Grieving Men: Thoughts, Feelings, and Behaviors Following Deaths of Wives." *Hospice Journal* no. 8 (1992): 33–47.

Byrne, Gerard J. A., and Raphael B. "A Longitudinal Study of Bereavement Phenomena in Recently Widowed Elderly Men." *Psychological Medicine* 24, no. 2 (May 24): 411–21.

Knott, J. Eugene. "Grief work with men." In *Handbook of Counseling and Psychotherapy with Men,* edited by Murray Scher, Mark Stevens, Glenn Good, and Gregg A. Eichenfield. Newbury Park, Calif.: Sage Publications, Inc., 1987.

Lister, Larry. "Men and Grief: A Review of Research." Special Issue: Men and Men's Issues in Social Work Theory and Practice. *Smith College Studies in Social Work* 61, no. 3 (June 1991): 220–35.

P. 194 THEIR PATHS THROUGH BEREAVEMENT ARE DIFFERENT. . . :

Feinson, Marjorie C. "Aging Widows and Widowers: Are there Mental Health Differences?" *International Journal of Aging & Human Development* 23, no. 4 (1986): 241–55.

Margolis, Otto S., Austin H. Kutscher, Eric R. Marcus, Howard C. Raether, Vanderlyn R. Pine, Irene B. Seeland, and Daniel J. Cherico. "The Forgotten Men: Concern for Widowers." In *Foundation of Thanatology Series,* Vol. 8, *Grief and the Loss of an Adult Child.* New York: Praeger Publishers, 1988.

Morycz, Richard K. "Widowhood and Bereavement in Late Life." In *Handbook of Social Development: A Lifespan Perspective. Perspectives in Developmental Psychology,* edited by Vincent B. Van Hasselt and Michel Hersen. New York: Plenum Press, 1992.

Bibliography

Bradburn, N. *Structure of Psychological Well-Being.* Chicago: Aldine, 1974.

Leary, T. *Interpersonal Diagnosis of Personality.* New York: McGraw-Hill, 1957.

Lieberman, M. A. "Bereavement Self-Help Groups: A Review of Conceptual and Methodological Issues." In *Bereavement: A Sourcebook of Research and Intervention,* edited by M. S. Strobe and R. O. Hansson. New York: Cambridge University Press, 1991.

Lieberman, M. A., and L. D. Borman. "The Impact of Self-Help Groups in Widows' Mental Health." The National Research and Information Center's *National Reporter* 4 (July 1981): 1–4.

Lieberman, M. A., and S. Tobin. *The Experience of Old Age: Stress, Coping, and Survival.* New York: Basic Books, 1983.

Lieberman, M. A., and L. Videka-Sherman. "The Impact of Self-Help Groups on the Mental Health of Widows and Widowers." *American Journal of Orthopsychiatry* 56 (1986): 435–49.

Lieberman, M. A., and I. D. Yalom. "Brief Psychotherapy for the Spousally Bereaved: A Controlled Study." *International Journal of Group Psychotherapy* 42, (January 1992): 117–32.

Mellinger, G., and M. Balter. Collaborative Project, GMIRSB Report, National Institute of Mental Health, Washington, D.C., 1983. University of Chicago.

280 DOORS CLOSE, DOORS OPEN

Mullan, J. "Parental Distress and Marital Happiness: The Transition to the Empty Nest." Doctoral dissertation, University of Chicago, 1981.

Pearlin, L. I., and M. A. Lieberman. "Social Sources of Emotional and Distress Research. *Community and Mental Health* (January 1979): 217–48.

Pearlin, L., M. Lieberman, B. Mennaghan, and J. Mullan. "The Stress Process." *Journal of Health and Social Behavior* 22 (1981): 337–56.

Rosenberg, M. *Society and the Adolescent Self-Image.* Princeton, N.J.: Princeton University Press, 1965.

Roser, A. "Stress and Maintenance of Self-Concept in the Aged. Doctoral dissertation. University of Chicago, 1968.

Veroff, J., R. A. Kulka, and E. Dowan. *The Inner American: A Self-Portrait from 1957 to 1976.* New York: Basic Books, 1981.

Yalom I. D., and M. A. Lieberman. "Bereavement and Heightened Existential Awareness." *Psychiatry* 54 (November 1991): 334–45.

Yalom, I., and S. Vinagradov. "Bereavement Groups." *International Journal of Group Psychotherapy* 48 (1988): 419–46.

Index

Gender, 233–34
and attitudes toward remarriage,
186–88
comparison of recovery issues, 213
and differing views of loneliness, 56,
191, 195
and disposal of personal belongings,
194
and loneliness within marriage,
195
and support, 213
Ginsberg, Genevieve Davis, 10–11
Grief-loss model, 9–10, 21–22, 23,
24–25, 38, 154–55
GriefNet (on-line service), 262
Grieving
and age, 240
attitudes and beliefs about, 224–25
changes in symptoms of, 209, 211
comparison of level by gender, 213
initial period of, 4, 25, 41–42, 108
measures of, 221
medical profession's views of, 11–12,
24–25, 110–11
pathological mourning, 11–12, 23,
110
patterns, 221–22, 231–33, 243–45
profound, 31–34
role of in recovery, 38–40
"timetables" for, 1–2, 22–23, 24–25,
110
types, 25–31, 211, 245
widowers and, 31, 190–91, 213
by younger widows, 80, 82
See also Average grievers; Limited
grievers; Postponed grievers; Prolonged grievers; Recovery
Growth, 136–55, 228–29
Guidance
comparison of by gender, 213
sources of, 211
as type of needed help, 102
Guilt, 223
comparison of by gender, 213
as grief symptom, 12

impact on recovery, 59–66, 77, 78
as personal growth factor, 153–54
psychotherapy to relieve, 120
as remarriage factor, 176
in younger widows, 82, 89, 90, 92

Health
comparison of by gender, 213
widowhood's effect on, 11, 12, 23,
40
Helplines, 259–60
Holidays, 55, 85–86
Horowitz, Sandy, 44

Idealization, of marriage relationship,
66, 67–70
gender differences concerning, 195
as recovery factor, 77
self-exploration and, 152
Identity, 156–69
See also Self-image
Independence, 66, 69
Information resources, 259–62
Internet, 261
Intimacy
comparison of by gender, 213
sources of, 211
as type of needed help, 102
widowers and, 187, 213

Liberation, 139–42
Life-course view, 3–9, 23
Life satisfaction
among young widows, 80
changes in level of, 22, 34, 210
Limited grievers, 221
case histories, 26–31
grief-type comparison, 211
grief-type description, 25
recovery by, 38, 39–40, 110
Loneliness, 222
gender differences, 56, 191, 195
as newly widowed's concern, 4,
54–56
self-exploration as factor, 151

A professor of psychology at the University of California San Francisco, Morton A. Lieberman is the author of many books, including his most recent, *Self-Help Groups for Coping with Crises* and *The Experience of Old Age: Stress, Coping and Survival.* He is currently director of the Aging and Mental Health Program and of the Alzheimer Center, in San Francisco. He was a professor at the University of Chicago for more than twenty years.

Donated by...

Tina Norton

in memory of
brother

Jim Norton

June, 1999